Values in Education

Also available from Continuum

Philosophy of Education – Richard Pring
Theory of Education – David Turner
Analysing Underachievement in Schools – Emma Smith
Private Education – Geoffrey Walford
Markets and Equity in Education – Geoffrey Walford
Education and Community – Dianne Gereluk

Values in Education

Graham Haydon

continuum

Continuum International Publishing Group

The Tower Building
11 York Road
London
SE1 7NX
www.continuumbooks.com

80 Maiden Lane,
Suite 704
New York,
NY 10038

British Library Cataloguing-in-Publication Data
A catalogue record for this book is available from the British Library.

ISBN: 0826492711 (hardback)

Library of Congress Cataloguing-in-Publication Data
A catalog record for this book is available from the Library of Congress.

Typeset by BookEns Ltd, Royston, Herts.
Printed and bound in Great Britain by Biddles Ltd., King's Lynn, Norfolk

Contents

Preface

This book is about the issues of values that anyone engaged in education is sure to encounter. It is a revised edition of my *Teaching about Values: A New Approach* which was published by Cassell in 1997. Although that book was well received, especially by people teaching on professional development and Masters courses, it subsequently went out of print. But its favourable reception encouraged me to produce this second edition, a decade later.

The new title reflects the contents of the book more accurately. We cannot reasonably discuss what we should be doing in values education, moral education and the like without reflecting on the ways in which values enter into our wider thinking about education. So while the book may be of special interest to teachers in the area of values education – including, in the English context, Personal Social and Health Education (PSHE), citizenship education and religious education – it is really for all teachers and student teachers, and indeed for anyone who wants 'to be able to reflect as clearly as they can on the nature of their enterprise, the values involved in it and the values they bring to it'.

The sentence just quoted is from the Preface to *Teaching about Values*. I shall repeat here, with minor changes, several paragraphs from that preface, because it still accurately summarizes the intentions of the book. Then I shall indicate the changes that have been made in this new edition.

The point that teachers actively bring their own values into teaching is important. Teachers (like all of us) are people who value and care about things; and society will not value teachers properly if it fails to recognize this fact, and merely sees teachers as passive repositories or transmitters of society's values. Hence the title of the final part of the book, 'Valuing Teachers'.

Of course, we are concerned not only with the values that teachers bring into education, but also with the values that pupils[1] take out of it. So a central focus of this book is on values as part of the subject matter of teaching. All teachers, regardless of whether they are specialists in a single curriculum subject or not, are likely to be teaching about values some of the time. But this book sets teaching about values into a broader context, which is also to do with values. Teachers do not grapple with questions of values only when they are concerned about the values their pupils have or will acquire: values lie behind any educational decision or policy.

Often, though, values are only implicit. Among the day-to-day pressures there is little time for reflection and discussion which is not directly geared to the next decision that has to be made. Unfortunately, this is increasingly the case even for student teachers: the emphasis is more and more on 'how to do it' and less and less on 'what it is all about'. I would like to see all teachers in training, and indeed all teachers in service – not to mention governors and inspectors – having ample time and opportunity to think through and *discuss* amongst themselves the kind of issues raised in the book. Reading a book is not a substitute for discussion or for anyone's own thinking; but the aim of this book is to help readers – whether teachers, parents, school governors or politicians – to think about questions of values which a concern for education inevitably raises. That aim, as I see it, is a thoroughly practical one. No book can tell teachers exactly what to do in a given situation in the classroom, and this book does not try to. But coming to a clearer understanding of what it is that one is trying to do, and engaging with others in deciding what to do, are activities of direct practical relevance; while trying to forge ahead in the interests of 'doing something practical', without stopping to think, can turn out to be thoroughly impractical!

The book cannot be comprehensive, but I have tried to say something, at least to stimulate further thought, on quite a number of issues about values that are likely to come up for practising teachers. Part I is introductory; it says more about the role of values in education in general, raising questions about the idea of education *in* values, and about aims in education, which will be followed up later in the book. Part II looks at values in general, and begins to ask what is special about moral values. It also looks at the way in which the diversity of values in modern societies can lead to conflict, and at the particular values of tolerance and compromise which may be a response to this diversity. Part III concentrates on the idea of 'morality': what is morality, and why are some people suspicious of it, or of the idea that teachers might impose it on pupils? Part IV, applying some of the lessons of the earlier parts, looks at some particular sources of controversy involving values – controversies that may occur in the staffroom and in the classroom. Part V, drawing together many of these threads, asks how we should understand the ideas of values education and moral education; and what it is that schools are best placed to do in this area. In conclusion, Part VI raises questions and makes some suggestions about the role of values in the professional education of teachers, and in the professional standing of teachers.

Topics are discussed in this book that are relevant to teachers of Personal Social and Health Education, of citizenship education, of environmental education and of religious studies – but the questions raised in this book are relevant to *all* teachers in primary and secondary schools, and indeed to a wider public. The public tends to expect schools to stand for and promote certain values; that expectation is right at least in this respect – the approach teachers take to values *is* of significance for the whole society. This book should help people both within and outside schools to think through just what it is, or is not, reasonable to expect of schools.

The book is written in a British context (and more specifically, as regards curriculum matters, the context of England and Wales in which the National Curriculum applies). This context is reflected in some of the examples and references to the curriculum, but the main arguments in the book are in no way specific to this context. It should, therefore, be helpful to readers in any country who wish to think carefully and systematically about the values that enter into the work of teachers and schools.

In preparing the second edition it is the references to the British context that have sometimes needed to be updated. Policies and initiatives come and go, but the underlying issues do not change so rapidly. Since the 1990s the British context has changed in ways that make a book of this kind all the more important. At the level of policy, questions of the aims of education (and hence of the values underlying the work of education) seem to be taken more seriously than they once were. The National Curriculum since 2000 has contained a much fuller statement of the aims and values on which the school curriculum is to be based. With regards to curriculum content, Citizenship is now firmly established, the importance of Personal Social and Health Education is perhaps more widely recognized, and more students than before are choosing to pursue religious studies in the higher levels of secondary education: all of these are curriculum areas in which explicit attention to values is essential.

I have, then, taken the opportunity to remove or revise references to the British context in the mid-1990s that would now be dated. The most egregious example was my use of a speech made in 1994 by the then Secretary of State for Education: I devoted some space in the first chapter to a critical reading of this, and referred back to it from time to time in later chapters. I wonder how many readers of this second edition would remember that politician, one John Patten, who has since that time sunk back into the obscurity (politically speaking) from which he briefly emerged. My reference probably seemed dated even when the first edition appeared in 1997.

In preparing the second edition I hope I have avoided the trap of trying to be up-to-the-minute. That is possible in newspapers and pamphlets but not in books, unless by luck. At the time of writing this preface, I would be guessing if I were to predict what issues affecting schools will be getting most attention in the media at the time of publication. So I have tried, not so much to update the book, as simply to remove anything that would be either hopelessly dated, or thoroughly ephemeral.

Instead of using a particular speech as an example of the discourse of values in education, I refer occasionally to the 'Statement of Values' that emerged from work conducted by the Schools Curriculum and Assessment Authority at about the time of publication of the first edition. At the current time of writing this statement is still extant within the documentation of the National Curriculum for England and Wales, and does in that sense form part of the context within which teachers in England and Wales are working. It is available as a resource and common reference point, though no doubt it is not used in that way as much as it might be.

One addition to the book is a section, within the final chapter, on values in educational leadership. We have heard even more about school leadership in 2006 than in 1996. To an even greater extent than before, the responsibility for what goes on in a school seems to be made to rest on the shoulders of heads and senior management. I wrote the original book in the belief that every teacher has a responsibility for values education, and I have not changed that belief. But at the same time it is more important than ever that we should recognize the responsibility of school leaders, not just in pursuing targets and delivering results, but in maintaining a positive climate of values in their school.

Another addition is a section on respect within the chapter that addresses the ideas of compromise and of tolerance. As it happens, at the time of writing the UK government is pursuing its own 'Respect Agenda', which may or may not still be active when you are reading this preface. If the section on respect still has topical relevance, that will be a bonus. But a far more important reason for adding a section on respect is that respect itself is a very important value, with a significance that in some ways is positive where the significance of tolerance may seem negative. There are also some smaller expansions of ideas, including a brief review of the notion of rights in Chapter 3.

While readers who know the original book will notice these changes, they will also find that most of the book is familiar. I have made small stylistic changes at many points, but these will not affect the substance of the exposition or argument. In resisting the temptation to make more substantial changes I have been mindful of the positive reception for the original. Whatever it was in the original that various readers liked, I would not want to risk their no longer finding it in this book.

I have kept the great majority of the references from the original book; ten years' passage of time has not made them irrelevant. I have added a limited number of more recent references, including some to my own more recent writings. Since writing the original book, I have developed my thinking on a number of topics, including: the idea of 'morality as a system' or 'morality in the narrow sense'; the distinction between rules and principles; the morality of violence; the nature of a rational form of moral thinking; the relationship between respecting persons and avoiding offence; the importance of the whole surrounding climate of ideas that we can

call 'the ethical environment'. To have tried to incorporate fully
my more recent thinking on these topics into this book would have
meant an unreasonable amount of borrowing from other pieces I
have written, and would in effect have created a different book
rather than a second edition. The developments in my thinking do
not amount to a fundamental change of mind on anything. And
even if I had changed my mind, that would not invalidate the book,
since its intention is to encourage readers to think for themselves
about the issues of values that everyone involved in education must
face.

[1] I need a term throughout for the people whom teachers teach and, in
general, it is not adult education I'm concerned with. 'Children' is inappropriate for many of the people whom secondary teachers teach, and
'students' sounds inappropriate (to English ears) for many of the people whom primary teachers teach. So I shall use 'pupils' without intending any connotation of didacticism.

Acknowledgements

In the first edition of this book, *Teaching about Values: A New Approach* (1997), I acknowledged that I had drawn ideas from other pieces I had published in the preceding years. The most substantial borrowing – from a piece on John Patten – is no longer included in this edition. The following acknowledgements still apply: to the editors of *Journal of Philosophy of Education* and *Journal of Moral Education* for permission to reprint passages from my own articles on secular society and secular schools, and on the cognitive content of moral education, respectively; and to the publishers who granted permission for the use of quotations from other authors: Harvard University Press and Rowman & Littlefield, for quotations from Gilligan, Ward and Taylor (eds), *Mapping the Moral Domain* (1988) and Kittay and Meyers (eds), *Women and Moral Theory* (1987) respectively.

Ideas are also still incorporated from an unpublished report that I wrote for the Oxford Project for Peace Studies in the early 1990s, on the role of values education in reducing conflict in society.

I repeat my thanks to the many students at initial training, Masters and Doctoral level whose concerns and questions I was responding to in writing this book. And I add thanks now to Alexandra Webster of Continuum Books for the enthusiasm with which she took up the idea of a second edition.

PART I: THE WIDER CONTEXT

This part is introductory and sets the agenda for the rest of the book. In Chapter 1, the Introduction, I show how questions about values cannot be avoided by teachers or, indeed, by anyone involved in education. In Chapter 2 I discuss educational aims; not only because questions about educational aims are themselves questions about values, but also because later in the book I want to ask precisely what the aims of teachers and schools should be where teaching about values is the focus of attention. I suggest that, in thinking about aims in education, we need to think especially about areas in which schools are best placed to make a distinctive contribution.

Chapter 1

Introduction: Teachers and Values

What place do values have in education?

A superficial reading of educational reporting and debate at most times in recent years might suggest that the role of values is rather limited. The talk often seems to be of management and funding, of competences and skills, of targets and testing. Certainly, from time to time there is explicit talk of values – perhaps in a school's prospectus, in a politician's exhortations or in the media when, in response to some particular event, there is a flurry of concern, soon to die down again, about the responsibility of schools for the moral state of the nation. But this talk will often come across as rather detached from the main day-to-day business of schools.

So the impression might be that, while there is evidence of concern about values in education, it is generally fairly low-key and rarely dominant. But this would be a superficial impression, and it is one partly created by the language we use. Though much of the day-to-day language of education is not explicitly about values, it does not follow that the discussions that go on are value-free.

Much of the discourse of education is framed in terms of the effectiveness of means towards ends, as if the ends can be taken for granted – as they often are – because it is assumed that the outcomes aimed at are of the kind that can be measured and reported in league tables. This kind of talk may not seem to be about values (other than value for money), but it is by no means value-free. Even the concern for efficiency is one of our values, and one rarely now questioned: if we think it better, other things being equal, that things be done efficiently rather than inefficiently, then we value efficiency. But, of course, this could hardly be anyone's only value, since it makes a difference what it is that is being done (if someone is propagating racism, for instance, you may think it would be much better that it be done inefficiently). The language of efficiency and achievement tends to neglect the question of the worthwhileness of the achievement. Talk of better results assumes that we know what will count as better results; in other words, it depends on what it is in teaching that is valued.

This is not a quibble. The educational language of recent years has been emphasizing the attainment of targets, grading by nationally set levels, examination passes and grades. This emphasis necessarily affects the factors that are seen as relevant in evaluating questions of policy, school organization and teaching method. Take an issue that is as current today as when the first edition of this book was published in the mid-1990s: the size of school classes.

If measurable results are the only criteria, then there is an apparently straightforward question that can be settled by empirical investigation into the relationship between class size and results (and as with any genuinely empirical investigation, the outcome will not be a foregone conclusion; it may turn out that larger classes produce, on average, somewhat better results). But to use the outcome of such investigation as a basis for favouring classes of a certain size is to take a value position, namely that the kinds of results measured are the only factors that matter significantly. In the process by which policy gets to be implemented on the basis of the research that is perceived as relevant, other possibly relevant factors may be neglected. It might be that in larger classes the methods used tend to be more formal or more highly targeted at individuals (through individual worksheets, for instance). Teachers in smaller classes may be more willing to try out and persevere with alternative approaches involving group interaction and discussion.

Suppose that is so (well-designed empirical research should be able to enlighten us on this also). And suppose that the methods used in larger classes do indeed produce better results of the sort usually measured. The crucial point is that effectiveness in producing such results does not have to be taken as the only relevant factor. One might think that people cooperating in some task and talking to each other is worthwhile in its own right, even if it is not the most effective way of producing a given result; one might simply think that the atmosphere in the smaller classes is pleasanter; or, it might be that the interaction does produce worthwhile results, but ones that are less easily measurable. If, for instance, as I shall suggest in this book (Chapter 12), a crucial element of education in values is discussion between pupils and between pupils and teachers, then limitations on class size might be worthwhile for the sake of facilitating such discussion, even if it does not produce better examinable outcomes. We are exercising our sense of values in deciding what factors to count as important.

The same applies for an issue that happens to be very prominent at the time of preparation of this new edition of the present book: school choice and school selection. Again, there is a tendency to make comparisons in terms of what is quantifiable. Does one school consistently come higher in the league tables than another? Then that is the school, it is assumed, that sensible and responsible parents will wish to choose for their child. Do schools that select by 'aptitude' (a rarely explained quality that is supposed to be something different from 'ability') produce better exam results than schools that do not so select? Then they are better schools. And so on. In all of this, questions about what it really is that we value in education are constantly being pushed beneath the surface of the debate.

It is not that there is no concern about the importance of other values, besides achievement and efficiency, in education. Many policies and initiatives (including in England those connected with Personal Social and Health Education, and with Citizenship) bear witness to this. But even in those areas, it is easy for debate to slide away from seriously thinking about what the values in schooling should be, and to slip back into concentrating on more quantifiable factors.

When our concern is (as the title of the first edition of this book had it) 'teaching about values', it is more important than ever that we should not take it for granted that we know what we are trying to do, and can concentrate on measuring how well we are doing it. In many ways we do *not* know what we are trying to do. We need to give more thought to such ideas as teaching about values, transmitting values, values education or moral education. But we cannot do this in isolation from the wider questions of what we think education is about, and why we think it matters. We need to think about how the concern with values fits into some wider set of aims for education – which will be the concern of Chapter 2.

Teachers and values

It is sometimes said that all teachers are teachers of values. That is broadly correct, and it is worth seeing why before we turn to some more specific issues about the kinds of values that should be developed in schools and the kind of contribution that schools can make. Whatever our aims for education may be, it is doubtful whether there are any educational aims that do not involve influencing the values of pupils in one way or another. Consider, say, mathematics. Could this be taught with the sole aim of enabling pupils to do certain calculations and get the right answer? There could be students who have that ability but do not take the trouble to use it; such pupils might be careless in their working out and often get wrong answers, even though they could get the right answer if they tried. A teacher of mathematics will surely hope that his or her pupils will *want* to get the answer right. That is, the teacher will want her pupils to *care* about accuracy. The point can be generalized: a teacher of any subject could pick out aspects of their subject that pupils have to recognize as important, have to care about, if they are to do well in their subject.

While it is true that all teaching, at least if it is done well, involves influencing pupils' values, if we speak of 'values education' we often have somewhat different kinds of values in mind. These can be illustrated in all their diversity, though not defined or exhausted, by a quotation from National Curriculum documentation in England and Wales.

> Education influences and reflects the values of society, and the kind of society we want to be. It is important, therefore, to recognize a broad set of common values and purposes that underpin the school curriculum and the work of schools. Foremost is a belief in education, at home and at school, as a route to the spiritual, moral, social, cultural, physical and mental development, and thus the well-being, of the individual. Education is also a route to equality of opportunity for all, a healthy and just democracy, a productive economy, and sustainable development. Education should reflect the enduring values that contribute to these ends. These include valuing ourselves, our families and other relationships, the wider groups to which we belong, the diversity in our society and the environment in which we live. Education should also reaffirm our commitment to the values of truth, justice, honesty, trust and a sense of duty.[1]

This sets a large agenda. In the next two sections I raise some questions (still using the situation in England and Wales as a reference point) first about how such a large agenda may be pursued within a school curriculum, and then about where such an agenda leaves the individual teacher.

Recognizing values within the curriculum – a perspective from England

One point we shall note in Chapter 2 is that, in school curricula in any country in the world, concerns that are more or less explicitly about values are likely to coexist alongside concerns that are explicitly academic or vocational. The concerns that are explicitly about values may themselves be expressed in a variety of ways. This can be seen in the context of the curriculum in England even within such a relatively brief time-span of two decades. The present section will illustrate this point in order to give an historical context for readers who have a professional, parental or political interest in education in England and Wales. Readers in other countries may want to reflect at this point on their own experience, in which they will almost certainly find some points of similarity and some significant differences.

A convenient starting point for a recent historical overview is the *Education Reform Act* of 1988. This included in its preamble a brief statement of the aims that schools were expected to pursue, among them the moral and spiritual development of their pupils. This might have been entirely a matter of rhetoric, except that the system for inspection of schools was reformed by the setting up of the Office for Standards in Education (Ofsted). Inspectors working under Ofsted were expected to pay attention to a schools' contribution to spiritual and moral development (later extended to 'spiritual, moral, social and cultural development').

The 1988 Act, however, is best known for introducing the National Curriculum for England and Wales, implemented from 1989. As is well known, the National Curriculum made compulsory a list of predominantly academic subjects. Questions about values were not neglected; in fact in several ways they were explicitly acknowledged. Initially this was done primarily through the setting up of a number of cross-curricular themes: economic and

industrial understanding; education for citizenship; careers education and guidance; health education; environmental education.
Each of these was meant to include a range of issues in which
questions of values were prominent. But these cross-curricular
themes never became an established part of the curriculum in
most schools, largely for the reason that schools had no legal obligation to teach them.

It was not just through the cross-curricular themes that schools
were supposed to be addressing issues about values. Explicit reference to value questions was built into the specifications for a number of the main curricular subjects, including science. However,
this aspect of the content of the National Curriculum subjects
tended to be reduced in subsequent years as it was found that syl-
labuses were too demanding. Then, too, there was still the subject
that some people considered to be the major player where values
were concerned: religious education (an anomalous subject in
England and Wales in that it was already compulsory but did not
become part of the National Curriculum). Outside the major academic and traditional areas of the curriculum, by the end of the
1980s many schools had programmes, often of their own devising,
in 'Personal and Social Education'. Such programmes continued
alongside the National Curriculum, and within them issues
around health became increasingly prominent (especially issues
concerning sex and relationships, smoking, alcohol and other
drugs) until, at the end of the 1990s, the standard term became
'Personal Social and Health Education'.

Meanwhile, in the early 1990s a number of politicians and educational spokespersons had tried to make issues about values
prominent in the agenda of educational debate and practice.
Among these individuals were the Conservative Secretary of State
for Education John Patten (who figured far more largely in the
original edition of this book); Professor Stewart Sutherland, an
academic philosopher who became the first Chief Inspector of
Schools within the Office for Standards in Education; and
Nicholas Tate, head of the School Curriculum and Assessment
Authority. The latter was influential in setting up in 1996 a
national forum which was charged with trying to reach a consensus on the values to which schools might be publicly committed.
This forum (of which the present author was a member) did produce a statement of values which was incorporated into later

National Curriculum documentation. There is no evidence that this list of values is being widely used in schools. Nevertheless, it is worth quoting here as a reference point for some of the concerns mentioned in this book. After a preamble, the list itself is divided into four categories, as follows.[2]

The self
We value ourselves as unique human beings capable of spiritual, moral, intellectual and physical growth and development. On the basis of these values, we should:

- develop an understanding of our own characters, strengths and weaknesses
- develop self-respect and self-discipline
- clarify the meaning and purpose in our lives and decide, on the basis of this, how we believe that our lives should be lived
- make responsible use of our talents, rights and opportunities
- strive, throughout life, for knowledge, wisdom and understanding
- take responsibility, within our capabilities, for our own lives.

Relationships
We value others for themselves, not only for what they have or what they can do for us. We value relationships as fundamental to the development and fulfilment of ourselves and others, and to the good of the community. On the basis of these values, we should:

- respect others, including children
- care for others and exercise goodwill in our dealings with them
- show others they are valued
- earn loyalty, trust and confidence
- work cooperatively with others
- respect the privacy and property of others
- resolve disputes peacefully.

Society
We value truth, freedom, justice, human rights, the rule of law and collective effort for the common good. In particular, we value fam-

ilies as sources of love and support for all their members, and as the basis of a society in which people care for others. On the basis of these values, we should:

- understand and carry out our responsibilities as citizens
- refuse to support values or actions that may be harmful to individuals or communities
- support families in raising children and caring for dependants
- support the institution of marriage
- recognize that the love and commitment required for a secure and happy childhood can also be found in families of different kinds
- help people to know about the law and legal processes
- respect the rule of law and encourage others to do so
- respect religious and cultural diversity
- promote opportunities for all
- support those who cannot, by themselves, sustain a dignified lifestyle
- promote participation in the democratic process by all sectors of the community
- contribute to, as well as benefit fairly from, economic and cultural resources
- make truth, integrity, honesty and goodwill priorities in public and private life.

The environment
We value the environment, both natural and shaped by humanity, as the basis of life and a source of wonder and inspiration. On the basis of these values, we should:

- accept our responsibility to maintain a sustainable environment for future generations
- understand the place of human beings within nature
- understand our responsibilities for other species
- ensure that development can be justified
- preserve balance and diversity in nature wherever possible
- preserve areas of beauty and interest for future generations
- repair, wherever possible, habitats damaged by human development and other means.

Even while the process of consolidating this Statement of Values was going on, political change in 1997 brought a change of emphasis in value-related concerns in schools. The first Education Secretary under the New Labour Government, David Blunkett, pushed the idea of Citizenship Education up the political agenda. A committee chaired by Professor Bernard Crick produced an influential report on 'Education for Citizenship and the Teaching of Democracy in Schools'[3] (commonly referred to as 'The Crick Report'), which was broadly incorporated into government policy. When the National Curriculum was revised in 2000, Citizenship became a statutory subject. Meanwhile, there had also been an advisory group on Personal Social and Health Education (PSHE)[4] but its report had much less influence. PSHE did become an expected part of the curriculum for all schools, but did not acquire the full statutory status of other National Curriculum subjects.[5]

None of the areas of the curriculum mentioned above is concerned solely with issues of values, but they do all have that concern in common. The fact that there are several areas of the curriculum that can plausibly be seen as heavily involving values reflects the fact that a school's contribution to the developing values of pupils can be interpreted in very different ways. One traditional way of thinking has seen religion as the source and major support of values, or at least of many of the most important values; to this way of thinking, it may seem natural that religious education should bear the major responsibility for education in values. Another way of thinking, which (to risk a very sweeping sociological generalization) may have gained influence to the extent that traditional religion has declined in certain countries, sees values as resting ultimately in personal choice. To this way of thinking, Personal Social and Health Education, precisely because it puts the emphasis on the personal, might be the natural home for attention to values. To yet a further way of thinking, the values that matter are the ones that affect, not so much an individual's personal choices, but the ways in which people live together with each other in society. To this way of thinking, education in values is essentially an education in good citizenship, and citizenship education will be its natural home.

There is actually no need for these different ways of approaching values to be at odds with one another, and a strong case could be made for all to complement each other within a school curriculum. This is not the place to take further in an international context the question of where within a curriculum a concern about values should be especially pursued, since the circumstances and traditions of different countries vary so much: some countries, for instance, have courses explicitly named as Ethics or Social Morality, which has never been the case in Britain. The point of the present section has been only to illustrate, through an historic overview of the situation in just one country, that there is no one obvious answer. Nevertheless, in whatever way the curriculum is planned, some issues about the responsibilities of teachers will remain common to all.

The responsibilities of teachers

There is a longstanding expectation in many countries that teachers themselves will stand for and transmit certain values on behalf of the wider society. This expectation still exists, alongside the talk of teachers as, in effect, competent technicians who are skilled in 'delivering' certain subjects. There is still something of the idea that teachers are to be moral guides and exemplars, whose standards perhaps ought to be just a little above the level of the rest of society. That is why, in some minds, the idea of teachers going on strike arouses a sense of betrayal only exceeded when nurses or midwives take similar action. And there is the idea that, whatever may be the responsibilities of individual teachers, schools should somehow be creating good citizens, if not 'good people' all round.

Teachers, of course, are on the receiving end of these varied expectations from the public and the media. But teachers may have their own ambivalence too, either individually or collectively. Many teachers will claim, with good reason, that they have been playing the role of teachers of values, or of moral educators, for years, even if they have not expressed it in quite those words. Others, especially many young people going into teaching, do not see themselves in that role at all. They see themselves perhaps as developing children's mental capacities or teaching a subject, not as inculcators of moral rules or preachers of virtues. That feeling is understandable; this book is for teachers and student teachers who feel that way, as much as for anyone who is in no doubt that teachers unavoidably must be teachers of values.

Even teachers who feel no qualms, in principle, about the idea of moral education may still feel they are not prepared, in practice, to take on that role. In a literal sense that may often be quite true: they have had no preparation for the role. In Britain, even when the professional preparation of teachers could be seen as part of the higher education of people going into teaching, and various aspects of educational theory were taught, little time and attention was given to reflection on how teachers should handle the inevitable influence they would have in the development of young people's values. Since the mid-1990s, there has increasingly been a move away from teacher *education* towards 'on the job' training with an emphasis on specified competences.

Even in Britain, the picture is more mixed than this might imply. Student teachers within certain subject areas will have given some attention to questions of values: this will be generally true for religious education and to some extent, often depending on the personal concerns of tutors, it may be true in, say, history, English, geography and technology. It will also be true for student teachers who are able to give systematic attention to citizenship or to Personal Social and Health Education, though at the time of writing the number of initial teacher education courses in citizenship is limited, and there are no such courses specializing in PSHE. There is now recognition by the General Teaching Council of the importance of values in the professional education of teachers, yet the idea that all teachers should have a systematic preparation for their role with respect to values as a standard and important part of their professional education is far from established.

Part of the reason for this lack of systematic attention is that there is no consensus – either outside the profession or within it – about what the job description should be for this aspect of a teacher's role. Some people – more likely to be outside schools than within them – do not see any problem: in their view, there are certain basic values to be transmitted, and teachers should get on with the job. I shall question in Chapter 11 the idea that teachers should, or could, function just as transmitters where values are concerned. Teachers would be quite right to be unhappy with that role, which is not a viable one within our society. And teachers should be suspicious of any rhetoric that asks them to endorse and pass on certain values without thinking for themselves about what they are doing.

Actually there is, within the profession, and perhaps especially within that part of it which is still located within institutions of higher education, a strong strand of recognition that teachers must be people who can think for themselves about their role, who can be 'reflective practitioners'.[6] And consistently with seeing their own role as not being that of passive receivers and transmitters of society's values, teachers will often not see children as passive receivers. Many teachers, in their training, will have been encouraged to think, not of transmitting values to pupils, but of encouraging children and young people to make their own choices.

But at the same time, they will probably have been told that there are some values they must enforce: they must not, for instance, allow racist remarks, or bullying, to go unchallenged. If any tension has been perceived between the idea that pupils should choose their own values, and the idea that there are certain values from which deviation will not be allowed, newly trained teachers will have had little enough guidance in resolving this tension. Indeed the widespread recognition, within teacher training and within the schools, of pluralism within society, right and necessary as it is, has not been followed up by any adequate preparation for the teachers who directly have to face the question of whether certain values are to be seen as matters of choice or as non-negotiable. Part of what I want to do in the following chapters is to offer to teachers more systematic ways of thinking about such questions as 'what is a matter of choice?' and 'what is negotiable?' But first it is necessary to follow up the point made earlier in this chapter: that we cannot think systematically about what is involved in the teaching of values without thinking more broadly about how the concern with values fits into the aims of education more broadly conceived. So the next chapter will be about aims in education.

That chapter will conclude with a set of questions which we should ask of any more specific aim which may be proposed. But before we can actually bring those questions to bear we also need a clearer sense of the various possible ways in which teachers might try to approach values, and that means that we need to reflect on the nature of values in general and of moral values in particular. That will turn out to be quite a complex task which will occupy Parts II and III of this book. Much in those parts will be directly about values and only indirectly about education; then in Part IV I shall concentrate again on education, looking, almost as case studies, at certain controversial issues involving values that enter both into teaching and into discussions about schooling. The issues raised in Parts II through IV, besides being of interest in their own right, will prepare the ground for asking, in Part V, which of all the possible aims concerning values in education teachers should actually be concentrating on. Finally, in Part VI, I shall look at how a concern with values in education can enter into the role of leaders and managers in education, into the professional education of teachers, and into the self-conception of teaching as a profession.

[1] See www.nc.uk.net/nc_resources/html/valuesAimsPurposes. shtml
[2] I have reflected on the process by which the Statement of Values was produced in Haydon (1998). The full text of the statement, including its preamble, can be found on the National Curriculum website www.nc.uk.net under 'Statement of Values' and is reprinted in Talbot and Tate (1997).
[3] Advisory Group on Citizenship (1998).
[4] National Advisory Group on Personal Social and Health Education (1999), *Preparing Young People for Adult Life.* London: DfEE.
[5] At the time of writing, in mid-2006, there are indications that the Qualifications and Curriculum Authority is beginning to turn its attention again to PSHE. For some background arguments about the importance of PSHE see Haydon 2005.
[6] The phrase was made popular in a number of professions by Schon (1983). For a more recent discussion in relation to teaching see McLaughlin (1999).

Chapter 2

Education and Aims

What is education about?

If we start from a lofty enough vantage point, we might answer that education is about keeping civilization going. Perhaps it is worth reminding ourselves of this before coming down to earth. The English philosopher Thomas Hobbes, in the politically unstable times of the seventeenth century, bewailed the conditions that people would endure if – so he argued – there were not a strong central government:

> In such condition, there is no place for Industry; because the fruit thereof is uncertain: and consequently no Culture of the Earth; no Navigation, nor use of the commodities that may be imported by Sea; no commodious Building; no Instruments of moving, and removing such things as require much force; no Knowledge of the face of the Earth; no account of Time; no Arts; no Letters; no Society; and which is worst of all, continuall feare, and danger of violent death; And the life of man, solitary, poore, nasty, brutish and short.[1]

Today, there are still prophets of doom who will suggest that, as regards the continual fear and danger of violent death, our present condition is not much better. There are parts of the world, shaken by civil wars or terrorism, where the description will seem to fit; and since September 11 2001 in New York, and atrocities since then in Bali, Madrid, London and elsewhere, we have to say that no part of the world can be free of the possibility of sudden violent death on a large scale. Nor, after the experience of three centuries and more since Hobbes' day, can we have much confidence in strong government as a solution.

Yet, many of us do live our day-to-day lives without continual fear. For the majority of people reading this, life is far better than Hobbes' 'state of nature'. There is an understandable tendency for public comment to focus on criminality and violence, and to suggest that schools should be doing something about this. Hence the calls for renewed efforts in moral education or citizenship education when particularly horrifying cases fill the media. But the broader picture is one in which we do have Technology and Science (clearly referred to by Hobbes, though not by those names), Arts and Letters and Society. We do have a degree of civilization.[2] For most people reading this, and even for most of the people going through schools in affluent countries today, the chances are (and statistics *are* relevant here) that life is not going to be solitary, poor, nasty, brutish and short.

In terms of material conditions, that has a lot to do, of course, with medicine, science and technology; and material conditions aside, arts and letters, science and technology provide many of life's pleasures and meanings. And these human activities, these social traditions of enquiry and practice, would not last from one generation to the next without education. We will not get far in thinking about values in education if we do not recognize how much of what is important in life depends absolutely on education – at least in its broadest sense (exactly how much depends on schools is a more detailed question). It is a commonplace that international development is partly a matter of educational development (which is not to prejudge the question of how far that development should everywhere follow a Western model). And try to imagine what your own society would be like after one or two generations if no knowledge or understanding was passed on from one generation to another. It is highly debatable how far the avoidance of Hobbes' so-called state of nature actually depends on any particular moral or political system, let alone on strong government; it is hardly debatable at all that it depends on education.

So, it is part of a civilized society to have arts and letters and science and technology; and not just to have them, but to care about what is good in these enterprises, and to recognize what can go wrong in them. In the modern world, education is bringing these values within reach of more of the population than ever before. Increasingly, people are becoming aware both of how much is wrong in the world and that the knowledge by which it could be improved is available, if only it could be harnessed. Education, when it is working well, enables people to appreciate what is of value, helps them decide what is going to matter in their own lives, and lets them acquire the skills and knowledge to do something about it.

It is in this sense above all that teachers have always and unavoidably been teachers of values. Indeed, this kind of teaching of values could exist in schools irrespective of the presence of anything that could be called *moral* education. As I pointed out in the previous chapter, teachers of any subject are inevitably and rightly seeking in certain ways to influence the values of their pupils.

So far, so good. But all this may seem to be just high-flown rhetoric. How do we make anything more usable out of it? By some more careful thinking, I suggest, about aims in education.

Aims and values

Thinking about aims is a way of getting a clearer picture of what it is we are trying to do, and about what would count as doing it well. Our aims are closely related to our values: we aim at things that we value, that we think are in some way worth achieving. (But not all of our values can underpin aims; there may be some things we think are good that we are powerless to bring about.)

John Dewey, the American pragmatist philosopher and educationalist, said 'education as such has no aims. Only persons, parents and teachers, have aims, not an abstract idea like education.'[3] There are two important points I want to take out of this. First, the fact that we have a certain notion of education does not, by itself, tell us anything about the aims we ought to pursue. Secondly, given that it is people who have aims, it may very well be that different people approach education with different aims.

To illustrate the first point, think of what the words 'education' and 'indoctrination' convey to you. As a speaker and reader of English, you recognize these words, and the chances are that they convey two rather different ideas to you. For instance, 'indoctrination' may suggest an attempt to get an individual to believe something regardless of evidence or reasoned argument; while 'education' might suggest that someone's opportunities for thinking and reasoning are being opened up and extended rather than narrowed down. If the words convey to you something like these two meanings, then you can use these words to express two different kinds of aim: the educator (in your vocabulary) will be aiming at something quite different from the indoctrinator.[4]

There would be nothing idiosyncratic about such an interpretation – these words, with *something* like these meanings, are common currency. But the fact that we have these words tells us nothing by itself about what we *ought* to be aiming at. If someone thinks that teachers *should* aim to inculcate certain beliefs (perhaps religious or moral ones) in people in such a way that the people concerned will never be able to question these beliefs, then the fact that you – and many other speakers of the language – would not call this 'education' does not necessarily mean that there is anything wrong with the aim. People are free to say that if education is about opening up people's minds, making them critical and enquiring and so on, then education is not what they think schools should be aiming at.

Of course, we often use the word 'education' to refer to a social institution, namely the enterprise that teachers in schools are professionally engaged in. But in that case it is an open question whether education (in this institutional sense) should be about *educating* people (in the sense of opening minds) rather than training them for jobs, or moulding their behaviour, or even just keeping them off the streets.[5] I shall in fact be using the term 'education' mostly in the institutional sense, to denote formal education or schooling; but I shall also trade on the common ambiguity of the word, so that when I argue in Chapters 11 and 12 that values education should, precisely, be *education*, I shall mean that it should not be indoctrination or (mere) habit-forming or training, but should be concerned, above all, with knowledge and understanding.

Teachers and schools cannot, then, establish what they *should* be aiming at just by appealing to the meaning of words. There is a real area for debate here, and the debate will turn on values. This brings us to the second point raised by the quotation from Dewey: that different people may have different aims for education. Even where many people may share the same underlying values (which is not something we can just assume) the fact that they are involved in education in different ways may give them (quite properly) different perspectives and hence different priorities. In their day-to-day work, teachers will often find that they are concentrating on relatively short-term objectives that could be articulated in terms of the learning outcomes that they hope their pupils will achieve. To a certain extent, those same learning outcomes will be part of what at least some pupils are aiming at for themselves; but at the same time, pupils may have many other aims of their own that are not necessarily compatible with those of the school (it is relevant here that schooling, from their point of view, is compulsory). Parents of pupils may have aims for their own children (that they get a certain kind of job, for instance) where it would not be right for a teacher to have specific aims of this kind for individual children (that this child should succeed in this particular way, for example). At the same time, as members of the staff of a school, teachers are likely to be involved with others in formulating the aims by which the school as a whole presents its conception of itself to pupils, parents and a wider public.

Among other concerns, a school's statement of aims may express some of the values that the school wishes to put into practice: one will often, for instance, find a reference to the school 'respecting the individual'. Notice what an aim of that sort does and does not do. It *does* set up a certain guideline or principle that members of the school can try to follow; what it does not do is tell anyone what the purpose of the whole exercise is. Such an aim may help the school both to respect broader ethical concerns and to do its work effectively; but an aim of this kind does not tell us what the work of the school is. If the school did not exist, we would not create it just for the purpose of trying to ensure that people within the school respected each other. If schools in general did not exist, this kind of aim – which we could call an internal aim – would not give anyone a reason for inventing them. So there is a different kind of question to be asked, namely, 'what are schools for?'

What are schools for?

The question of what schools are for is, in a sense, one for a whole society, though it is still one on which anyone, whether teacher, parent, politician or pupil, may have a view. It is a question that takes for granted a certain context, namely that schools exist, and as such it is not an abstract question about the aims of education *per se*. In fact, the reader approaching this question is likely to be asking it in a still more specific context: what is to be the role of teachers and of schools in the twenty-first century? (As always in this book, where I refer to a British or English context for illustration, readers elsewhere will be able to take the illustrations as exemplifying more general points.)

Wherever there is an education system regulated by the state, teachers work within a context in which some aims have been either explicitly set or implicitly assumed by legislation. For England and Wales, as was mentioned in the previous chapter, the *Education Reform Act* of 1988 included a brief statement of aims. But the actual aims assumed in the legislation seem to have been largely derived from a context of tradition and existing institutions. There was no argument even in the preamble to the Act to suggest that the subjects included in the National Curriculum were derived from the statement of aims. Instead the legislation seemed to appeal to what, in practice, has become a canon of subjects that is recognized across most of the world. This includes: the dominant language of the society in question; mathematics; sciences (generally dominated by an established core of physical and biological sciences); historical and geographical studies with a content often highly relative to the particular society; literature, music and arts to various degrees, and again with a content that is at least partly culturally relative; useful second languages; various practical, technical and vocational skills.

The revision of the National Curriculum in 2000 included a more extended account of the aims of the curriculum (in the previous chapter I quoted a paragraph about the values underlying education, which forms part of the discussion of aims). But it is still far from clear that the actual range of subjects included in the curriculum, or the detail of their content, has been systematically derived from the stated aims.[6] The traditional canon of subjects still seems to be, to a large extent, taken for granted, and such is its influence that it tends to structure the aspirations towards mass schooling of countries around the world.

In mentioning this canon of subjects I do not mean to suggest that it cannot be challenged. Far from it. I mean only that if I am to say something here of practical relevance, I cannot start with a clean slate. Yet even the traditional canon of subjects is surely not as firmly entrenched in the thinking of most of us as is the institutional form in which we tend to expect that canon to be delivered: schooling. Legislation can be repealed, our ideas about the curriculum of schools *could* be radically altered, but the fact of the existence of schools and teachers would be, in modern societies, much harder to change.

The existence of schools can be challenged, of course. The 1970s saw a brief flourishing of deschooling literature, which suggested that universal compulsory schooling was not the answer either for modern societies that already took it for granted, or for developing societies that were following their model.[7] The intellectual case for that position can still be made, and perhaps the fact that at the beginning of the twenty-first century there seems to be little talk about deschooling society only demonstrates the power of the school that writers such as Ivan Illich were seeking to expose. But whatever the arguments, the chances are that we are stuck with schools in something like their present form (within which the disputes about comprehensive or selective intake, large or small size, even state-run or private, are details). It is this established fact of schooling (more even than any assumptions about the curriculum) that provides the context for our questions about aims. Notice that the context of which I am speaking is one in which for the vast majority of children attendance at school is, in effect, compulsory, even though there may be provision in law for alternatives such as education at home.

It is perhaps surprising, then, that we do not more often ask the question: given that we have a system of universal and compulsory schooling, how can we best use this system? What should we try to do with it? What does it enable us to achieve that we could not achieve without it? Is what we can achieve through this system so important that it would justify creating the system now if we did not already have it?

The way I have set up those questions might suggest that I shall be concentrating on the ways in which the institution of schooling may be of value to a society as a whole, to the neglect of any consideration of what it can do for the individual. But it can be very misleading to think in terms that set up an opposition between what is good for society and what is good for an individual. If we had to make a choice, say, between on the one hand developing in people the capacities that will enable them (individually) to lead fulfilling lives, and on the other hand giving them the skills and attitudes that will equip them to be efficient cogs in an impersonal machine, then there would be a real divide between aiming at the good of the individual and aiming at the good of society. But it is not necessarily like that. If, for instance, your view of a good society is that it is one in which all individuals can lead unrestricted and fulfilling lives while at the same time feeling a positive sense of belonging to the society, then no contradiction would exist between aiming at individual good and aiming at the good of society. In fact, even without being idealistic, it is clear that many aims do cut across the individual/society division. Giving people skills that will enable them to get productive jobs, for instance, will in many cases be of benefit both to the individuals concerned and to others within society.

Without, then, worrying too much for the moment about what is good for society and what is good for individuals, it may be more fruitful to look at some of the different kinds of aims that can be suggested for education. If we think again of what I have called the traditional canon of subjects in the curriculum, we can see that this has not only faced challenges recently from other concerns competing for a place in the curriculum, but has also in fact always faced challenges to its dominance.

Moral and political concerns

Perhaps the longest-standing of these concerns outside of the traditional canon appear in the moral and political area. Society has often looked to schooling to make people morally better, but approaches to this concern vary greatly. In some societies it has been widely assumed, at least until recently, that the moral aims of schooling are to be achieved largely through religion. Perhaps for that reason religious education, as noted in the previous chapter, was a compulsory subject in English schools well before the advent of the National Curriculum. But as we know, in other countries, such as the USA, religious education, or at any rate instruction in any particular religion, is excluded from the curriculum of state schools, so that moral aims perforce have to be pursued in some other way. Some countries do include courses in ethics or morals explicitly in their curriculum. To the extent that morality is treated as a matter of public rather than private concern, such courses are likely to overlap with the concern to promote good citizenship. This highlights another of the very common concerns that societies expect their school systems to address: that education should enable people to be good citizens, and perhaps, in democracies, politically active citizens.

Some of the moral and political aims of schooling reflect perennial concerns: the moral and social functions of education were recognized in the Greece of Plato and Aristotle and the China of Confucius, as well as in the practice of many societies in which there was little systematic reflection on education. But in addition to these concerns, and often on the basis of the same underlying values, there are specific issues that appear urgent at a particular time: for example, that education should foster a multicultural non-racist society; that it should advance the cause of equal opportunities between the sexes; and that it should promote citizenship in a wider context than that of the nation state.

Then there are claims arising from perceived dangers that an educational response may do something to mitigate. One such is 'education for natural disaster reduction', which involves preparing people to cope with earthquakes, floods and other catastrophes in the hope that this may reduce the scale of the *human* disaster.[8] In a similar way, HIV/AIDS education has been promoted in some countries as a way of reducing the spread of AIDS by influencing the choices that people make in their personal lives; and sex education more generally is often perceived in part as a way of tackling high rates of teenage pregnancy. Within recent decades in some countries, and especially at the height of the Cold War, there were strong calls for peace education, which was advocated in part as a response to the perceived threat of nuclear war.[9]

How are we to assess all the varied calls for this or that issue to be addressed in education? Can we say, for instance, that given certain real threats, then it follows that we should do whatever we can in schools to reduce the danger? Actually, the amount of controversy generated around peace education or sex education shows that the argument cannot be so simple. In cases that have proved controversial, people on both sides of the controversy have been appealing to their sense of values. Yet if we look deep enough, we may well find that there is some common ground.

Most people would agree that formal education should in some way improve people's lives, whether individually or in societal or even global terms. Even the view that the mass of the population should be educated so as to serve more effectively the interest of a

privileged class would be an attempt to justify education by its contribution to *some* people's quality of life. But differences between
classes are not now the most important reason for disagreement
on educational aims within the broad and usually implicit consensus that education should improve lives. More important is that
there is room for many different interpretations of what constitutes a better life: that people should acquire intellectual interests
that make their lives richer; that they should develop skills that
enable them to achieve worthwhile aims of their own; that they
should be less at risk from the antisocial behaviour that *other* people might engage in if they were not taught how to behave; that
they should keep the wheels of the economy turning; that they
should live in harmony with nature; that they should live in obedience to divine law. All of these and many more are possible opinions about the benefits of education. Here again, our values
necessarily come into our assessments of what makes one kind of
life better or more worthwhile than another.

We cannot look here at all the possible permutations of values
that can come into such assessments. Instead, I shall pick out just
one difference that seems to underlie many actual disputes over
the aims that should be pursued in schools: the difference
between, on the one hand, values that traditionally have been
specifically associated with the idea of education, and on the other
hand, values that might be seen as necessary to any kind of worthwhile life. Education has often been seen as especially concerned
with knowledge and understanding, rationality, and the more
elaborated and refined kind of appreciation, both of the natural
world and of human creations, that becomes possible only
through education. But schooling may also promote what in a
sense seem more basic values: health, a sense of security, adequate
nutrition and shelter, freedom from injury and in the end, sheer
survival (possessing the skills necessary to support oneself will be,
at least, instrumental in enabling individuals to secure these basic
values). The difference between 'educational' values and 'basic'
values, as it enters into actual debates, is likely to be one of emphasis. It is not that some people care only about one set of values,
others about the other kind, but that, where schooling is in question, people will differ on the balance to be struck between one
kind of value and the other. In that way, the question about the
aims to be pursued in schooling could be seen as a question of

priorities, between those who seek to promote the 'higher' or more specifically educational values, and those whose aim is to promote the more basic values.

But to see it this way is actually misleading. These are not two independent sets of values; rather, they are in a symbiotic relationship with each other. The basic values are fundamental to almost anything else that is of value in human life, including educational values. If, for instance, individuals perish, whether through disease, natural disaster, the despoliation of the environment or war, their opportunity to realize any higher values is simply deleted; and when societies are thrown into chaos by events, whether natural or humanly contrived, there is little chance of enjoying the satisfactions of the life of the mind that education can make possible. The relationship also holds good the other way round: without knowledge and rationality, and technologically informed skills, we have little chance of doing much to mitigate the assaults that the world, both natural and human, can make on our most basic values.

If the question were only a theoretical one of priorities, it could be endlessly debated. But the interrelationship between these values is not only theoretical; it is mediated, in the most practical way, through the actions of persons in their own lives. This is true at more than one level. It is clearly true in the case of those whose education leads them into specialized fields. It would not, in the modern world, be realistic to try to equip every individual to meet every one of his or her needs independently; we are all of us dependent to varying degrees for much of the basis of our quality of life, and schooling has a large role to play in promoting an environment in which the production of specialists can flourish.

But the relationship between the promotion of educational values and the promotion of more basic values is not only mediated through the actions of specialists but also through the skills and capacities that any individuals may exercise in their daily lives; and through the actions of all persons in their capacity as moral and political agents. Since the exercise of these capacities will involve the working out in practice of values that have been partly formed through education, we shall need in this book to look not only at the way in which values underlie any conception of aims in education but also at the way in which values may enter explicitly into the *content* of certain aims. In what way should the promotion of values be part of the aims of education? And which values should these be? As I said at the end of Chapter 1, we need more clarity about values in general before these questions can be answered. But first, can we suggest any guidelines that might help to resolve differences about educational aims in general? I think we can at least list some questions that it would be worth asking about any suggested aims.

Some questions about educational aims

1. *Is the aim for something of positive value?*
2. *Is the aim for something that can feasibly be realized or at least promoted through formal education?*

Taken together, these two questions perhaps capture the minimum requirements for any aim of formal education. There are some things that schools are likely to be able to achieve (such as subjecting the majority of pupils to years of boredom) that are not likely to be seen as of positive value, and which therefore should not be taken as aims. There are other things that we would generally regard as uncontroversially positive but which it is unlikely that schools can do much, at least directly, to influence, so that there would be no point in trying to treat them as aims of education (such as an optimal combination of rainfall and temperature from the point of view both of the production of food and of people's pleasure in the weather).

3. *Is what is aimed at something that can be seen as both good for individuals and good for society, or at least as not merely benefitting the few at the expense of many others, or the majority at severe cost to a few?*

A fault of the first kind, arguably, might be a concentration on the academic achievement of high-flyers if this meant that everyone else received less benefit from their education than they would have in other conditions. A fault of the second kind, which might arise unwittingly, could be the formulation of aims in terms that assume normal oral communication, thus disadvantaging those whose speech or hearing is impaired.

4. *Is the aim of broad relevance rather than narrowly specific?*

Since it is unrealistic to expect schools to accomplish everything we might like them to do, we should give priority, other things being equal, to goals that can be realized in conjunction with other goals that are also worth achieving. Those aspects of the curriculum, whether in content or in method, that can serve more than one worthwhile purpose will have a preferential claim over aspects that can only serve one particular purpose. This suggests that some broad overarching concern, such as promoting the capacity for rational and critical thinking, will have a stronger claim, other things being equal (but see Question 7 below), than specific aims like, say, education for natural disaster reduction or HIV/AIDS education, because the overarching aim can contribute, even though less directly, to the same goals as the more specific educational endeavours, as well as to other goals.

> 5. *Is what is aimed at something that teachers and schools are particularly well placed to promote? Or is it perhaps something that would come about anyway, independently of formal education?*

In the education profession we perhaps slip too easily into thinking that if something is worth doing, it must be worth teaching – or in some way laying a foundation for – in schools. There are many other sources of learning and experience (a point the deschoolers were right to emphasize), and many desirable things that may happen even though teachers do nothing about it. There is at least a case for saying that schools should concentrate on things that schools are necessary for.

> 6. *Is what is aimed at something that it is important for everyone to have (or to achieve, be exposed to, etc.)?*

This is not to rule out the existence of options within any individual's career in formal education, but it is worth remembering that one of the things a system of universal compulsory schooling can do is to ensure that everyone is exposed to similar experiences. There may be nothing else in modern society that can do this. Ten or twenty years ago it might have been thought that television could come as close as schooling to exposing all children to certain ideas. But with the proliferation of television channels and the increasing tendency of young people to spend time not watching television but at their computer screens (where again the range of individual choice is vast), there may be no way of, as it were, getting a message across to all young people, unless it is built into a compulsory curriculum.

I do not mean to take it for granted here that it *is* a good thing for the same message to be put across to all young people. That is a genuine question. My emphasis here is on the relevance of that question for the aims of education. Are there things that everyone *should* be exposed to? (And if not, should there be a common curriculum, or universal compulsory schooling, at all?)

7. Is what is aimed at something that has a justified place in education because of its sheer importance, regardless of the other questions above?

It is not inconceivable that we might consider a particular aim to be so important that we should devote all possible means, educational and otherwise, to realizing it. Some people have probably thought at times that the avoidance of nuclear war came into such a category, and the avoidance of global environmental disaster might now be a plausible candidate. If formal education were really to be devoted to one overriding aim above everything else, it might be radically different from what we are used to. Actually there are probably few people who would want to see education subordinated to just one goal, however important it may be. In other words, we recognize in education as elsewhere a plurality of values.

8. Can what is aimed at be pursued without violating any moral values in the process?

If a particular aim, however valuable, could only be achieved by subjecting all pupils in school to half an hour of severe physical pain every day, most people would rule out that aim. The means would be seen as immoral and not justified even by a valuable end. Closer to concrete reality is the situation in which a certain aim – perhaps getting people to believe that a certain kind of behaviour is wrong – could only be achieved through methods that some people, but not all, would count as indoctrinatory, so that some, but not all, would count those methods as immoral and so rule out such an aim.

If we ask how far education (in the formal institutional sense) should be concerned with aims that fall under the headings of moral education and/or the transmission of values, and what more precisely the aims should be, these questions may be helpful. I shall use the questions for this purpose at the end of Chapter 11. We may not need a positive answer to every question before we can consider that a particular aim is justified, but certainly an aim ought to be called into question if it yields negative answers to most of these questions. The first two questions, which set up a minimum requirement, direct us to ask what it would be desirable for schools to do in the area of values, and what would be feasible. Before we can say more even on those questions, we need to clarify what we are talking about when we speak of values in general, and of moral values in particular. That is the task I shall start on in the next chapter.

[1] Hobbes, *Leviathan* Part 1, Chapter 13. See Hobbes (1968: 186). First published 1651.

[2] Of course, as with most broad-brush statements, to call a society 'civilized' is only partly a factual description; it is also an evaluation, albeit one that most readers of this are likely to share. But we should be reminded from time to time of Gandhi's comment when asked what he thought of English civilization: that it would be a fine thing.

[3] Dewey (1916), Chapter 8. John Dewey's classic *Democracy and Education* is still well worth reading. Dewey is often recognized simply as an advocate of child-centred education. In fact, his educational theory is part of a well worked out theory of the relations between individuals and society, and of the nature of knowledge and thought. See especially Chapters 1–4, 8 and 9.

[4] A classic philosophical analysis of the concept of education, which in a sense stands at the beginning of the modern history of the philosophy of education, is in Peters (1966). With reference both to the nature of education and to the values within it, see Walsh (1993). Much work on indoctrination has lasted less well, but see Snook (1972), and Spiecker and Straughan (1991).

[5] Among the classic attempts within philosophy of education to analyse the concept of education, Barrow (1981), Chapter 2 was unusual in clearly distinguishing education from schooling and arguing that education was just one among many possible aims of schooling.

[6] See Bramall and White (2000); White (2004).

[7] The most famous item in this literature was Illich (1973). I contributed to the literature on the justification of compulsory schooling in Haydon (1977).

[8] There would have been fewer deaths from the Indian Ocean tsunami of 26 December 2004 if more people had been taught to recognize the signs that a tsunami was approaching. On the aims of education for natural disaster reduction, see Haydon 2004.

[9] Peace education was never entirely about reducing the risk of nuclear war. It was partly also about understanding the many ways in which people can come into conflict, and partly about practical methods of non-violent conflict resolution. It would therefore continue to have relevance even if the use of nuclear weapons by states could reliably be avoided. Peace education is relevant to the issues discussed in Chapter 9.

PART II: VALUES

My intention in this part is not to give a definitive account of values; I am more concerned with emphasizing their variety. Not only are there moral and non-moral values, there are different interpretations of moral values.

While the notions of a plural society and of a multicultural society do not appear in the title of this book, they are part of the context assumed throughout – a context that surely has to be assumed by any book on values in education. That is why, after making some distinctions between moral and non-moral values in Chapter 3, I turn in Chapter 4 to conflict of values, and in Chapter 5 to the values of compromise, tolerance and respect that may especially come into play when other values conflict.

Chapter 3

Values and Moral Values

A variety of values

If we ask the question 'What are values?' it is much easier to draw up a list of examples than it is to give a general account of what kind of thing a value – any value – is. Suppose we take as a convenient source of examples the Statement of Values from the English National Curriculum. Every item in the list begins with the phrase 'we should . . .', and each of these items could be construed as a statement of a value, expressed in a rule or a principle. But often, when asked for examples of values, people will answer with single words (or hyphenated phrases) that are taken to be the names of values. If we look for examples of this sort in the Statement of Values we can find at least the following:

- self-respect
- self-discipline
- care (for others)
- goodwill
- respect (for others)
- loyalty
- trust
- cooperation
- love
- commitment
- truth
- integrity
- honesty
- balance
- diversity
- beauty

Many of these may strike you as 'moral values', though some – including perhaps balance, diversity and beauty – would not

naturally occur on many people's list of moral values. It is easy
to add more words for values that may not be moral values, such
as:

- security (a sense of security)
- comfort
- cheerfulness
- convenience
- intelligence
- efficiency
- cost-effectiveness
- neatness
- reasonableness

We shall come back to the question of what makes a value a
moral one. First, one obvious thing to notice about all these examples, whether moral or not, is that they are abstract ideas rather
than concrete objects. This does not mean that it is not possible
for people to value concrete objects; it clearly is. You may value
your house or your car or your watch (I do not mean in the sense
of 'putting a specific monetary value on it' but in the sense,
roughly, of 'caring about it'). All sorts of things can be important
to us, can matter to us, and in that sense we can value them. But it
seems (as a fact at least about the English language) that we tend
to use the word 'values' for the more abstract ideas.

Many of these ideas are of qualities that can characterize objects
or institutions, or indeed whole societies, or that can characterize
individual persons. Take 'tolerance': we can speak of a tolerant
society or of a tolerant person. Several of the examples mentioned
in the first list above pick out personal qualities – such as loyalty,
honesty or integrity; they are ways that persons can be (or fail to
be) in their thinking and action. As it happens, we have in English
an old word that we can use as roughly equivalent to 'a (morally)
good way a person can be in their thinking and action'. The word
is 'virtue'. Though it has rather fallen out of use in everyday language it is a useful word for picking out the kinds of personal quality that we find morally desirable or admirable. So we can say that
tolerance, unselfishness or integrity are virtues. (Of course, you
will only say this if you do think the qualities in question are good
ones. If you thought that a particular quality – say 'loyalty' – was

not a good quality for people to have, or perhaps if you thought that, while positive rather than negative, its importance is over-rated, then you would not see it as a virtue.)

Our values, including moral values, do not have to be expressed by speaking about virtues. We may, for instance, say that honesty is a virtue, but we can also speak about what people should do (such as 'tell the truth') or should not do ('don't tell lies'). We can speak of unselfishness as a virtue, and we can also say 'you should not pursue your own interests at the expense of others'. Speaking of a personal quality and speaking of what is to be done or not done are not exactly equivalent (I will have more to say about this in Chapter 6) but they do seem in some sense to be referring to the same underlying value. Reference to rules allows us to be fairly specific about the kinds of behaviour we want to praise or to criticize. For example, 'Do what your teachers tell you' is – for better or worse – more specific than the idea of respect for authority. Reference to personal qualities tends to put some weight on the motivation behind a person's behaviour, as we shall see in Chapter 6. So in some contexts it will make a difference whether one thinks in terms of personal qualities or in terms of rules. But since people sometimes express their moral values by referring to rules or principles, I want to use the term 'values' in a broad enough way to include talk of rules or principles as well as of qualities. As already noted, the National Curriculum Statement of Values, while it often mentions personal qualities, consists largely of sentences beginning 'We should . . .'

There is a further distinction that is worth making, though often it is not marked consistently in everyday language. Rules, as noted, can be quite specific in what they tell someone to do or not do. But if we say something like 'be truthful' or 'don't be selfish' we are not laying down anything at all specific about what a person is to do or not do. If we call such cases 'rules' at all, we should not confuse them with rules that are much more specific. It may be useful to use the term 'principle' for the more general norms that leave a great deal open to interpretation. So 'be generous in help-ing others' would be a principle; 'give ten per cent of your income to charity' would be a rule. Both could be ways in which some-one's values were expressed. No doubt the difference will be one of degree. With regards to the Statement of Values, its sentences beginning 'We should . . .' are generally ones that are not very specific about what a person is to do or not do in order to follow the norm; so these are more like general principles than rules.[1]

People have values

I hope that by this point my meaning when I speak of values is clear enough for practical purposes. For such purposes, we do not need to raise metaphysical-sounding questions about the real existence of values. *People* value things, and prominent among the things they value are the qualities of people (themselves and others) and the ways that individuals can be and act. Since we are concerned in this book with issues that people think about and discuss when they are formulating educational policies or planning teaching strategies, it makes good sense to concentrate, not on the question 'what *are* values?' but on the role of values in people's thinking and behaviour. For whatever else may be true of values, it is true that people value things (using 'things' in the widest possible sense, to include personal qualities, states of affairs, anything that people can be aware of or have a notion of). In that sense at least we can be sure that people have values, or acknowledge values.

You might wonder whether there is not something more than this to values, more than just the fact that people value things. Many people have an idea of values as somehow lying beyond or being deeper than everyday human thought and action in the mundane material world. Later in the chapter I shall look more systematically at the ideas that values may be objective or universal. At this stage it is worth indicating two things: first, that the idea of values as having some kind of reality independent of human thought is quite problematic; and second, that we do not *have* to think of values in that way in order to address important questions about values in education.

The idea of values as having an independent reality is sometimes expressed by saying that values – or perhaps just certain particular values – are timeless or eternal. It is not obvious that this is so. We can recognize that one generation may value what another generation does not. Take an example that may not be a *moral* value at all, though it is mentioned in the Statement of Values: our ideas about natural beauty in the environment. We are told that prior to the romantic movement in poetry and paint-

ing, Europeans saw rugged landscapes of bare rocks and mountains as hostile (to human purposes) rather than beautiful.[2]
Assuming that we can accept some such broad generalization, we
could say that our ideas of beauty have changed: people began to
put a certain positive value on things they had not previously valued in that way. If we give no more than this kind of account, the
idea of timeless values is unnecessary (in relation to this example). But some people would want to give a different account,
insisting that the beauty of rugged natural landscape is a timeless
value, but that it is only in recent centuries that people have
begun to recognize this, whereas previously they were blind to it.

If some people would give that kind of account about aesthetic
values, more will probably feel compelled to think of moral values
as timeless. If we believe that slavery is wrong, it does not sound
very plausible to suggest that it only became wrong when people
(some people, most people?) began to think it was wrong. We are
more likely to say that its being wrong is a matter of values that are
themselves timeless (perhaps the values of freedom or dignity, or
the value of personhood), even though it may have been only in
recent historical times that most people have either recognized
these values or accepted the full implications of them. If we call a
certain value timeless in this way, we are not, I suppose, saying that
it has always existed, which would commit us to saying, for
instance, that the value of human dignity has always existed, even
before there were any human beings. We are saying, rather, that
the value is somehow independent of time altogether.

If we concentrate in an educational context, for certain purposes, on *people holding values*, that does not preclude speaking of
values as embodying some kind of independent existence or reality. That is why I used the idea a few paragraphs above of people
'acknowledging' values, which suggests that the value is already
there to be recognized. If we think of human dignity, say, as a timeless value, we are acknowledging not only that some people do in
fact value human dignity, though that is true, but also that they are
right to do so (and that people who do not are in some way mistaken or blind to this value). Already here some difficult questions
are emerging about the sense in which values could have a real
existence or an objective truth about them.

I shall not give much space here to these questions, as it would
be impossible to resolve them to every reader's satisfaction (or

even to my own). Even to survey the arguments that have occu-
pied moral philosophers for centuries would turn this into a quite
different kind of book. The book is premised, rather, on the
assumption that something worthwhile can be said and done
about values in education without a stand having to be taken on
questions of objectivity or subjectivity of values and the like. No
doubt some people will continue to think that there are objective
values, and others will insist that all values are subjective, while
many people may be confused about the whole issue. *That* is the
situation that teachers have to work in.

So, while I do not attempt to settle questions about the timeless-
ness or reality of values, I do take seriously the fact that many people
(I suspect most of us some of the time) do *treat* many of their values
as being more than just the preferences they happen to have or that
society imposes. I am also aware that people can get seriously mud-
dled by some of the terminology in this area: objectivity, subjectivism, relativism, 'absolute' or 'universal' values, and so on. Hence
the note about such terms at the end of this chapter.

Before turning to the question of what distinguishes people's
moral values from any other values they may hold, there is a possible ambiguity we should clear up about what counts as a person
having certain values. Do a person's values lie in what they profess to
value, or in what they actually put weight on in their behaviour, or
(if we are talking about personal qualities) in what they are actually
like? Probably the answer is all of these. You might say that a person's real values are shown in what they do, since when people talk
about their values they may be insincere or self-serving. Yet what
people say about their values – their professed beliefs about values –
should not be neglected; on the contrary, it is the origin of much of
the conflict that people get into over values, as we shall see in the
next chapter. In any case, if somebody fails to be, say, as kind as they
would like to be, that does not mean that they do not genuinely
value kindness. Our values can provide us with ideals; someone who
fails to live up to their ideals may still genuinely hold those ideals.

Which values are moral ones?

Accepting that people's values are revealed both in what they say
and in what they do, our next question – since people's concern

about values in education so often seems to be a moral concern –
is to ask what it is about some values that makes them moral ones.

Notice first that we are not asking about the distinction between
moral and immoral (or morally right and morally wrong). We are
talking about the distinction between moral values and values of
other kinds, be they aesthetic, or purely personal, or whatever.
Suppose, for instance, you think (a) that no twentieth-century
European music is as good as some music of the eighteenth and
nineteenth centuries; and (b) that it is wrong for people who are
not married to each other to sleep together. Then (a) expresses
an aspect of the aesthetic values you subscribe to and (b)
expresses an aspect of your moral values (probably – though as we
shall see in the next paragraph it depends on the reasons you have
for your views). Suppose someone else thinks (a) that some rock
music is (musically) as good as any classical music and (b) that
there is nothing wrong (in itself) with unmarried people sleeping
together. Then you may think that the other person's musical
judgement is depraved or uninformed and that their moral views
are corrupt. But it remains true that the distinction between (a) as
aesthetic and (b) as moral holds in their case as much as in yours.
That there is nothing wrong with unmarried people sleeping
together expresses (or may follow from) an aspect of *that person's*
moral values (the relevant aspect in this case may be that they do
not see this as a moral issue at all).

This also shows, I think, that we cannot distinguish someone's
moral values from the other values they hold merely by the *content*
of the values – by what these values say or what they are about. It is
true that when asked to name some moral values we may mention
notions like honesty or truthfulness, or, if our thoughts turn to
rules, we may mention 'don't steal' or 'don't tell lies'. But even
these *might* not be moral values, at least on one quite commonly
held view of what makes something moral (a view that we shall see
a lot more of in Part III). 'Honesty is the best policy' is a piece of
advice appealing to a person's own self-interest; some would say
that this means it is not a matter of morality at all (similarly the
near-equivalent 'Don't deceive people because you might be
found out'). 'Don't sleep around' might well be a moral view, but
it could also be a piece of health advice aimed at the avoidance of
sexually transmitted diseases. Similarly, 'don't eat meat' could be a
moral view (from an ethical vegetarian) or, again, advice on a

healthy diet. Even a criticism of rock music, while it is most probably an expression of aesthetic values, could be a moral judgement on the message put across by some of the lyrics. So what makes someone's views moral ones may not be, so to speak, their surface content, but the kinds of reason a person has for them. That, of course, leads us to ask what makes a reason a moral reason. We shall come back to that later.

There are other features, too, that may help to distinguish people's moral values from other values they hold. (Incidentally, whether a person actually uses the term 'moral' of some of their own values is only one factor, and probably a rather minor one. Some people have reasons of various kinds, as we shall see in Chapter 6, for not liking the *word* 'moral'; they may not want to think of themselves as making moral judgements. But it would be surprising if even these people did not recognize some moral values, whatever they choose to call them.) Which of your values, then, will count as moral ones? Let me mention some features that may distinguish some of your values from others, and let me suggest, very roughly, that the more of these features your values exhibit, the more clearly those values will be moral ones.

Some of your values have to do with the way people behave; not all of them do. What kinds of music you appreciate, for instance, will have a lot to do with your aesthetic values, but these may say nothing about how people are to behave. From your preference for a particular kind of music, for instance, it will not necessarily follow that you think everyone playing or listening to music *ought* to play or listen to music only of that kind, or that they are doing something wrong if they do not.

Following on from that, some of your values (unlike aesthetic ones, probably) may be ones that you are inclined to express by using words such as 'ought' and 'ought not', 'right' and 'wrong'. So far, this only begins to narrow down the field; using these words does not in itself mean that you are making any kind of moral judgement ('You ought not to do the calculation that way; you have got it wrong').

Some of your values may be ones you consider to be particularly important, ones that in the end you would have to stand by, even if you were to give up or compromise on all sorts of other things. (But see the remarks on compromise in Chapter 5.)

Some of your values may be ones that seem to you to make

some sort of claim on you 'from outside', as it were, independently of how you happen to feel or what is convenient for you at a particular time. You might realize on a particular occasion, for instance, that it will smooth over a difficulty if you tell a lie; but the idea that you ought not to tell a lie may still be there, and you may feel that you cannot decide just to ignore it.

Some of your values may be ones that you think apply not just to yourself but to everyone (a point that you might express by saying that you take these values to be universal). Perhaps this will be the case just because you do feel that these values make some sort of claim 'from outside' (and therefore cannot be making that claim only on you). Because you can see such values – examples might be the wrongness of torture, or of racism – as having a claim on everyone, you can think that everyone *ought* to recognize these values, even if not everyone does in fact recognize them.

Some of your values may be ones that you do not think can be at bottom a matter of your preferences, choices or tastes. Other values in contrast may seem, even to you, to be at bottom matters of preference or taste – if not just your personal preference or taste, then a cultural one. This may be true, for instance, of your views about the quality of music of various kinds. We are well aware, after all, that there are different musical traditions, and some of us acknowledge our ignorance about most of them. It is also true that there are different moral traditions. But you may very well think – and with good reason – that your idea that it is wrong to kill people is not just a matter of preference or taste, either personal or cultural.

When trying to think in general terms about values, some people do *say* that ultimately moral values are a matter of choice or subjective preference. It is actually quite difficult to maintain this position when you think about something that, for you, exhibits many of the features just mentioned. Think of something that you feel strongly opposed to. I shall take racism as an example, but you could substitute another. Can you seriously think that your position on racism amounts to no more than an expression of a preference? Could that be all there is to it: that you just happen to prefer an environment free of racism, as you might prefer an environment free of ugly buildings?

If you really thought that all values, including moral ones, were nothing but subjective preferences, you could not argue with anyone about any of their values, and you would have no basis for disapproving of their actions. (I presume that, if you prefer coffee, you do not disapprove of someone else exercising their preference for tea.) Now, you may say – as some people do – that you do not disapprove of other people's values. Perhaps you want to say that everyone is entitled to his or her own values, that they are all equally valid, or something of that sort. Many people now do think like this about various matters – sexual preferences, for instance – that, in an earlier generation, people thought of as in no way a matter of choice. But my example of racism was intended to suggest that, perhaps, there are some things that you cannot sincerely treat in that way. If the example of racism does not work for you in this way, you can think of torture, or child abuse, or anything else that seems to you quite clearly wrong. It is difficult at the same time to think of this as just a preference you happen to have, or to think that any people who disagreed would have an equally valid point of view. (To think that other people's position is *not* equally valid – that it is actually wrong – does not mean that you have to go around condemning people. Whether people should ever be condemned because of the values they hold is a quite different issue, which we shall touch on in Chapters 6 and 7.)

What does this argument show? It does not show that moral values *are* objective; to show that would take a great deal more argument, if it could be shown at all. (It would also need some more careful sorting out of ways in which it can even make sense to think of values as objective – on which I shall say more below.) The point just made is only that people – probably most people, at least some of the time – tend to think and talk about certain values as if they are objective. This in itself is an important point for education. The tendency to think of certain values as objective reflects the significance that the values have for the people whose values they are. I am suggesting that it is the kind of significance values have for a person that largely determines whether they are among a person's *moral* values.

At this point the argument would be simpler if we could say that there is just one kind of significance that values must have for a person if they are to count as moral values. But the situation is more complicated than that, because different people have different conceptions of what moral values are (even if most people's conceptions are only implicit, never spelt out even to themselves).

So we can say that there are different kinds of significance that moral values can have for people. It would be a mistake to think that the variations are only on an individual level. Having certain ideas of the nature and significance of moral values may be shared quite widely across a culture, and may indeed be part of what differentiates one culture from another; but for convenience I shall speak in this chapter of the significance as it appears to individuals.

A person, for instance, who thinks in terms of simple and general rules of behaviour, which admit of no exceptions, has a different conception of morality from one whose approach, explicitly or implicitly, is in terms of a plurality of values that have to be realized as fully as possible within a given situation (there will be more on this contrast in Chapter 5 and again in Part III). A person who sees the values they recognize as being both objectively and universally valid attaches a different significance to those values from someone who sees their values as the conventions of a society of which they happen to be a member. The difference is not necessarily that one person attaches *greater* importance to their values than the other; the difference is qualitative rather than quantitative. The person who sees their values as the values of their culture, rather than being universally valid, may still be very attached to those values, and care greatly about them. Conversely, the person who sees their moral values as being universally valid may nevertheless in practice not care very deeply about them. (For all those people who pay lip-service to the idea of universal human rights, there must be relatively few who are actively trying to do something about ensuring that they are respected everywhere).

Probably the most striking difference, and one that is very important educationally, is that for some people moral ideas are intimately tied up with religious ones, while for others they are not. The most obvious difference this makes is that people who have no religious belief cannot attach any religious significance to their moral values. They may see certain values as having some special kind of importance, but they are likely to have more difficulty than religious believers in saying much about the nature of this importance, whereas for religious believers it is likely that the special importance of certain values will be spelt out in religious terms. There is still room, even given some religious connection, for different kinds of significance: for instance, the idea that moral requirements simply are commands of God is only one kind of account, which (to many Christians at any rate) would not be the most plausible. Yet in one way or another it remains true that in the thought and experience of a believer it is possible for an offence against moral value to be at the same time an offence against religion, whereas for a non-believer this, obviously, is not possible. (There will be more in Chapters 4 and 8 about the ways in which moral values can have religious significance.)

I suggested above that one kind of difference between moral and non-moral values would rest in the kinds of reason that can be given for them. We can now see the importance of recognizing at least two different kinds of reason that can back up moral values. For religious believers, the fact (if there are such facts) that something is against the divine order of things – against what is experienced or believed to be the divine order – may be sufficient to make it morally wrong. For non-believers, it may be that the only kind of reason that can make something morally wrong is that it is in some way bad for other people (or animals), hurts other people (or animals) or shows disrespect for people. Both these kinds of reason appeal to something outside of the individual's own interests and preferences. But their differences are important too, and underlie a lot of disagreement about values in a plural society, where for many liberal and secular thinkers the *only* question of moral relevance about anything is 'does it do any harm?' For some religious thinkers, on the other hand, that question would be largely missing the point.

Some secular thinkers may want to confine the notion of moral values to ones that they can justify in their own particular way. I think they do not have good reason for that, any more than religious thinkers would have good reason for not counting as moral values anything that was not backed up in *their* way. 'What kind of values count as moral values' is a question that may be answered, in various contexts, by an appeal to any of the features I have mentioned above. As a matter of empirical fact, it will be the case for many people (though perhaps a minority in the UK) that the values they see as most important, as making claims on them independently of their own preferences, and so on, will be experienced as having a religious significance. Furthermore, the reasons they would give, if pressed, for the importance of these values would be couched in religious terms. At the same time, they may use the word 'moral' of these values. Where the connotations of the word 'moral' are established by long usage, there is no more justification for secular thinkers to try to wrest it away from religious believers than there is for religious believers to try to deny the word to those who use it within a secular framework. This does not, of course, prevent secular and religious thinkers from disagreeing in some cases, from their different perspectives, about what is right and what is wrong.

Objectivity, relativism and rights – a cautionary note on terminology

Specialized terminology is often indispensable for specialists when they are talking to each other, and where there can be a precise definition of terms. But while there *are* people who specialize in talking and writing about moral matters – including moral philosophers, moral theologians, psychologists studying moral development, and others – they do not share a specialized, agreed vocabulary. Instead, there are terms that have either been borrowed from everyday language in the first place or have made their way back into it, terms that anybody may use when they get into talking about moral values, but which have no agreed technical definition. I mean terms like 'absolute', 'relative', 'subjective', 'objective', and 'universal' – to which we can add the idea of 'rights'. It may be useful to say more about such terms here – but only to show how easily they can be misleading, and as a guide to your own thinking if you still feel the need for these terms.

Of the examples mentioned, objective/subjective and absolute/relative provide a useful pairing, giving us two dimensions with two opposing positions on each. But sometimes people use 'objective' as more or less equivalent to 'absolute', and 'subjective' as more or less equivalent to 'relative', while they may use 'universal' as more or less equivalent to 'absolute' too – in which case five terms are only serving to mark one distinction, which seems a waste of resources.

'Objective' and 'subjective'
'Objective' may be used of claims or beliefs that can be true (or false) independently of the thoughts, feelings or viewpoint of the person who makes the claim or has the belief. The simplest and least controversial examples we can give of objective truths will be

descriptions of states of affairs in the physical world: for example, the structure of the solar system. We can use the term 'objective' here because we assume that there is an actual state of affairs, a part of reality, which is independent of what anyone thinks. Notice that the idea that something is objectively true (using the term in this way) is not the same as the idea that we are *certain* of its truth. Things we are certain of may turn out to be false (many people used to be certain that the sun revolved around the earth). The point about objectivity (as I am using the term now) is that the truth or falsity of something does not depend on what we think or feel about it – and that means, among other things, that it does not depend on whether we feel certain or uncertain about it, or even on whether we agree about it. There is (we assume when we speak of objectivity in this way) a fact of the matter, even if we do not know what the fact of the matter is. That there was a time when people disagreed about the movements of the earth and the sun does nothing to show that their movement is not a matter of objective fact.

So what is 'subjective'? My preference for sugarless coffee is surely subjective – it is literally a matter of taste. But already we need to be careful. It is a fact that I prefer coffee without sugar. That it is a fact specifically about me – about an individual person – does not by itself make it any less a fact. Like other facts, I can tell it to you, and you can learn it. What is *not* a fact is that coffee tastes better without sugar, full stop.

What, then, of values, and moral values in particular? There are many facts about people's values, just as there are facts about people's tastes. And one fact is that, on some matters, different people think different things: for example, some people think that capital punishment is right in certain circumstances and some people think that it is always wrong. But just as in the earlier example of the time when people disagreed about whether the earth revolved around the sun, the fact that people disagree does not by itself mean that the whole matter is subjective. When people say that capital punishment is wrong, they usually mean to convey, or they simply assume, that its being wrong is *not* dependent on what they, or anyone else, thinks. If they really think it is wrong in this way – objectively – they will be willing to say 'it will still be wrong, even if everyone – including me – misguidedly comes to think it is right.' Or when someone changes their mind about the morality of capital punishment, they do not think it is the morality of capital punishment that has changed; they think that they were mistaken about it before. There is no inconsistency, then, in someone recognizing that people have different views about the rightness or wrongness of capital punishment, and still maintaining that there is an objective truth of the matter.

But suppose someone says that while there might be an objective truth of the matter, we have no *objective procedure* by which we can find this truth. Here we are shifting towards a different sense of 'objective':[3] when someone says that there is no objective truth in moral matters, they could mean *not* that there is no truth of the matter at all but (merely) that there is no truth *that can be established in the way that the claims of science are established.* If that is what someone means when denying objectivity to values, their claim may not be very controversial. I said that the simplest examples we can give of objective matters of fact are of states of affairs in the physical world. If values have a real existence, they do not manifest it in the way that trees and rocks do, or even in the way that electrons and electromagnetic forces do; if there is an objective fact of the matter about values, we do not have the same kind of procedure – sense perception, hypotheses and the experimental testing of hypotheses – for establishing it.[4]

But there is quite another and perhaps more promising way in which it might be possible to establish an objective truth about moral values without having to say that they exist in the world. If this sounds paradoxical, think of mathematics. At least at the level taught in school, there are plenty of objective truths in maths: '7 + 5 = 12' is correct, and is about as objective as one can get; there really is not much room for dispute over it. But to say that is not to take any particular position about *how* there can be objective truths in maths, and it certainly does not commit us to believing that numbers, or sums or answers really exist in the world in some way that is quite independent of the fact that there are people doing mathematics. If intelligent beings had never evolved on earth, would it still be true that 7 + 5 = 12? What to make of that question, what sort of reality mathematical truths have and whether they are timeless, is open to interpretation and argument (pursued within one of the more esoteric branches of philosophy). But we do not have to be able to understand the philosophy of mathematics in order to treat maths as a field in which there are objective truths. In effect, we can here run the first two senses of 'objective' together. We do have objective procedures for establishing answers in mathematics – not the same procedures as those of empirical sciences, but if anything more clear-cut – and that may be enough to entitle us to speak of objective truth here.

In the same sort of way, the question 'if human beings had never existed, would it still be true that human dignity matters?' is one that it is difficult to make sense of. (Perhaps it would be possible to make sense of it within a theological perspective by referring to the timeless perspective of God.) But we do exist, and we do have moral ideas and systems, and *if* within those systems we have procedures, ways of thinking, by which we can arrive at answers about certain values, then that may be enough to entitle us to speak of objectivity. It would make a difference here whether we thought that we had ways of thinking that would, if they were properly followed, lead everyone to the same answers. In the case of truths about the physical world, as we have seen, we can make sense of the idea that while everyone agrees, everyone *could* be wrong. In the case of mathematics, however, it is not clear that we can make sense of this (could everyone be wrong in thinking that $7 + 5 = 12$?). What, again, of moral values? If *everyone* had reasons for thinking that, say, torture is wrong, could everyone be wrong about this?

Perhaps it would still depend on what *kind* of reasons people had for thinking this. This brings us to yet a third (related) sense of 'objectivity': the idea of persons being objective in the way they look at and think about something – that is, adopting an unbiased standpoint detached from their own particular preferences and inclinations. It is very plausible that objectivity in this sense would form part of any way of thinking that would be able to lead people to agree on moral values. I shall refer again to this third sense of objectivity in Chapter 7 when I defend morality against some of its critics.

'Relative' and 'absolute'

As with 'objective' and 'subjective' it is probably best to clarify the terms 'relative' and 'absolute' in contrast to each other. But first, I want to put on one side the fact that people sometimes use the word 'relative' to make a contrast, not with 'absolute' but with 'universal' in one of its meanings. It is a matter of fact that different people in different parts of the world, at different times and in different cultures, hold or have held different moral beliefs (on infanticide, for instance, or even on head-hunting).[5] Sometimes when people say that values are relative they intend no more than to report this fact of actual variation. The contrast to that would be to say that some values are universal, meaning that everyone shares them. Whether there are any values that are universal *in this sense* is a question of fact, which could be settled by reports from anthropologists, sociologists and so on. It may be that there are no values that literally *everyone* holds (since 'everyone', if we mean it literally, would have to include, for instance, psychopaths). But there may be some values that exist in every human culture. And it is consistent with this that there may also be considerable variation. In this factual sense, we can say that some values are universal and others are relative, and neither statement should be very controversial.

What I said above about objectivity should show that the fact that there is variation in the values people hold does not by itself mean that there is no objective truth of the matter (faced with the fact that some people think it is right and meritorious to cut off the heads of people from the next village, we still have the possibility of saying that they are wrong). The word 'relative' has a more distinctive role when we use it to say that there are some truths that are objective *but also* relative to the context. That July is one of the summer months is true, but this truth is relative to geography (it is true in the northern hemisphere but not in the southern). When a weather forecaster, standing in front of a map of England that shows a temperature of 35°C says 'it will be hot today', this is not a subjective report but it *is* relative. It is relative to what the inhabitants of England have come to expect, and it is also, in a wider sense, relative to the range of ambient temperatures that human beings are adapted to (inside an oven 35°C would be rather cool). Judgements of hot and cold are always relative to something, with the exception of the physicists' 'absolute zero'.

That scientific phrase illustrates the best use for the term 'absolute' – to indicate that something is not relative to anything else at all. Unfortunately, where values are concerned the same values might be relative (and therefore not absolute) in respect to some things but not others. The least misleading use for the idea of values being relative is to say that they are relative to cultures. This is very different from saying that 'anything goes'; rather it is saying, quite objectively, that there are some things that go and some that do not, but that what these things are is relative to culture or tradition. If, for example, you were to say that it is wrong (and you meant that it *is* wrong, not just that it is considered wrong) for a Muslim girl to marry someone her parents do not approve of, but not wrong for a non-Muslim girl, you would be expressing a relativist view of this kind.

The most thoroughgoing account of values as absolutes is, I think, that of the philosopher Kant (whom we shall encounter again from time to time). He held that there are moral imperatives that are binding on any being capable of following them – that is, on any rational being, not just on human beings. It would, for instance, be wrong for any being that is capable of communicating truth or falsehood to tell a lie (so if you meet aliens from a flying saucer, you know that it would be wrong for them to lie to you). Many people probably consider that there are moral values that apply to all human beings by virtue of something to do with human nature; Kant could have labelled these people as relativists. For his own part, Kant was the most uncompromising kind of absolutist, holding that there are moral truths that are not relative to anything to do specifically with human nature or the human condition.

In Kant's account it was also the case that the application of a moral imperative could not be relative to particular circumstances – in other words, if it is wrong to tell a lie, it is wrong full stop, without exceptions. Yet it does seem possible to distinguish here two notions of absolute values, which correspond to different respects in which values can be relative. We might want to say that truthfulness is always and everywhere an important value – in that way it would be absolute, not dependent on culture – but at the same time, we may want to stress that its importance could in a particular case be outweighed by other values (such as saving life).[6] Thus, the rule 'never tell a lie' would *not* be a rule with no exceptions (the distinction between rules and principles can be helpful here: while we may not accept 'never tell a lie' as a rule without exceptions, we can still say that truthfulness is an important principle that should never be treated lightly).

Unfortunately, when people speak of moral absolutes, it is often unclear whether they mean that there are values that are not relative to culture, or that there are rules that can never admit of an exception. The second position – that rules such as 'don't tell lies' or 'keep your promises' or even 'don't deliberately take the life of an innocent person' could *never*, under any conceivable circumstances, have a justified (even if tragic) exception – is one that probably few people hold.

'Universal'

We have already looked at one definition of the term 'universal values' – namely, the rather implausible belief that there are values that are actually held or recognized by everyone. But another sense of 'universal' is to say that a value *applies* to everyone (which makes it almost equivalent to 'absolute' in the sense of 'not relative to culture'). For example, the right not to be tortured is *not* a value that is universal in the first sense, since there are apparently people who do not recognize or respect it. But if you say that it is universal in the second sense, you mean that it applies to *everyone*, that everyone (regardless of race, religion, culture and so on) has the right not to be tortured. It follows from this that everyone *ought* to recognize and respect the right not to be tortured, but that is quite different from saying that everyone does in fact recognize and respect it.

Rights

Since the notion of human rights is so often associated with the idea of universality (as in the Universal Declaration of Human Rights), this is an appropriate place to say a little more about the notion of rights, which will figure again from time to time in these pages just because it is such a common part of contemporary moral discourse. Talk of rights as such does not necessarily imply any kind of universality. There are plenty of cases of recognized rights that do not apply to everyone in the world: a British citizen's right to vote in elections for the UK Parliament, for instance.

Nor are rights necessarily *moral* rights. In fact the clearest cases of rights are the legal rights that are established within particular legal systems, and these are open to moral criticism. Thus, slaves in the southern United States, or Jews in Nazi Germany, had severely curtailed legal rights, but this does not commit us at all to saying that they lacked the same moral rights as other people.

Whether we are thinking in legal or moral terms, a useful distinction is between rights that are matters of people's freedom to do what they want, and rights that involve claims on other people to make some positive provision. If you are unmarried you have (in the view of most but not all cultural traditions) a right to decide whether to marry and if so whom to marry; but you do not have a right to have a suitable spouse supplied for you. On the other hand, a child's right to education is not, or not only, that child's right to seek out education for himself or herself; it is a right to have educational facilities provided.

There are many other important distinctions and clarifications to be made in understanding the idea of rights, but this is not the place for an extended discussion, partly because any adequate discussion would have to go some way into legal and political, not just moral, philosophy. Perhaps the most important point in this context is to recognize the way that talk about rights tends to function: it is used to block other kinds of reason that might be given for some decision or policy. So, for example, calculations of convenience and cost might indicate to a government that the best educational policy would be one that (unfortunately) left some disabled children without adequate educational provision. The claim that these children have a moral right to an adequate education functions as an argument that the considerations of convenience and cost should not be final.

Even the little that has been said here is enough to show that talk about rights, like talk about objectivity, subjectivity, relativism – and indeed talk about moral values generally – needs to be treated with care. Like so many other notions, the notion of rights can cause confusion or stalemate unless the parties to discussion are clear about how they are using the term. Human rights, children's rights, citizens' rights, animal rights, the right to life, a woman's right to choose (whether to continue with a pregnancy), the right to holidays with pay, the rights of trees, and the rights of criminals to be punished – all and many more rights have been claimed. To go no further than bare assertion about rights – as when one side in the controversy over abortion asserts a woman's right to choose and the other asserts a foetus's right to life – leads only to an impasse. In such cases it is better either to avoid the word, or to be prepared to look in detail at what it means to attribute a right to someone or something, at who has which rights, and how we can decide that.[7]

What I have said here about some difficult notions will hardly have cleared them up, but it may at least have shown why they can cause trouble (and why my arguments in this book will rarely rely on them, although I shall find it useful in places to refer to the different senses of objectivity, and mention of rights will be unavoidable). I would suggest that before embarking on any discussion of moral values in which notions of relativism, moral absolutes, moral rights and so on are likely to come up, you should establish the extent of people's understanding of these terms. If there is clarity and agreement about the meaning of the terms, well and good: these terms will then serve as useful tools for the discussion. But if, as is more likely, the meanings are unclear, or the words mean different things to different people, then spend some time, if there is time available, trying to get some shared understanding on how you are going to use the terms. But to do that adequately does take time and care. If there is too little time available, then it is probably better to avoid these terms altogether. It should be possible for anyone to convey the meaning they wish to convey in a more straightforward language that makes fewer assumptions.

[1] I have developed the distinction between rules and principles further in Haydon (1999b), Chapter 9.

[2] See, for example, Schama (1995).

[3] There are intelligible connections between the different senses I am picking out, but to trace them here would be too complex a process for this context.

[4] I say little here about the question of whether moral values have some kind of real existence in the world, and if so, what kind. This is because, so far as I am aware, the notions of moral 'realism' and 'non-realism', in that terminology, are largely confined to philosophical debate. (This technical notion of 'moral realism' is, of course, different from the sense of a realist as someone who takes pride in not expecting very much by way of moral behaviour from actual human beings in real-life situations.) I am doubtful whether we can make sense of the notion of values having a real existence independently of human thought unless we are seeing values as in some way attributes of a (really existing) God – and even then the interpretation may be difficult. I have a little more to say in Chapter 8 about whether a denial of the real existence of moral values need make any difference to our sense of morality.

[5] 'A European peasant, beheading a woman from a neighbouring village whom he happened to encounter on his way home from the fields, would be locked up as a criminal lunatic; whereas in a Naga village a

youth returning with a human head captured under similar circumstances earns the insignia of a successful headhunter.' Von Fuerer-Haimendorf (1967:1); see also *ibid.* pp. 97–101. No doubt 'earns' ought now to be in the past tense.

[6] I have in mind here an example of Kant's, which I shall refer to in Chapter 5.

[7] For more on rights, see Waldron (1984, 1993); and in an educational context, Snook and Lankshear (1979); Wringe (1981); Haydon (1993a).

Chapter 4

Conflict and Plurality in Values

What do values have to do with conflict? The first answer is that they may help to reduce conflict; the second is that they may cause conflict. We shall look at both connections here, and in doing that there will be more to be said about value-pluralism.

Values as a conflict-avoidance device

In Chapter 2 I mentioned Hobbes' claim that human beings, left to their own individual devices, would lead a life that was 'nasty, brutish and short'. In Hobbes' view, the world being as it is and human beings as they are, the potential for conflict is always there and has to be restrained.

What are the sources of this potential conflict?[1] Some of the sources lie in the nature of the world we live in: what we want does not automatically come our way; we have to make efforts to acquire what may be in short supply, and in demand by others as well. This by itself would not necessarily lead to conflict, if it came naturally to human beings to resolve amicably and cooperatively any difficulties which the nature of the world lays upon them. But in fact it may seem[2] that human beings are essentially concerned with their own individual interests, and often take a short-term view of those. Besides, while the pursuit of individual self-interest is enough to produce conflict, there is also among the motivations of human beings sometimes an active malevolence towards others. And, further, there are limitations in human capacities: in knowledge and intelligence, understanding and imagination.

If this is the human condition, something is needed to prevent human life being always and everywhere 'nasty, brutish and short'. Morality, in this picture, is part of what is needed. Not that an established moral system would be sufficient in itself to prevent conflict: for Hobbes, only a human authority, endowed with enough coercive power to keep people in check through the making and enforcement of laws, would suffice. But there are many forms of self-restraint that can hardly be enforced by law; moral prohibitions, and not only legal ones, can deter people from doing what, in the absence of the moral prohibitions, they would do at others' expense. I shall refer to this as the Hobbesian picture of morality; it approximates to what elsewhere, following several other writers, I have called 'morality in the narrow sense'.[3]

This, then, is the sense in which moral values can be seen as one factor in reducing the level of conflict among human beings below what it might otherwise be. If everyone were to pursue his or her own advantage or immediate desires amorally, there might be far more overt conflict between people than we actually experience. Morality on the Hobbesian picture is that set of values that is necessary in order to contain the potential conflict: it will consist of basic prohibitions on killing, assault, theft, lying, promise-breaking and the like; or perhaps of an all-purpose set of virtues.[4] This picture is still quite powerfully operative in our culture. It is there, for instance, when public figures, condemning, say, an increase in vandalism and theft among young people, call on parents and schools to reinforce moral values as the way of reducing anti-social behaviour. (The conflict here may be seen as between individuals and society, or between different groups of individuals, as when rival gangs clash in street fights, and the harm to the wider society is, from their point of view, a by-product.) The more firmly moral values are instilled in people, the less, in this view, will be the conflict. It is a simple picture, and one that seems to give a clear-cut role to education – or at least to schools.

Values as a cause of conflict

Unfortunately, this picture is far too simple. Education in modern societies has to take the existence of a plurality of values into account, and so it cannot neglect the fact that there can be conflict *between* values. Indeed, values will sometimes be the very factors that lead people into conflict. So if we put a positive value on avoiding conflict between people, we have very practical reasons for seeing whether education can prepare people to live in a society in which there are different values in play. The first step will be to understand more about how people's values can lead to conflict.

That possibility may seem paradoxical if we start by taking the Hobbesian picture for granted. How can moral values, which have to do with restraining one's own wants and putting weight on the interests of others, actually bring people into conflict? It is a clear fact of experience in plural societies that some conflicts arise because of differences in the moral values to which people adhere. In clarifying this point, I need first to say something about the sense of 'conflict' that I have in mind; then I shall go on to give some examples and look at what it is about moral values in particular that can lead to conflict.

There is a sense in which we can speak of conflict between values themselves. It is often said, for instance, that there is a conflict at a social level between freedom and equality, meaning that equality cannot be realized within society without (too much) restriction on people's freedom (I am using this as an example of the kind of thing that is said, without necessarily endorsing it).[5] There can be a conflict at an individual level between honesty and kindness, as when we wonder whether to tell someone an unpleasant truth. It seems a familiar part of experience that values can conflict in this way,[6] though it is worth noting that this brings some complication to the simple Hobbesian picture; if morality is viewed as a kind of device for reducing conflict between persons, there would seem to be a deficiency in the 'design' of the device if it cannot work without producing its own internal conflicts. Conflict of values in this sense, though, which may be experienced by a single person, does not necessarily lead to interpersonal conflict. Here I am going to concentrate on conflicts between persons which arise because different people adhere to different moral values.

That such cases of interpersonal conflict do frequently occur is part of what it means to speak of a plural society. We can, if we like, say that there is an inevitable kind of conflict here (as when we speak of conflicting opinions or conflicting points of view). Since there are many reasons for welcoming the existence of plural societies, we do not have to say that conflict in this sense is undesirable. Indeed, with the benefit of hindsight over the longer term, we can recognize that conflict of moral positions can be a positive advantage to a society. Changes which would now almost universally be recognized as constituting moral progress – the ending of slavery, the enfranchisement of women – would not have come about if everyone in society had remained content with the *status quo*. Such changes generally have begun with a minority whose views conflict with those of the majority, or with those whose entrenched positions favour the old order. But while, with hindsight, there might be general agreement that a particular conflict over values had been resolved in the right direction, at the time it is part of the essence of the conflict that the persons in disagreement cannot at the same time stand back and take a common view on what would be a satisfactory resolution. In such cases there will sometimes be a resort to violence – as we have seen in the cases of abortion in the United States and the treatment of animals in Britain. (In Chapter 9 I shall ask whether the resort to violence can ever be justified.)

What is it about values, and moral values in particular, that is liable to lead to conflict? We can establish at least part of the answer to this by looking back at some of the features that distinguish moral values from other kinds, which I picked out in the previous chapter. For instance, that moral values are perceived by people as important: if that were not so, conflict about them would be less likely, for people are less likely to fight about what they themselves see as trivial. (Some people, as I have suggested, do not spontaneously think of what they *call* 'moral' values as important; such people may be liberals of a certain kind, and their tendency to disclaim the importance of 'moral' values, which to other people seem vital, may be part of the difficulty that some liberals have in seeing why anyone should fight over moral values. But, to repeat, liberals who take this view are likely after all to have some values – perhaps not the ones that immediately occur to them as examples, but values such as tolerance or respect for diversity – which do function for them as moral values.)

Moral values are perceived by people as not just a matter of individual preference. If they were, conflict over them would again be less likely. Examples like that of coffee with or without sugar may suggest that this is the same point as the one about importance; but it is different. Some matters of individual preference may be very important, even central, to the lives of the persons concerned. This may be true, for instance, of a career or lifestyle or lifelong ambition. But there is a sense in which what is important in my life may still be something that I do not think is particularly important in itself. ('It may be of the greatest importance to Henry that his stamp collection be completed with a certain stamp, but even Henry may see that it is not, simply, important' – or important, full stop.[7]) Someone whose life would seem meaningless without risk and adventure might still recognize that this is a personal preference, and need not think that it should be shared by everyone (he might indeed acknowledge that it is better that it is not shared by everyone). But a man who thinks it important that unborn children should not be killed does not (just) think this is important *for him*. People are more likely to get into conflict over things they think are *important*, full stop, than over things that are just important for them (at least if they do not see other people as restricting their pursuit of what is important for them).

The sense that moral values have some kind of objectivity means that one person can consider another to be wrong. 'Wrong' can have a double sense here. First, it can mean morally wrong, immoral; in this sense, when one person thinks that another is acting wrongly, there is not necessarily any *conflict* of moral values. It is commonly acknowledged that people sometimes act against their own moral values, doing what they themselves believe to be wrong. In the person acting this way there may be an internal conflict, perhaps between self-interest and moral obligation, but there need be no conflict of values between this person and another who criticizes her conduct; they may both share the same standards.

But secondly, 'wrong' can also have the sense of 'incorrect'; the person criticizing may think that the other's values are wrong. And the two kinds of judgement can be combined: the critic may think not merely that the other's values are incorrect, but that the other is culpable for having the wrong values. Perhaps it is this kind of judgement more than any other (particularly when linked with religious belief, a link we shall come back to) which has led people to believe they are justified in persecuting others over their moral differences.

I said too that moral values, unlike some values, are to do with how people behave. Moral values are values that people at least to some extent live by, or think they ought to; and (because these values are seen as making some sort of claim independently of preference) people tend to expect others to live by them too. This means that differences over moral values are not like some differences of opinion, which may have no practical consequences even when expressed in conversation. Differences in moral values are to some degree differences in ways of living; and differences in ways of living are a more potent source of conflict than differences in opinion as such. For example, someone who can tolerate the expression of an opinion with which they disagree may find it more difficult to tolerate the fact that other people are actually living in ways they disapprove of.

But what is probably more important is that much of morality concerns a person's conduct towards others. The conduct that a critic believes to be wrong may be conduct that (in the critic's eyes) has victims. (Some liberal-minded people find it difficult to see any conduct as wrong if it has no victim.) No one suggests that someone who believes there is nothing wrong with murder should be allowed simply to live out this alternative policy. But perhaps it is too often forgotten by liberal-minded people that the person who believes that abortion is murder can hardly view policies that are favourable towards abortion as innocent expressions of an alternative lifestyle; and much the same goes for the person who condemns vivisection. (This will be relevant in Chapters 5 and 9 when we look at the scope for compromise over different kinds of moral issues.)

Moral values, culture and religion

If the features of moral values that I have mentioned are ones that are liable to lead to conflict over differences in values, it hardly follows that such conflict could be avoided by doing away with these features. For such features seem to be central to much of our experience of morality; and there is probably enough truth in the Hobbesian model to suggest that a world lacking in morality would be unlikely to be a world with less conflict in total (a question to be followed up in Part III).

But one thing we must now notice about the Hobbesian model is that it purports to pick out features of the human condition, tending to lead to conflict, which are universal; and hence the kind of morality looked to as a remedy would also be universal. If the simple Hobbesian picture were correct, we should expect to find moral values the same everywhere. I shall not here try to resolve the debate, mentioned briefly in the previous chapter, on how much in actual human values is in fact universally shared; but it is certainly true that there are cultural differences. Possibly the most plausible way of looking at these differences is to note that while there may be universal features of the human condition that are likely to lead to problems in the absence of a recognized moral code, there may be more than one possible code that will serve to mitigate these problems. Thus, it is certainly something about the nature of human sexuality which leads to every culture (even the most liberal) having some set of moral conventions about what sexual conduct is or is not acceptable; but there is more than one possible set of conventions that can prove more or less workable (where what is 'workable' is largely a matter of what enables the culture to continue).[8]

It should not be surprising then that different cultures have different conventions; or rather, different conventions have developed in different human populations, and it is such differences that in part define different cultures. This is not in itself any kind of problem; even the possibility of its leading to problems only arises when cultures come into contact with each other, and particularly when members of different cultures are living in proximity (this is not intended as an argument for trying to keep societies culturally homogeneous, even if there were any possibility of doing that). As the possession of a particular set of moral values is one of the factors that constitute a human culture, so it is one of the factors that constitutes the cultural identity of individuals. Sharing a common set of values is part of what gives members of one culture a sense of belonging together; and recognizing differences between their values and those of others is part of what can give a sense of other cultures being alien. In a plural society, this fact is perhaps one of the most potent ways in which differences in values turn into conflict between persons. People's moral values can be of central importance to them, not just because these are the values that they as individuals hold, but because these values partly define their being the kind of persons they are. When people find that some of their values are opposed by others in their society, they may feel that they themselves and their culture are threatened – especially if they are already in a minority in their society.

What has just been said applies especially when the values in question are integral to a person's religion. It would be greatly oversimplifying, of course, to suggest that actual conflicts in the world which we may identify as religious are entirely about religion. Whatever example we take, we are likely to find a variety of political, historical and often economic factors (Northern Ireland is a case in point). But sometimes a degree of simplification can be an aid to understanding, and I want here to make just such an initial simplification by focusing on the religious aspect of certain conflicts, in order to ask the question, difficult enough in itself, of how far a religious conflict is a conflict over values.

I think it would be widely agreed that to have a religion is not just a matter of holding certain beliefs about the existence of God or other metaphysical matters; it is also a matter of being committed to particular values (where the commitment, naturally, does allow of degrees). It is rather artificial to speak of beliefs and values as if they were separable, but it does allow us to recognize that it is not just because of differences in beliefs, as such, that people are likely to come into conflict. Some people believe that there is intelligent life on other planets, others that there is not; we do not find rival groups fighting over these beliefs.

If it is largely because of their differences over values that adherents to different religions sometimes come into conflict, then the points already made, about why values can bring people into conflict, will be part of the explanation of religious conflict too. No doubt this is too crude a way of putting it; it would be better to say, without suggesting that beliefs and values can be separated, that the beliefs already carry evaluative import. Or we could turn this round and say that the values are given their particular significance by the beliefs. Either way, the point is that the religious context of values can make a difference not only to the content of people's values but also to their significance.

It may come naturally to assume that conflict over values arises because of differences in the *content* of people's values – such as the difference between the orthodox Roman Catholic position on artificial contraception and a standard liberal position – but what may be even more likely to generate conflict is not that people's values tell them to do different things, but that the values have different sorts of significance for different people. I pointed out some of these differences in the previous chapter, but we need now to see how they can lead people into conflict. For the most part, differences between various non-religious interpretations of values do not tend towards conflict, though there is an argument, long made by some theorists of liberalism,[9] that conflict is more likely to ensue when people see their values, not simply as being the values of their own culture, but as having objective and universal force, since they must then see others as wrong and are thereby going to find it difficult to tolerate them. But this danger of intolerance, though it can apply independently of any religious interpretation being attached to values, may itself be heightened where values are perceived as having religious significance. So it is to the potential for conflict in the perceived religious significance of values that I now turn.

To repeat, the differences over values between religious believers and non-believers are not necessarily differences in the content of the values. A Christian and an atheist, for instance, may to a large extent be in favour of and against the same things. And it is also, of course, possible for both of them either to follow the values they acknowledge consistently or sometimes to go against their own values. But going against one's own values cannot, for the atheist, be disobedience to God, or violation of a divinely ordained order, or *sin*. And this in turn affects the perceived importance of the values. It is not that the moral values of the atheist cannot be, to the atheist, of supreme importance, for they may well be paramount within his or her scale of values; it is rather that the very nature of supreme importance is different for the religious believer: right and wrong – at least on matters on which the religion pronounces – will have a cosmic significance that they cannot have for the non-believer.

This difference in significance would not by itself yield the potential for conflict, but it can when coupled with two other factors that are particularly associated with a religious point of view (though they are not exclusive to it). One is the degree of confidence with which one's moral convictions are held. The secular moralist, aware of how much people can differ in their values, and that other apparently reasonable people hold values different from their own, may always retain some room for the thought that others might be right after all. But the believer who has a quite unshakeable religious faith may by the same token have the strongest possible conviction of the correctness of certain moral positions. The second factor is having the strength of motivation to act on the values one acknowledges. In part, this interacts with the first factor: the stronger the conviction the stronger may be the motivation to act. And there is also another way in which the different significance of moral values for the religious believer can make a motivational difference, in that there are motives, whether love of God or fear of God, that are only available to the believer. To the extent that the believer's relation to God is the most important facet of the believer's life, so it may furnish the strongest possible motivation.

In pointing to differences between religious and non-religious interpretations of values, I should not neglect the differences between different religious interpretations. Within the theistic religions, perhaps the most significant difference is between the outlooks of those who regard moral values, in the end, as a matter of individual conscience (though it would be misleading to call them in this context a matter of individual choice[10]) and those for whom moral values are essentially a matter of authority. To approach a moral dilemma as one on which we must ultimately make up our own mind, or to approach it as one on which we can look to scripture or a spiritual leader, are two very different understandings of moral values. Of the major world religions it is probably Islam, in its more fundamentalist tendencies, that has gone furthest in stressing the need for the believer to submit his will to God's. Within Christianity, however, even in its Protestant manifestation, there is all the variation from the most fundamentalist attempt to rely on the words of the Bible to the most liberal stress on the decision of individual conscience in the actual circumstances at hand;[11] but by and large there has been a cross-fertilization between Christianity and modern moral and political liberalism that might not be possible to the same extent within Islam. As regards the non-theistic religions, necessarily they cannot have the conception of moral action as being in conformity with the will of God, but it can still be true that for Hinduism or Buddhism, under their non-theistic interpretations a moral life will be a life that is in conformity with the true nature of the world; and that significance is not on the face of it available to a secular and materialist worldview.[12]

But while there are differences between religions, it is possible that in modern plural societies their importance is outweighed by the differences between religious and non-religiously based interpretations of values. This is reflected, for instance, in the choice that British Muslims not infrequently make, when an Islamic school is not available, to send their children to a Roman Catholic rather than a secular school, and in the fact that non-Christian religious communities in Britain by no means necessarily support the disestablishment of the Church of England.[13]

It would be a mistake, of course, to think that all the differences in values between, say, Muslims of Asian origin and secular liberals within Britain correspond to the religious or non-religious basis of the values. There are values that demand an explanation in terms of broader cultural patterns, rather than by reference to scriptural authority: for example, some aspects of the role of women in South Asian societies, and of the status of children in different communities. There are cultural outlooks in which obedience is a major virtue and ones in which, outside of special cases, it may be looked on even with some suspicion, and this again does not seem to be primarily a religious difference. In parts of the Western world teenagers are almost expected to rebel against parental authority at some point; autonomy of the individual is a central value in some cultures and only a subordinate one in others. And there is a long-standing, though possibly overdrawn, anthropological distinction between cultures where moral thinking revolves around the idea of shame and those where it revolves around the idea of guilt.[14]

Even where a dispute arises explicitly in the context of religion, the values brought into play may be of broader cultural relevance. In general, the only way that liberals can make sense of offences against religion is to see them as causing offence to persons. They can then bring them under the general liberal principle that the law should only interfere in people's conduct in order to prevent harm being caused to others.[15] There are problems in interpreting offence as harm (as shown also in the debates over obscenity and pornography) but at least this perspective appears to bring offences against religion under the same conceptual scheme as other cases the liberal is used to dealing with. This appearance may, however, be superficial, since it may be difficult for the liberal to understand the nature of the perceived offence without sharing conceptions of honour and shame which have become relatively unimportant in Western society.[16]

I began this chapter by referring to the Hobbesian picture, by which moral values are essentially those which, if put into practice, will prevent the conflict which otherwise would arise among human beings pursuing their interests amorally. We can see now that this picture omits a large part of the total range of moral values; and that the values it omits are not merely at the periphery. It omits values which can for many people be fundamental to their moral outlook, indeed to their life.

[1] My answer here is not purely Hobbesian. Accounts that have some features in common include Hume (1888), Book III, Part II, Section 1; Hart (1961), Chapter 9; Warnock (1971), Chapter 2.

[2] I say 'may seem' because it is certainly open to dispute. Hobbes took himself to be an objective observer of human nature; a Marxist would point out that the human life that Hobbes observed, and the perspective from which he observed it, were those of a particular socio-economic context (early English capitalism). Marx, as we shall see in Chapter 6, thought that this context could be transcended: the motivations and behaviour appropriate to that socio-economic context were not a fixed part of human nature.

[3] For more on the idea of 'morality in the narrow sense' see Haydon (1999b), which refers to other writers including Bernard Williams and Charles Taylor who have written about morality in the narrow sense.

[4] See Warnock (1971), Chapter 6.

[5] For a discussion of whether equality and freedom in a political context must conflict, see Norman (1987), Chapter 7.

[6] See Hampshire (1983), Chapter 7; Taylor (1982); Williams (1981).

[7] Williams (1985: 182).

[8] See Hampshire (1983), Chapter 6.

[9] A classic argument is in Berlin (1969). There will be more on liberalism in Chapters 5 and 11.

[10] 'Conscience' here refers to an individual's own capacity for judgement. On why the exercise of an individual's capacity for judgement need not amount to individual 'choice' of values, see my comments on the ethics of Kant in Chapter 7.

[11] The situation ethics of Joseph Fletcher (1966) is an example.

[12] Some ethical positions within an ecological perspective may be an exception: see Chapter 8.

[13] Cf. Modood (1992), Chapter 11.

[14] The distinction was first drawn by Benedict (1946).

[15] This is the 'harm principle' that was given its classic expression by Mill (1962a; first published 1859).

[16] On the notion of honour see Berger (1983), and Chapter 12 below.

Chapter 5

Three Important Values: Compromise, Tolerance and Respect

In Chapter 4 I discussed the way that conflict can arise from the differences between people's values. In a plural society, education may have a potential for mitigating such a conflict, not by trying to demolish or weaken the potentially conflicting values, but by promoting still other values that help people to coexist with the values in which they differ. Two values that are often mentioned in this connection are tolerance and respect; another that is perhaps less often mentioned but nevertheless important is the willingness to compromise.

How we (nearly) all compromise on values

Attitudes towards compromise are ambivalent – not only within one society, but also often within one person's thinking. When we look in the next chapter at why some people are suspicious of the very idea of morality, we shall find it is partly because morality may be seen as rigid and uncompromising. Yet this can also seem an essential feature and strength of morality. While we can in some circumstances see a willingness to compromise as a positive value, we may also sometimes see a willingness to compromise on what one stands for as a sign of weakness; indeed, we will sometimes admire an uncompromising stand on moral principle.[1] We need, then, to look further at compromise in relation to values.

What I want to suggest here is that compromising over values should not cause us any special qualms, because there is a sense in which as individuals we all very frequently, and quite properly, compromise between different values. I shall start with these individual cases.

If all situations in which values come into play were ones in which just one value clearly applied, life would be much simpler than it is, and the question of compromise might not arise. In fact, cases where just one value applies are the exception. The first point to note is that it is easier to construct examples if we think in terms of rules, for it is these that can be most directly construed in an absolutist way ('absolute' in the sense of 'allowing no exceptions'). The rule 'never tell a lie, under any circumstances' at least makes sense in itself. By setting up this rule as an absolute, Kant was able to reach a notorious conclusion in a particular (imagined) example. Suppose a person seeks refuge in your house from a pursuer intent on killing him. The would-be murderer comes to your door and asks 'Is he here?' In Kant's view, you must not deny that he is in your house, for you must not tell a lie (though refusing to answer might be an option).[2] (As I shall make clear in Chapter 7, I do not by any means want to dismiss Kant's view of morality, but I think that we can hold on to what is central to his view without going along with this kind of absolutism.)

Many people react against Kant's conclusion, finding it absurdly rigoristic. Surely in such a case (many people will say) it would be justified to tell a lie, if this was the only way in which a murder could be avoided? What is going on when someone reacts in this way? I would say that, whether one sees it explicitly in these terms or not, one is recognizing the validity of a compromise. Kant's conclusion is uncompromising; he is not prepared to compromise the absolute imperative of not lying for the sake of any valuable end. Most people will think that other values must be allowed to come into play here, chiefly the value of the life of the victim (and also perhaps the value of preventing the would-be murderer from committing a heinous crime and sin). They will think that these other values take precedence in this case, as they outweigh the importance of not telling a lie. But this does not mean that the rule (or as we might better say, the principle) of not telling a lie ceases to have any force at all.

In one respect, this example is not a good one for my argument, since to many people it will not seem to constitute a serious dilemma, precisely because it will seem obvious that one ought to tell a lie in these circumstances. So I shall take an example that most people would recognize as a dilemma.[3] Frances, who trained as a research chemist, cannot get a job. She has two small children who are dependent on her. At last she is offered a well-paid job, with convenient hours, in a laboratory where research is being done on chemical weapons. On the one hand, she is opposed to chemical (or any other kind of) warfare, and dislikes the idea of contributing to it in any way. On the other hand, she is living in very difficult circumstances and she knows she will be able to give her children a better life if she takes the job. The director of the laboratory tells her that if she does not take the job it will go to another researcher whom she knew at university, and who she knows would have no compunction about working on chemical weapons; he can be expected to pursue this research with all possible efficiency. If she took the job, perhaps she would do it less effectively and, since she would rather the weapons were not produced at all, that would be better than letting her acquaintance do it. There is a dilemma here, of course, because more than one value comes into play. If it were clear that one consideration outweighs any of the others, the dilemma would be resolved. But often this is not clear. What people then tend to do is to try to balance the different considerations against each other, and take whatever course seems to allow due weight to all of the considerations (so far as possible). In other words, people effect a compromise between different values, the best they can see in the circumstances. In some cases, there will be one course of action available which in itself constitutes a compromise; if, for instance, you have to decide between devoting a long time or a short time to some activity, there may be some intermediate period of time you can opt for. Even in something like a choice of career, where you might start by considering two quite disparate alternatives, you might think of a possibility which combines some of the best features of each.

There are other cases, however – and the most serious dilemmas will often be of this type – in which so far as the outcome is concerned there is nothing that constitutes a compromise in itself. There is no intermediate between having and not having an abortion. But even in a case like this, the total context of relevant considerations and possible outcomes may be one in which compromise is not irrelevant. First, even an either/or decision is not necessarily made by the straightforward application of a single principle; many factors may be weighed up in arriving at it, and the alternative decided on may be chosen because it seems to satisfy rather more of the considerations than the other. Secondly, the dilemma may not present itself to the person concerned in such a sharp way. Even if having an abortion seems like one unitary course of action, not having an abortion could in a sense be many different things – depending on whether the child is kept or not kept and so on; and the woman who is not applying a single principle could well conclude that not to have an abortion would be the right thing *provided, but only provided*, she can be sure of various other factors.[4]

Sometimes it is suggested that the person who is willing to compromise is the one who tries to decide by weighing up which course of action will have the best consequences overall; while the person who will not compromise is the one who thinks that certain things are right or wrong in themselves, regardless of consequences. This characterization seems to fit Kant's example, but it is misleading. The person who genuinely thinks that he should always do what will have the best consequences in the circumstances is not a compromiser at all; he is, in the jargon, a strict consequentialist, or in slightly more familiar but less precise language, a strict utilitarian.[5] Such people are probably quite rare, and this no doubt has something to do with the fact that a strict consequentialism is among the most *uncompromising* moralities there can be. For it holds to just one principle: that what should be done is always the thing that will have the best consequences. If the consequences of some action involve, say, breaking a promise or telling a lie or even someone's death, these factors will not have any independent weight of their own; they can be taken into account, but only as some among the totality of consequences. The strict consequentialist does not compromise between the promotion of the best consequences overall and anything else.

In contrast, many of us are partial consequentialists and by the same token are constantly compromising. We do think it important to take the consequences of our actions into account, but there are other considerations to which we tend to give independent weight; we would rather avoid telling a lie or breaking a promise if we can, and this is not just because we think that telling lies and so on tends to lead to bad consequences. At least sometimes, we may give most weight to one of these other values; we may decide, for instance, that we had better tell the truth, even though we think the consequences would be better if we told a lie. Most of us do, I think, give weight to a number of values in this way, and so it is inevitable that we often have to make the best compromise we can between them. The person who would give to any single value the kind of overriding weight that Kant gave to the principle of not telling a lie (though even here I am simplifying Kant's position) is probably about as rare as the strict consequentialist. It is worth noting, too, that even if we try to avoid all reference to consequences we shall not evade the possibility of facing conflicts of values; for principles which do not themselves refer to consequences can come into conflict. You may find yourself in a situation in which you can avoid telling a lie, or avoid breaking a promise, but not both.[6]

These points about compromise do not depend on whether we talk about principles, or virtues or simply values. If, instead of talking about a principle of not telling lies and a principle of not breaking promises, we put it in terms of the virtue of honesty and the virtue of fidelity, or if we talk simply of the value of telling the truth and the value of keeping one's word, in all cases the substantial point remains. But it does seem to be true, as I said above, that the language of moral *rules* lends itself more easily to the impression that there is no compromise to be had. If we think, on the other hand, in terms of honesty and fidelity, we can think of these as qualities which we try to exemplify so far as we can, and we are less likely to feel that if we allow an exception in one case, we have betrayed the value in question altogether. We can care about these values without making exceptionless rules out of them. If, instead of saying to myself 'I must never tell a lie' and 'I must never break a promise', I say 'it is important, other things being equal, to tell the truth' and 'it is important, other things being equal, to keep my promises', then I am more likely to think that what is the best thing to do in particular circumstances is something that does not, so to speak, realize one of the values as fully as it might be realized ideally.

To some people it may seem that to move away from thinking in terms of absolutes is already to have compromised too far; though, as I have suggested, it is easier to say in theory that one would never compromise than to achieve this in practice. What we have here is an instance in which the way in which one sees one's own values, the kind of significance they have for one, will affect one's attitude towards compromise. But instead of illustrating this any further in the individual case, I want to turn to the cases in which the values in question are those being upheld by different persons.

Compromising with each other

Suppose first that some set of persons are members of a collective entity; they identify themselves as members of the group, and at least sometimes they think of themselves collectively as making decisions that are the decisions of the group. Many sorts of groups or institutions can be collective entities in this sense: the staff of a school, for example, or members of a parent–teachers association or residents of a local community. Suppose that the members of the collective entity have to make a decision that they see as raising moral issues. And suppose (as a simplification of greater complexity in real life) that each member puts forward just one moral consideration that he or she sees as being the one on which the decision should be based. Moreover, each member puts forward a different consideration, and the considerations pull in different directions. Since (I am supposing) they can meet face-to-face, they have the possibility of attempting to reach a consensus; but it is clear that a consensus will not be reached by fastening on just one consideration and ignoring all the rest. What they can do is to try to arrive at a decision that gives some weight to all of the considerations and tries to find a balance between them all.

Depending on the circumstances, it may or may not be possible to achieve this; but what I am interested in asking is whether there is anything irrational or reprehensible about the attempt to arrive at a consensus in this way. So far as I can see, there is not. It seems that what is happening here is in principle just the same as what happens when one person, having to come to some resolution of a moral problem, weighs up a number of values which come into play and arrives at some compromise between them. In the case of the group, the compromise is between values that happen to be held by different persons; but that does not seem to me to make compromise any less reasonable. It may be even more reasonable, since in the collective case there is the added incentive to avoid, not a personal dilemma, but interpersonal conflict.

I was assuming in that example that the members of the collective entity do identify themselves as members of it. In effect, though probably not in so many words, they see themselves as constituting a collective person (a notion readily recognized in legal contexts). At least to this extent, I am supposing that they share a common interest in reaching a decision; and perhaps I am also implicitly supposing that there is no fundamental antagonism between them as individuals which could outweigh their interest in arriving at a common decision. If we change these assumptions, the position becomes more problematic. If a decision has to be made on behalf of a whole society (which is the standard case, for instance, with legislation), we cannot so readily apply the idea of a decision being arrived at through compromise. While the large number of people in question, and hence the impossibility of their all meeting face to face, is a significant factor, I suspect that the most important difference lies in the fact that members of a large society are likely to have a much weaker sense, if any at all, of themselves as members of a collective entity whose decision the decision will be. So the importance attached to seeing one's own values 'win' will be correspondingly greater. Nevertheless, we know that on the broader political scale compromise can be effective. While the procedure of voting on a bill in parliament, say, is not itself a method of reaching a compromise (since in a given vote the decision is an either/or one), it often happens that a good deal of compromise has gone on in the drafting stage or in the committee stage before a final decision has to be made.

It still seems, then, that in moving from the individual level to the level of decision making within a large community many of the factors which may make compromise between values possible, desirable and often unavoidable remain unchanged. In some respects, the move to the larger scale often gives more scope for compromise. There is no halfway house between having and not having an abortion, but there are all sorts of intermediate possibilities for a society between complete prohibition of abortion and complete freedom to choose on the part of individuals, and any one of the intermediate possibilities might be a compromise between a number of the values that come into play.

It may seem to some readers that I have been weighting the scales too heavily in favour of compromise. It is sometimes suggested that it is only if we already assume a liberal point of view that compromise is possible, and that while this liberal point of view may be open to secular thinkers and also to many Christians, it might not be open, for instance, to a Muslim, for whom Islamic values will be non-negotiable.[7] Here again we need to be careful in interpreting what is at issue. In a sense it is clearly true that Islamic values are not negotiable because they are not open to compromise. If the Qur'an informs Muslims that God has commanded that something not be done, there is no room for negotiation about the truth of that belief (many Christians would take a similar view about the authority of the Bible). So the value deriving from that belief is not negotiable. But this does not mean that even fundamentalist Muslims, and other fundamentalists, cannot, alongside other groups within a plural society, negotiate and if necessary compromise over what the guiding principles of that society are to be. For any fundamentalist believer living in a plural society has reason to accept, if only on pragmatic grounds, that the society as a whole cannot be governed by the principles of his or her own religion. For such a person, some compromise is inevitable in living in a plural society.

Every Muslim father who would prefer to send his daughter to a single-sex Islamic school but who for lack of one available has to send her to a mixed and predominantly secular school, is involved in a compromise. Even for a father in this position, the values in play will not be all on one side. If he thought that his daughter ought not to be educated at all, and he allowed her to acquire something of an education only because he feared the penalties which the law would inflict if she did not go to school, this from his point of view would be a pure case of coercion by the state; it would not be compromise. But such a case is unlikely. We can assume rather that the father does want his daughter to have an education, he does want her potential (or aspects of it) to be developed. There are, in other words, values in play which weigh in favour of her going to school, but there are other values which weigh against her going to the sort of school which may in fact be the only sort available. If proposals for abolishing compulsory schooling were ever to become a live political issue, the father I am imagining would be unlikely to vote for them, for he does value education, and he does realize that many children, including perhaps his own, might be worse off if there were no free and (effectively) compulsory schooling. So he is not unwilling to compromise if compromise he must.

Of course, none of this means that the compromise presently available is the best possible, either for him or for the society as a whole. In fact, policy on schooling – what is to be the scope of free and compulsory provision, whether single-sex schools must be available, whether schools attached to particular religions must be available within the state system,[8] and so on – is eminently an example of the sort of large-scale policy issue on which negotiation and compromise do make sense as ways of coming to an agreed policy. The current *status quo* owes much to historical developments that minority groups within our society have often been expected to adapt to with little opportunity of influencing the arrangements. When a minority begins to feel that the existing arrangements are not acceptable to it (and this will, of course, be a perception through the lenses of its own values) a process of change in which their own voice is fully heard, even if it can only lead to compromise, is still likely to be better for all concerned than out-and-out conflict. Even though there may be no institutional arrangements by which a formal process of negotiation between different groups can lead to change in the governing values of a whole society (a parliamentary democratic system can at best be a very imperfect approximation to such an arrangement), the process by which values (or perceptions of values) do over time change within a plural society can be seen as a kind of informal negotiation (though one that may be weighted too much in favour of the dominant majority), as various groups put forward their claims and others gradually come to have more understanding of them. To engage in such a process does not mean that the minority group is ceasing fully to hold its own values; the fundamental values remain the same, though it is recognized that the outcome, within a plural society, will not fully conform to those values.[9]

Tolerance

The idea that education, especially in a plural, multicultural, society, should promote tolerance (among other aims), is one that I shall endorse in Chapter 11. But as with so many of the values with which education has to concern itself, there are questions about tolerance which we need to think through if we are to take a coherent educational stand. As with compromise, these questions will take us a little way into thinking about issues of politics and the state. The distinction made earlier between virtues, which are personal qualities, and rules that tell us to act in certain ways, is relevant here. Tolerating someone is an action; or rather, it is a deliberate refraining from action, that is, refraining from interfering with the conduct of others even though one disapproves of it. It makes sense to have a rule – or law, or political policy – that says we should tolerate, or put up with in practice, some of the things we may disapprove of. Laws tell us what we should do or should not do; they do not in general tell us what attitudes we should have, provided our behaviour conforms to the law. 'Toleration' is a word often used for deliberate forebearance from interfering with something that is disapproved of; 'tolerance' can be the name of an attitude, which for many liberals will be a virtue in its own right. This distinction between 'toleration' and 'tolerance' is probably not marked consistently in everyday speech, but it is a useful distinction nonetheless.

Consider the question: is British society more tolerant of homosexual relationships than it used to be? So far as the law goes, same-sex partnerships have been tolerated since 1967. That was the year in which the *Sexual Offences Act* removed homosexual acts between consenting adults in private from the list of offences. Basically, so far as the law goes, something is tolerated if it is not illegal. The *Act* of 1967 introduced toleration of what had not previously been tolerated, but it did not attempt directly to legislate for people's attitudes. Whether there is, and should be, legal toleration of same-sex partnerships is one question; what attitudes people do and should have towards homosexuality is another. (This is not to say that the questions are unrelated; the fact that something comes to be legally tolerated may have a gradual affect on people's attitudes, just as the fact that something – such as smoking in public places – comes to be not legally tolerated may affect people's attitudes towards it.)

As regards to the first question, there are probably still in modern society some people who think that if society generally disapproves of something, it should be illegal. But the view that has prevailed for the most part is one going back to the liberal philosopher John Stuart Mill in the nineteenth century: that the only justification for using the law to restrict people's freedom is to prevent people doing harm to others. Most of our criminal law now has this basis. Thus, the change in legal status with respect to homosexual acts in Britain in the 1960s is a good model of what toleration, strictly speaking, means. Many people disapproved of homosexuality, but decided that it should be allowed anyway.

If we say now, in the first decade of the twenty-first century, that society has become more tolerant of same-sex relationships, we may be referring not to personal attitudes at all, but to legal permissibility and to legal recognition of equal opportunities (as in recent British legislation on civil partnerships between same-sex couples). If we *are* referring to attitudes, there are still two possible interpretations:

First, we may mean that people who disapprove of same-sex relationships (who might still be numerous) have less tendency than before to put their disapproval into practice. Second, we may mean that fewer people disapprove of such relationships at all.

Think about people who do disapprove but do not put their disapproval into practice. We have to say (if the word 'tolerance' is not to lose any connection with its original meaning) that they are exercising tolerance. Then what of the people who do not disapprove at all? We have no reason to call them *intolerant.* They may be very broad-minded; perhaps they do not much mind what people do, so long as they are not harming others. In some ways this liberal broad-mindedness can be an easy position to take, since it avoids thinking seriously about where to draw lines between what should be accepted and what should not. It is an attitude that in many respects fits a liberal society. But a liberal society cannot expect the same degree of broad-mindedness from everyone. There may be some people for whom tolerance, in certain circumstances, is actually a difficult quality to exercise.

Consider the circumstances in which people who have been on opposite sides in a hard-fought conflict are brought together. This happened famously with the Truth and Reconciliation Commission in South Africa, and something similar on a much smaller scale has been attempted in Northern Ireland. When people who are on opposite sides in a political dispute are speaking to each other, no one expects that one side does not mind or care about what the other side has done. Tolerance is exercised simply in being willing to stop fighting and to listen to what the other has to say. The ability to do this can be considered a virtue – the virtue of tolerance – partly *because* it is difficult.

But there is still a question about why we should admire tolerance: what makes it a good thing? *If* we think that what someone else is doing is morally wrong, how can it be right to put up with it rather than trying to stop it? The problem was expressed well in this passage from David Raphael (notice that Raphael draws on some of the same points about what is involved in holding a moral position that I used in Chapter 3):

> to disapprove of something is to judge it to be wrong. Such a judgement does not express a purely subjective preference. It claims universality; it claims to be the view of any rational agent. The content of the judgement, that something is wrong, implies that the something may properly be prevented. But if your disapproval is rationally grounded, why should you go against it at all? Why should you tolerate?[10]

In other words, why should you not try to stop people from going against the values that you believe to be right? Why not prevent them from acting in ways that you disapprove of? And if that leads to conflict, why should that not be justifiable, especially as the avoidance of conflict is not necessarily the highest value for people who are defending the moral values they are committed to? Why *should* people in this position be tolerant?

Some liberals would respond to this challenge by presenting an argument of principle. Tolerance will be displayed as a virtue in its own right, a higher-order value which takes precedence (at least sometimes) over the particular values that support disapproval of particular things. For the liberal-minded person, an attitude of tolerance may – if it is not simply a lazy acceptance of 'anything goes' – be linked with a certain humility, an acceptance that one's own views might possibly be wrong. But then it is not easy to argue for tolerance with someone who does not take seriously the possibility that their views might be wrong. It may be better in practice to rely on a more pragmatic kind of argument for toleration, as a policy and practice, even when tolerance as a virtue in its own right is difficult to defend.

Some religious communities, for instance, do not see the state that exercises liberal toleration as an ideal. Their ideal would be a state governed in accordance with the principles of their own religion. The enforcement of the principles of their religion by law would not be against *their* values but in accordance with them. It would not be fanatical, for instance, for a Muslim to take this kind of view; it would be consistent with Islamic principles.[11] But in a plural society the only realistic option for the foreseeable future is a liberal state that allows and even supports a wide variety of beliefs, practices and values. It is perhaps on this basis that tolerance is often spoken of as an essential virtue in a plural and multicultural society.

However, we should be careful not to speak of tolerance too glibly. If the question of tolerance only really arises when you disapprove of something or someone, then talking of tolerance between different groups *implies* that they disapprove of each other, and are, perhaps rather reluctantly, putting up with each other. But that suggests that we might disapprove of someone just because they are different: because they have a different skin colour, or live in different ways, or have different religious beliefs.

Here again there is a lazy kind of tolerance that is the easy option; it allows you to have some kind of underlying attitude of *disapproval* of other people because they are different, so long as you let them get on with their lives. And that avoids the challenge with which people ought to be faced: *why* should we disapprove of others just because they are different? If we accepted the differences in the first place, the need to tolerate people for their differences would not arise. It is not surprising, then, that people do not like to feel they are merely being tolerated by others. On that basis, many people will claim that they want and deserve, not tolerance, but respect.

Respect

'Respect' is a term so widely used, in so many contexts, that we may rarely stop to reflect on what it involves. To some people, respect for persons is central to any moral outlook; but in everyday language we speak also of respect for many other objects besides persons. In the National Curriculum Statement of Values, for instance, we find the following mentions of respect: that we should

- develop self-respect and self-discipline
- respect others, including children
- respect the privacy and property of others
- respect the rule of law and encourage others to do so
- respect religious and cultural diversity.

In addition to such ideas, the phrase 'respect the environment' is often heard. The Statement of Values, though it does not use exactly that phrase, does refer to our responsibilities to the environment in a way that is consistent with the idea that it merits our respect.

If there are so many things that we can and should respect, is there any core meaning to the idea of respect? For many people, respect for *persons* is central, and everything else derives from that.[12] In modern moral philosophy, respect for persons is often associated with the ethics of Kant. One of his formulations of the central demand of morality – the 'categorical imperative' – was that we should never treat other people purely as means to our own ends, but always as 'ends in themselves'. Of course, we cannot avoid using other people as means to our own ends in all sorts of ways: we do this, for instance, whenever we engage in any commercial transaction with another person. The point is that we should never treat others as if they were simply objects there for our benefit; we should always recognize that other persons have value in their own right, independently of our own amusement, convenience, or benefit.

Many young people do have an understanding of this on an intuitive level. The UK government's 'Respect Action Plan', for instance,[13] quotes the following responses from children who were asked what respect means to them:

> 'Treating others in the way that you would like to be treated.'
> 'Being able to be the way I am without being bullied or skitted. And vice versa.'
> 'Not offending or damaging someone else's feelings or property.'
> 'Appreciating someone, even though they're from another country and they're different.'
> 'Consideration for others.'

One point that is implicit in these comments is that respect is seen as a matter of attitudes and relationships between equals. This is not respect as deference. In the world portrayed, for instance, in many nineteenth-century novels and the television period dramas based on them, respect had a lot to do with class and authority: looking up to those who were superior to you. But 'respect for persons', as a fundamental moral idea, is about recognizing the basic moral worth of every person.

To respect someone, then, we do not have to look up to them as superior to ourselves. We do not have to share their way of life, their religion or their politics. We do, though, have to be prepared, not to ignore them, but to make some effort to understand the way they see the world. Even if we do have some intuitive understanding of what respect for persons is, in a multicultural world we have to *learn* about the ways of behaviour that count as respectful – or that should be avoided because they would be seen as offensive – in other people's eyes. It is an educational task to enable people to understand how best to show respect.[14]

If respect for persons is a fundamental moral idea, does that mean that all other kinds of respect derive from it? Not necessarily. It may be true that we should respect the law because indirectly that is a way of respecting persons: the law exists for the benefit of the persons who share a life in society. But what of respect for the environment? If this is at bottom a form of respect for persons, it means that we should look after the environment because to damage the environment is not to recognize sufficiently the importance of the *persons* – all of us – whose quality of life ultimately depends on the environment. No doubt that is part of the reason why we should look after the environment – I shall touch on this again in Chapter 9 – but the notion of *respect* for the environment conveys more than that. If respecting persons is a matter of recognizing that persons have value in their own right, independently of our individual aims and preferences, then we can understand respect for the environment – or for anything else – in a similar way. To respect the environment is to recognize that it is of value in its own right – not just because we happen to appreciate it and depend on it – so that we have responsibilities towards it.

Something similar, I think, needs to be said about respect for cultures. It is partly that to respect another person – and to know what this demands of us in practice – we have to understand something of how they see the world, that is, we need to have some appreciation of their culture. But we can also have respect for the whole complex of ways of life, values and beliefs that make up what we call a culture. Just as we can respect a person without having to agree with everything they say or approve of everything they do, so we can respect a culture without thinking that everything about it is good. Any culture – including, for each of us, our own – has features that are open to criticism, but we may well think that the enormous diversity and richness of human cultures – like the diversity and richness of the natural environment – is something we should respect.

[1] See Day (1989).

[2] Kant's discussion is in Kant (1927), first published 1797.

[3] The example is taken, slightly adapted, from Bernard Williams in Smart and Williams (1973: 97–98).

[4] I return to the abortion question in Chapter 6 in connection with the perspectives of caring and justice.

[5] A consequentialist holds that the rightness or wrongness of actions depends only on their consequences. A utilitarian is a particular kind of utilitarian who holds that the value of different consequences should be assessed in terms of the pleasure, happiness or well-being of persons and of sentient beings generally. Strictly speaking, there can be consquentialists who are not utilitarians, because they assess consequences by some standard that has nothing to do with pleasure or happiness. Here it is the consequentialist aspect that I am concerned with.

[6] Ross's notion of prima facie duties is relevant here (Ross 1930, 1939). Ross's conception is cited in connection with compromise by Day (1989: 479). On Ross's notion, see also Dancy (1992).

[7] See Halstead (1992).

[8] See Chapter 10 for more on this issue.

[9] Chapter 9 includes a discussion of how far there is scope for compromise over one particular controversial issue: the treatment of animals.

[10] Raphael (1988: 139).

[11] In fact, of course, as in any religion, there are different interpretations of what the principles of the religion require.

[12] For a general account of the ethics of respect for persons see Downie and Telfer (1969).

[13] See www.respect.gov.uk

[14] A difficult aspect of this is to know how to avoid offending people, and when causing offence may be justifiable and compatible with respect. See Barrow (2005) and Haydon (2006a).

PART III: MORALITY

While the idea of morality has already been present in Part II, the discussion of values and moral values did not concentrate on the notion of 'morality' as such. As compared with the whole field of values, morality seems narrower, more systematic and less open to choice – as if, while people may to some degree choose what values to put weight on, they have to be initiated into morality. But if morality is a pre-existing system and moral education is initiation into it, in some people's eyes this will go against the grain both of pluralism and of education. The issues raised by the notion of morality need attention in their own right.

In Chapter 6 I consider the objections that some people have to the very idea of morality; in Chapter 7, what can be said in its favour; and in Chapter 8, whether we can make sense of it independently of a religious framework.

Chapter 6

What's Wrong with Morality?

In Part II we saw something of the complexity and variety of values – non-moral and moral values, different understandings of moral values, and religious and non-religious interpretations. To some people the variety, while it may set a challenge, is not unwelcome, and the ideas of compromise, tolerance and respect may set us on the right road to handling the complexities. But there may be other readers who feel that so far I have avoided the heart of the matter. Are there not, they will say, some values that education should simply set out to teach? If asked which values, these readers might turn back to the Hobbesian picture of morality which I sketched in Chapter 4. I suggested that, ignoring all the surrounding complexities and variety, the Hobbesian picture tries to set up a minimal morality – now sometimes referred to as morality in the narrow sense – which, if it does not play a major role in enriching our life or giving it meaning, should at least enable people to co-exist without conflict. A minimal morality of this kind could be very important for education. If education cannot do everything in the area of values that might be desirable, a minimal social morality might well be what it should concentrate on.[1]

But if we suggest that it is the business of education to promote even a minimal morality, there may be other readers – perhaps the same ones who will be attracted to the ideas of compromise and tolerance – who will be uneasy. Some teachers, and others who are about to go into teaching, are reluctant to see themselves as teachers of morality. What is it that underlies the worry here? It may have a lot to do with the connotations of the *word* 'morality'. As Standish has said 'For many the very word 'morality' has become tainted, suggesting the stiff correctness of Victorian behaviour, sexual repression (if not hang-ups), timid subjection to conformity, and a certain starchiness of tone.'[2] We need to explore what the notion of morality means to people; and we need also to ask the substantive question of whether morality is a good thing at all. Could we be better off without morality?

Many teachers are liberal-minded people – that will often be part of the reason why they have gone into teaching. By calling people 'liberal-minded' I mean to say something about their values: that they think it is good for people to have freedoms and opportunities to live their own lives and to think for themselves. Liberal-minded people are likely to be unhappy about the idea that they might be imposing certain ways of thinking – certain values – on other people. But when they think about the teaching context, these liberal-minded people may well agree that there are certain rules that it will be essential for a school to maintain – rules of order and non-violence without which a school could hardly function. Maintaining these rules may not be seen as imposing anything; and not everyone will see it as a matter of morality. Some teachers will say that it is only for pragmatic purposes that these rules have to be upheld inside the school; how people behave in the rest of their lives, what *values* they hold, is not (on this view) the teacher's business. And a liberal-minded teacher of this kind may, in particular, recoil from the idea of imposing *morality*. In this reaction I think there is more than just the liberal-minded person's dislike of imposing anything; there is a sense also that morality is itself a kind of imposition.

I shall defer to the next chapter the question of whether there is any way in which teachers can teach morality without imposing on their pupils. For this chapter, I want to ask whether there is any substance in the idea that morality as such is an imposition.

Morality and sex – a side issue

First, but only to get it out of the way, there is no doubt that morality has become associated in some people's minds with a rather narrow set of concerns – specifically, who sleeps with whom. This tendency to think that morality is about sex may, as many people have suggested, be a particularly English phenomenon, with cultural roots that can be traced back to Victorian times. It has, if anything, been reinforced recently by media attention to the private lives of politicians (though any argument as to why politicians should be expected to observe different standards in their private lives from those of media celebrities is rarely spelt out).

There are many people, particularly young people, who do not have much time for 'morality' if this is all it is supposed to be. As I suggested in Chapter 3, though these people may not have much use for the *word*, this does not mean that they do not have moral values. That people should have the freedom to choose their lifestyle, provided they do so without harm or disrespect to others, may well be among their moral values; and in recognizing what would count as harm or disrespect to others, their values will tell them that emotional as well as physical hurt is bad, that fidelity to promises is good and betrayal bad. But they will see no reason why consensual sexual relations between adults should necessarily violate any of the positive values here.

This is surely a reasonable view. It means not just that morality is not especially about sex, but that there is no special 'sexual morality'. Sexual relations may well lead to hurt and betrayal, and young people will not always realize how readily this can happen. There is a kind of consciousness-raising to be done about this, as part of what is quite rightly in England now called not just sex education but 'sex and relationships education'. But the standards by which hurt and betrayal are judged wrong are not special to sexual relations. Some people, too, would see the attempt at even a well-meaning 'sexual morality' – where it is not concerned with the consequences to third parties – as paternalistic. Heterosexual relationships, of course, can have enormous consequences for 'third parties' by bringing them into existence; relationships that have this potential can certainly not be seen as morally neutral. So when I describe 'morality and sex' as a side issue I do not mean at all that sex is a morally unimportant matter. I mean that to link morality especially with sex is misleading, because the moral values that come into play where sex is concerned are not unique to it. Those who say that sex education should be conducted within a moral framework are right, but perhaps not in quite the way they think. It is not that sex education should, as it were, have moral values added on to what is taught about the biological and social aspects of sex, but that sex education should take place within a school where values education as a whole is taken seriously. (There are some people who will say that sex education should take place in the family, not in schools at all; but can they be sure that every family is a place where values education as a whole is taken seriously?)

Whether you agree or not with the idea that there is no special sexual morality, this idea is likely to be one to which many young adults subscribe; and some of them will be going into teaching. Thus, anyone who expects teachers to be moral paragons, yet cherishes this restricted conception of morality, is being unrealistic. There will be people in teaching, just as there are outside teaching, who in their private lives are involved in all kinds of sexual relationships. This does not mean that the public can have no legitimate concern at all about how teachers behave when they are not in school, but it does mean that this concern should not be misdirected. It may well be true (I shall raise the question again in Part VI) that it is better for pupils if they have teachers who are morally admirable people, or at least no worse than average. If this is right, then we should expect teachers to have a sense of moral values themselves and be prepared to live by them. But we should not demand that they conform to certain traditional rules of lifestyle when those rules may not be justified by the teachers' own moral values. The fact, for instance, that a teacher is living with someone in a relationship not sanctioned by marriage is not, in itself, any reason why that person cannot be a good teacher.

So I shall now put concerns about sex on one side and turn to a somewhat less restricted notion of morality. This will allow us to say (again in accordance with tradition, but not such an artificially restricted tradition) that keeping promises, not hurting people, not telling lies, and so on, are questions of morality. We can now ask why some people still regard morality as some sort of imposition.

Morality as social control – can we do without it?

When we speak of morality in this way, as if it had an upper case M, we are not just speaking of the sum total of an individual's moral values. We are speaking of something that is wider than any one individual – something more like a *system* of demands to which individuals are subject. Some of the features of this system coincide with features of an individual's moral values that I mentioned in Chapter 3. Morality is seen as making demands on people independently of their preferences or inclinations, and perhaps also demands of a generalized kind that do not take account of the circumstances of particular individuals and situations. But *where* do these demands come from, if not from the preferences, or even from the values and commitments, of individuals? For some religious believers it will come naturally to think of these demands as issuing from God; and that may indeed be a way of making sense of them. We shall come to this possibility in Chapter 8. But what is the person without any religious belief to make of this system of demands?

One likely answer is that the demands are those of society. This fits with the idea that morality is a system over which individuals have no control, but which attempts to control them. On this view, morality is one more form of social control, less formalized than law and not backed up by an institutionalized system of punishment, but still a way in which entrenched opinions and traditional ways of doing things exercise tyranny over individual lives. It exercises this tyranny partly by making people feel uncomfortable, perhaps guilty, about actions that might otherwise seem to them natural or harmless. It sets up rigid categories and tells people 'you must not do this' (because it falls under a certain category that attracts disapproval), and thereby does not allow people to make their own decisions, even though they may know their own circumstances best.[3] This conception of morality may explain why some liberal-minded teachers do not want to see themselves as promoters of morality: they do not want to be regarded as agents of social control (even if the sociology of education tells them that they cannot avoid this).

In the next chapter I shall suggest that we do not have to see morality as a system that is imposed on people. But having seen why some people take a negative view of morality, it will be worth asking whether we could do without it. Would we even be better off without morality?

One who thought so was Karl Marx. In fact Marx provides a good illustration of the way in which someone can have moral values but not subscribe to the *system* that is recognized as morality in a particular society at a particular time. There was certainly what we can call, in the terms of Chapter 3, a moral impulse behind Marx's criticisms of nineteenth-century capitalism. In his view, it stunted and confined human capacities, and Marx seems to have valued the free development and flourishing of human capacities almost above everything else. Yet *morality* to Marx was a form of alienation (as was religion, in much the same way). This meant that even though morality was something that had been created by human beings as part of their social form of life, it had come to be seen as having an independent existence, putting objective constraints on people. It functioned ideologically: it induced false consciousness in those who believed in the external reality of this human construct, and it served the interests above all of the ruling class in society (this is particularly clear in the case of moral rules about property – notably the prohibition on stealing – which did far more for those who had property than for those who did not).[4]

That morality served some interests rather than others is the key to Marx's belief that human beings would be better off without morality – that is, in conditions in which morality was no longer needed. Morality presupposes economic and social arrangements in which people's interests are in conflict with each other. (We encountered in Chapter 4 this idea that morality is about conflict and how to contain it.) Once that conflict of interests was overcome, and communist society fully established, people's interests would be in harmony. They could develop and exercise their human capacities without restricting the same development and exercise on the part of others. This does not mean that individuals would be living in isolation from each other; quite the reverse. They would be cooperating with others rather than competing; promoting others' interests rather than undermining them. The most rigid moralist would find nothing to complain of in their behaviour. The difference would be in their motivation. People in this fully developed human society would not assault others, would not tell lies, would not break promises: not because they felt themselves constrained by some external system of rules, but because they would have no interests that could be served by doing so, therefore no reason to do so, and no wish to do so.

Marx never went very far in attempting to work out what personal and social relations would be like in a fully communist society – in his own terms, it would have been pointless to try to predict what choices people would make when they were genuinely free to make them. (In the fully communist society the State would have withered away; therefore it hardly needs saying that the so-called communist regimes that were in command in much of eastern Europe until the early 1990s were very far from being fully communist societies.) My concern here is not to defend or to criticize Marx's thinking. I am extracting one point, which is by no means special to Marx: the idea that morality, as a system of constraints, would be unnecessary if people's motivation was right – or if social conditions were right, because if you take seriously, as Marx did, that human beings are social animals, people's motivation will depend on social conditions.

Morality and bad motives

The conception of morality we have been looking at incorporates a certain kind of motivation – a sense of being bound by constraints not of your own making, with the prospect of suffering guilt if you go against these constraints. What is by no means special to Marx is the thought that if that kind of motivation were unnecessary, morality itself would be unnecessary. This idea is present in the Christian tradition, for instance in St. Augustine's 'love God and do what you will' – for if you love God, you will not *want* to do the things that morality tells you not to do.[5] The idea is there too in the emphasis that some moral theorists have put on virtues, from Aristotle to the present day.

At the beginning of Chapter 3 I referred to the idea of virtues: personal qualities that we think it is morally important for people to have, or that we feel are morally admirable. There is more than one interpretation of the sort of quality that we are talking about here. Take as an example unselfishness. What are we saying about a person when we say that he or she is unselfish? One answer might be that the person does not behave in ways that further their own interests at the expense of others. But this by itself could hardly be enough, because it only tells us about the actual effects of the person's behaviour, and nothing about why they behave as they do; so it is not really attributing a personal quality at all. To call a person unselfish is not just to say that, as a matter of fact, their actions do not benefit them at the expense of others. That might be purely accidental as far as the person is concerned, and nothing to do with what they are aiming at. It could even be that some people are so incompetent at pursuing their own desires that they end up benefitting other people when really they only wanted to do the best for themselves.

In calling a person unselfish, we are saying something not just about the effects of their actions but about their motivation. But there are still two different kinds of motivation that may be relevant.

First, suppose that what one person is really most concerned about is their own interests, but that they also had it drummed into them throughout childhood that one ought not to be selfish. So they do their best to follow this rule, and most of the time succeed. This person deliberately sacrifices their own desires to those of others, not because they really care about others, but because they want to do what is morally right. So the person helps others but does so rather reluctantly. Another person might be one who really does have the interests of others at heart. This person does not *want* to pursue their own interests at the expense of others.

So there are different motivations here. We could raise the question of which motivation genuinely constitutes unselfishness, but there would be little point in this. Our language is flexible enough to allow us to refer to either as unselfishness; the important point is to be as clear as we can about what qualities it is that we value. Think of other words that we have for virtues. Courage, for instance. The courageous person stands up to dangers – it could be physical danger, as in facing a bully in the playground, or it could be the courage to stand up for one's convictions; it could even be the courage to stand up to the taunts of others when refusing to fight the bully. But we can ask again what motivates the person to stand up to such dangers. Is it that they are only too aware of the reality of the dangers, fear of which would normally motivate people to avoid them; except that they would be ashamed to avoid the dangers, and so make an effort of will to face them? Or do they see the dangers positively, as challenges that they actually want to face?

What of truthfulness? The truthful person does not tell lies (and may even go out of their way to tell as much truth as possible). Is this because, while the person often sees that it would be more convenient or profitable to tell a lie, their moral compunction restrains them? Or is it that it would never occur to them to tell a lie – they seem to be just 'naturally' truthful?

You could perhaps add to the examples yourself. The point is that whenever we treat some personal quality as a moral virtue, there are likely to be at least two possible accounts of what it involves. On one account, the person's underlying motivations – self-interest, laziness, fear, perhaps a degree of callousness or maliciousness – will be of a kind that needs to be restrained by an awareness of the requirements of morality. The motivation to do what morality demands will have to overcome other, non-moral motivations. On the other account, a person will not have a particular virtue at all unless their underlying motivation is of a kind that is consistent with morality, so that it does not need to be restrained or overcome. On this account, a person is not a kind person if there is any callousness or maliciousness in them, even if they successfully overcome that and always manage in practice to be helpful. The person is kind only if the good of other people – or rather, the good of the particular people they encounter – is itself one of their underlying values.

Faced with examples like these, many people think that it is better, more admirable, for people to have underlying motivations that will make for peace and harmony, rather than having contrary motivations that have to be restrained by a sense of morality. If we interpret the idea of virtues in such a way that the underlying motivations will themselves work in the same direction as morality, then it is possible to hold that if people have the right virtues, there will be no need for morality – in the sense in which I have been using the word here.

This conception of virtues, as having a lot to do with one's underlying motivations, and very little to do with deliberately restraining oneself according to moral rules, goes back at least to Aristotle (though it would be misleading to suggest that there is no place for rules or principles in Aristotle's ethics). Among contemporary moral philosophers, approving references to Aristotle are quite common, and criticisms of the system of morality by no means rare. Bernard Williams, then Professor of Moral Philosophy at Oxford University, argued in the 1980s that we would be better off without what he called 'morality, the peculiar institution'.[6] One of the leading British philosophers of education, John White, influenced in part by Williams, took a similar line in the context of education, arguing that we would do better to abandon 'moral education' as such in favour of education in altruism, which he saw as preferable in a number of ways. Morality, he suggested, brings with it rigidity, a tendency to fanaticism, an unwillingness to compromise, and the pervasive tendency to blame oneself and others for moral defects. Our ethical life, says White, 'does not *have* to be as unlovely as this'.[7] So rather than teaching morality, we should on White's view be trying in various ways to develop altruistic motivation in pupils.

You can see now why I could not go straight from discussing the aims of education in general to asking what place moral education should have among those aims. The whole notion of moral education has been brought into question. We need to be clearer about the place of morality itself among our values before we can expect any answers about the place of morality in education.

Is caring better than justice?

A further twist to this story of the defects of morality has emerged since the 1970s from a different quarter: psychological research into moral development. This field was dominated for many years by the work of the American researcher Lawrence Kohlberg. He claimed to have found that as people grew up they would go through a sequence of stages in their moral thinking and that, while some individuals in any culture would progress further through these stages than others, the *order* of the stages was the same in any culture.

The fact that a certain way of thinking comes later in a person's life does not mean that it is better; given some standpoint from which to make the assessment, we cannot rule out, without further evidence or argument, the possibility that people's ways of thinking will deteriorate as they get older and more experienced but not necessarily wiser. (The idea that formal education tends to corrupt people's earlier moral innocence has been with us at least since the educational writings of Rousseau.) Kohlberg, well aware of this point, tried to present philosophical arguments to show that the later stages in the sequence of moral development were indeed morally better than the earlier ones.[8] But the main point for the present argument is the nature of the later stages. Kolhberg's stages of development progressively move further from the individual's immersion in his own immediate circumstances (you will see below why I use the masculine pronoun here) towards the individual making consciously abstract judgements about situations, and appealing to universal principles of justice. The final form of moral thinking – Kohlberg's 'Stage Six', which his research indicates only a minority of the population reach – is one of consciously endorsing universal[9] principles, and judging the rights and wrongs of particular situations in the light of those principles.

Kohlberg's associate Carol Gilligan noticed that his claims about the sequence of stages did not fit very well with the results of her own research on women's moral thinking. Kohlberg had apparently not been inhibited in his generalizations by the fact that his subjects had been predominantly male. But apart from the gender of the subjects there was also another important difference between Kohlberg's research and one early research project of Gilligan's. Kohlberg conducted his research by presenting subjects with hypothetical dilemmas. Given the bare outline of a situation, with a minimum of detail, subjects would be asked whether it would be right for a person to do such-and-such. Gilligan, on the other hand, studied the moral thinking of women facing a genuine dilemma in their own lives: whether to have an abortion (she contacted the women through an abortion clinic).[10] Now it may not seem at all surprising that women in this position will not think in quite the same way as people, male or female, asked about a hypothetical case; but what we need to follow up here is Gilligan's characterization of the ways in which the women did think.

Gilligan in fact argued that there are two significantly different orientations in moral thinking, and that one is more associated with males, the other with females. What are these orientations? So far as labels go, one has been commonly called the justice or the rights perspective, also sometimes the perspective of separateness, as opposed to connectedness; the second, in addition to the idea of connectedness, has been named the perspective of responsibility or, most often, that of care. Look at the responses of two adults to the question 'What does morality mean to you?'

1. Morality is basically having a reason for or a way of knowing what's right, what one ought to do; and when you are put into a situation where you have to choose from among alternatives, being able to recognize when there is an issue of 'ought' at stake and when there is not; and then . . . having some reason for choosing among alternatives.
2. Morality is a type of consciousness, I guess, a sensitivity to humanity, that you can affect someone else's life. You can affect your own life, and you have the responsibility not to endanger other people's lives or to hurt other people. So morality is complex. Morality is realizing there is a play

between self and others and that you are going to have to take responsibility for both of them. It's sort of a consciousness of your influence over what's going on.[11]

It is not difficult to align the first of these with the notion of morality as a system; whereas the 'sensitivity to humanity' which the second respondent talks about does not sound like an acknowledgement of morality, in *that* sense, at all. But for bringing out the difference in the orientations, one of the clearest illustrations is itself a hypothetical dilemma that has been used in research on adolescents' moral thinking. It is rather an unusual dilemma in that it is not even presented as a story about human beings. Be prepared to put the book down for a minute or two after you have read the next paragraph.

A group of industrious, prudent moles have spent the summer digging a burrow where they will spend the winter. A lazy, improvident porcupine who has not prepared a winter shelter approaches the moles and pleads to share their burrow. The moles take pity on the porcupine and agree to let him in. Unfortunately, the moles did not anticipate the problem the porcupine's sharp quills would pose in close quarters. Once the porcupine has moved in, the moles are constantly being stabbed. The question is, what should the moles do?

Before reading the continuation of the quotation, consider what you think the moles should do.

On the one hand, subjects answering according to the rights perspective point out that the moles own the shelter and are therefore entitled to throw the porcupine out. When asked what the moles should do if the porcupine refuses to leave, some of these respondents favour shooting the porcupine. On the other hand, subjects answering according to the care perspective suggest solutions like covering the porcupine with a blanket. These respondents devise compromises that defuse conflict and secure everyone's interest.[12]

The reference to defusing conflict is worth following up, since we have already looked at the potential for conflict growing out of

people's adherence to different values. On the face of it, the justice orientation seems more likely to lead to overt conflict, or is at
any rate less likely to defuse it. Notice that some respondents suggested the porcupine should be shot if he refused to leave. It may
well be that some subjects (one suspects boys) were giving a consciously macho response here. Even so, it is significant that the justice orientation, but not the care one, allows scope for this. In this
dilemma a justice approach starts by setting off the claims of the
moles and of the porcupine against each other; a *conflict* of claims
is seen as the chief feature from the beginning, and the assumption is implicit that the solution must be all or nothing, one way or
the other. Since this will inevitably mean that one side loses, within
this orientation what counts as a solution to the problem is not
necessarily a *resolution* of the conflict. The alternative orientation
sees the conflict between individuals as *constituting the problem*, so
that a solution is not reached until the conflict has been resolved.

It might look as if the differences shown up here are differences
in the content of people's values: some saying, in effect, 'the most
important thing is to uphold justice and respect people's rights',
others that 'the most important thing is to maintain relationships,
defuse conflict and secure everyone's interests if possible'. But if
these are differences in content, they are not like the relatively
specific difference between yes and no answers to the question 'Is
abortion wrong?' The different perspectives do not so much give
different answers to the same question as display an interest in asking different questions. Faced with a given problem, some people
try to approach it by thinking at the level of general principles,
asking whose rights are at issue, and what it is that justice
demands. For these people, any reasoning about a moral issue
starts from principles that are expressed in a very general form
and seen as universal – in the case of the moles and porcupine it
might be the principle that people have a right to control access
to resources that they have created for their own use – and then
draws from the general principle a conclusion for the specific
case. Others tend to approach the specific problem without working from the general level first. They ask what is at stake in the
relations between the persons involved: who might be hurt and
how can hurt best be avoided?

Consider the abortion issue again. If we think in terms of
rights, we ask whether the foetus has a right to live and whether

the mother has a right to choose whether to have the baby or not. If this is the question, then we have to answer in favour either of the foetus or the mother, or else we are simply faced with an impasse. For many people, especially if they are thinking at the level of state politics and legislation, this *is* the question. But for many women, if they are pregnant and there are reasons of some (serious) kind for not having the child, the issue about rights will not be what is in question. Their question will not be about the rights of foetuses in general or about the right of women to choose. A particular woman's (or teenage girl's) question is about what to do in this situation, in this particular relationship, or lack of relationship, with the father, with her parents, with others who might or might not be involved in caring for the child. In fact, the woman's dilemma only arises because a general answer in terms of rights is not sufficient either way. If a woman really thought that a foetus had a absolute right to life[13] that would immediately settle the question against an abortion. But it is not surprising that a Catholic mother in Gilligan's study, even though she had always thought of abortion as murder, found that this thought, rather than removing the dilemma, merely added another aspect to the whole problem. If, on the other hand, a woman thought that she had an absolute right to choose – to choose either way, for any reason at all, or for no reason – then she could toss a coin. But, of course, the problem only exists for the woman because she recognizes other values besides wishing to claim her own rights. Having the child or not having the child is going to make a great difference, not only in the existence or non-existence of an individual human being – to whom the mother may already feel some sort of relationship – but to the mother herself and to other people who are part of her life.

So taking one perspective or the other does not predetermine a particular answer to a dilemma. The rights orientation will tend to set off the rights of the mother against the rights of the foetus, but different persons using this orientation may come down on one side or the other. The care orientation focuses more on an ongoing complex web of relationships, unique to each situation. So it is even more clear that to take this focus does not predetermine what the answer will be.

While much of the recent attention to these different orientations arose from research on women's moral thinking, it would be an oversimplification to suggest that men think in terms of the rights or justice orientation, women in terms of the care orientation. Rather there appears to be a predominant focus to the thinking of each individual, which may be either of justice or of care. For most males the predominant focus is that of justice, as it is also for a considerable number of females (in other words the justice orientation seems to be predominant, irrespective of gender, in the North American culture where most of the research has been done). But for many females (and relatively few males) the predominant focus is that of care. At the same time, most individuals seem to be able (perhaps with a little prompting) to appreciate the alternative orientation to their own predominant one.[14]

In my own experience of talking to teachers about these orientations, I find that most, males as well as females, tend to find the care orientation more congenial.[15] It seems to embody more concern for the individual person (which surely is one of the values that motivates many teachers), whereas the perspective of justice or rights appears, in contrast, abstract and impersonal. Of course, the fact that a person finds one orientation more attractive when the two are described (where the description itself may not be neutral) does not show that the same person will tend to use that orientation in their own thinking. I cite the apparent attractiveness of the care orientation here only because it forms yet another angle of attack on the idea of a system of morality.[16] (In Chapter 12 I shall ask whether teachers should be trying to promote the use of one orientation rather than the other.)

So far we have encountered several lines of attack on morality, which all seem to portray it as a rather unattractive, even alienating, idea. The kind of motivation it can involve (doing something not out of love or fellow-feeling for other persons, but out of a sense of obligation, perhaps backed up by feelings of guilt if one fails); the sense that it is abstract and impersonal; the impression that it is imposed from the outside – all of these can add to the unattractiveness of the idea of morality. In addition, many people are uneasy about passing moral judgement on others. This uneasiness may be expressed in the pejorative terms 'moralizing' or 'being judgemental', suggesting a censoriousness that is unattractive in itself, and may too often be linked to hypocrisy.[17]

If the arguments of this chapter held sway, we would have to agree with John White that we should be trying to move 'beyond moral education'. Taking Bernard Williams' conclusion seriously, we ought to be trying through education to prepare people for a world without the system of morality, attempting instead (the 'instead' here is important) to cultivate in pupils altruism and caring. But it may be premature to reach that conclusion. Having examined what there is to be said against the system of morality, it is now time to see what there is to be said for it.

[1] On the idea of a minimal morality in an educational context, see White (1982: 78–88); White (1990: 43–5). On morality in the narrow sense see note 3 to Chapter 4.

[2] Standish (1997: 50).

[3] From a present-day perspective, there is nothing very new or radical about this view. There was something of it, for instance, in the writings of the Victorian liberal and utilitarian John Stuart Mill; see especially Mill (1962a), first published 1859.

[4] See Lukes (1985).

[5] It is worth remembering in this context that Jesus of Nazareth is often portrayed as one who was more concerned with quality of motivation than with strict adherence to the letter of the conventional morality of his day.

[6] Williams (1985), Chapter 10.

[7] White (1990: 53).

[8] Kohlberg (1981).

[9] In the sense of 'universal' meaning 'applying to everyone' – see Chapter 3 above.

[10] Gilligan's report of this and other studies, and her interpretation of the results, is in Gilligan (1982).

[11] Lyons (1988: 21). Reprinted by permission.

[12] Meyers (1987: 141). Reprinted by permission. Copyright 1987, Rowman & Littlefield.

[13] In the sense of 'absolute' meaning 'without exceptions' – see Chapter 3 above.

[14] See Gilligan *et al.* (1988). It is worth noting that any realistic dilemma is likely to give scope for thinking within either of the perspectives. Think, for instance, of the dilemma of the research chemist in Chapter 5.

[15] I have found the same with nurses, again with no obvious gender difference. Probably the commonest response I have encountered to the story of the moles and the porcupine among teachers and nurses is that the moles should make their burrow bigger.

[16] Dancy (1992) helps one to see how Ross's notion of prima facie duties may be illuminating in making sense of the justice/care distinction, and

thereby links this topic with that of attitudes towards compromise, though he does not himself use the language of compromise.

[17] For more on 'moralizing' and on popular suspicions about morality, see Hare (1992) and Midgley (1991).

Chapter 7

What's Right about Morality?

In Chapter 6 we looked at a number of problems that arise in the idea of morality as a system of restraints on people's conduct: that the sort of motivation it appeals to may not be desirable; that it is abstract and impersonal; that it involves the imposition on people of something alien (the last point in particular is one that many teachers may worry about). I suspect that while some readers will be sensitive to these points, others will wonder what the fuss is about; for them, morality is just there, and it is right, and it has to be passed on to each new generation. This diversity among the reactions of readers reflects one more aspect of the pluralism of our society: it is not just that people have different ideas about what is right and wrong, but that the very ideas of 'right' and 'wrong' mean different things to different people.

The question for education

In view of this diversity, one strategy that it would not be very helpful for me to try to take in this chapter is the one that says 'morality is just there, and it's right, so we have to pass it on'. It is true that if there is an objectively right moral system, then it would seem sensible to pass it on; just as, if certain beliefs about the existence and nature of a God are objectively right, it would seem sensible to communicate them (though in each case there is a further question of whether it should be schools that are responsible for the passing on). But first it would have to be established that certain identified beliefs are correct or, in the case of morality, that a certain understanding of its nature and content is objectively correct. Philosophical arguments that attempt to establish this are plentiful, and inevitably spawn disagreement about the nature and content of morality. So if I were to try to use the strategy that morality should be transmitted because it is right I would have to establish, to every reader's satisfaction, the correctness of a particular interpretation.

The book would then become a treatise in moral philosophy, and whatever the conclusion of my argument, it would still be controversial.

We need a more pragmatic approach. There is room for disagreement about the nature and content of morality, but what is less controversial is that morality as a system does have a degree of social reality. Some people, at least, do still speak of moral obligation, or of certain things as morally wrong. People will sometimes refrain from doing something because they think it is wrong, or conversely, will do something because they believe they ought to; and sometimes people will express moral approval or disapproval of what others are doing. To some degree, thinking in this way elicits social approval, though the picture is ambiguous here: making moral judgements about others also quite often arouses *disapproval.* In any case, since some people do grow up using words like 'right' and 'wrong' in something like a traditional sense, it must be the case that this way of using language, this way of thinking, is being passed on from the older generation to at least some of the young.

But none of this can be taken for granted – not even the language in which morality is characteristically expressed. Morality, as such, is after all a phenomenon only of language-using animals. That is not to say that it does not have biological roots. Among non-human animal species, one individual will sometimes act in a way that benefits other individuals of the species at its own expense (evolutionary theorists, begging a lot of questions, have labelled such behaviour 'altruism'). And it would be taking the refusal of anthropomorphism too far to deny that some animals can feel (something like) what we would label 'care' or 'concern' for others; at the very least, we can accept that female animals in many species may feel this for their offspring.[1] Much of our language of morality might appear intangible if we could not sometimes link it to *feelings* and motivations that may well be biologically programmed into us and which (by the same token, according to evolutionary theory) we share with other species. But what other species certainly do not have is the *language* of morality. They cannot say things like 'that is wrong' or 'I have a moral obligation to do this'. And since they cannot say these things, they also cannot think them; there is no non-linguistic feeling or experience that could be *equivalent* to these thoughts, even if certain feelings may characteristically underlie them. No animal, for instance, could experience a sense of moral obligation without having a concept of obligation, and this involves knowing that word or a close equivalent of it.

The language of morality is something that has developed within human communities, and like other parts of language it is spoken by each generation only because it has been passed on by the older generation. But language does not, of course, remain static; whole areas of it may undergo a change in significance, or may fall out of use altogether. It is not impossible that this could happen with morality. It is already likely that some children grow up with little sense or morality (which is not, of course, saying that there is no altruism of empathy in them). Where there is a degree of scepticism about morality, and a diversity of conceptions of what it involves, a plural society cannot just assume that it will survive come what may. In these conditions, formal education, rather than everyday conversation and family upbringing, could be the major agency by which morality survives. But, as we saw in the previous chapter, not everyone thinks it good that morality should survive. If we would be better off without morality, then we should not be using education to promote it. Rather than engage in moral education, if that means education in morality, we should be educating people to live without morality.

So there is an important decision facing formal education: to try, deliberately, to promote morality, or not? In Chapter 6 I indicated some of the problems with morality; I want to suggest here that there are still some things that are right about it. In doing this, I shall address the problems outlined at the beginning of the present chapter: the criticisms about motivation, about abstractness and impersonality, and about the imposition of something alien. And I shall add a further question (to be followed up in Chapter 8): can we make good enough sense of morality to see how it can be promoted in present conditions?

Moral motivation again

Take first the question of motivation. One kind of motivation is shown by helping someone who is in distress because their welfare matters to you; another kind by helping out of a sense of moral duty. Most people reading this will probably feel that the first kind of motivation is preferable. But it does not follow from this that there is never any place for the second.

The philosopher Kant, in his writings on morality, was concerned to distinguish a sense of right and wrong from all the other motivations that could move people. He wrote, for instance, of 'spirits of so sympathetic a temper that . . . they find an inner pleasure in spreading happiness around them and can take delight in the contentment of others as their own work'.[2] These are people to whom altruism is second nature: in spreading happiness around them they are doing what they want to do. And precisely because of that, there is nothing specifically *moral* in their motivation (where 'moral' is contrasted with 'non-moral' rather than 'immoral'): they are simply following their inclinations rather than acting out of a sense of *morality*. Now it is surely a good thing that there are people like this; that is not, I think, in dispute. It may even be that if everyone were like this, all the time, there would be no need for morality (though what I say later about justice may make us hesitate before accepting that conclusion). But if as a matter of fact many people are not like this, it is still important that people are capable of being moved by considerations that go against their own inclinations.

Kant, speaking of the type of person who enjoys spreading happiness around, formulated the following hypothesis:

> Suppose, then, that the mind of this friend of man were over-clouded by sorrows of his own which extinguished all sympathy with the fate of others, but that he still had power to help those in distress, though no longer stirred by the need of others because sufficiently occupied with his own; and suppose that, when no longer moved by any inclination, he tears himself out of this deadly insensibility and does the action without any inclination for the sake of duty alone . . .[3]

This person is capable of helping someone in distress despite his own worries and depression, because he is able to say to himself (and mean it) 'this is what I ought to do'. Think of the good Samaritan. In the biblical story (Luke 10), he was moved by compassion or pity for the man who had been mugged and beaten. But if he had been moved by a sense of moral duty, the victim would still have received his help. The importance of the moral motivation, I am arguing, is that it can operate even where fellow-feeling does not.

Take another case: a real, though artificially constructed, one. A number of experiments by the psychologist Stanley Milgram have gained a certain fame or notoriety. In these experiments, the subjects were led to believe that they were inflicting electric shocks on other participants – people who were innocent victims, except that they were not doing very well in the supposed learning experiment. On the experimenter's instructions, the subjects were supposed to inflict what they had been told were high-voltage shocks to the point of causing severe pain and distress. Relatively few subjects refused to go along with the experiment.[4]

What sort of motivation could have led to more people refusing to be party to this infliction (as they saw it) of suffering? In reply, we might say 'altruism' or 'compassion', and certainly we can suppose that if the experimental subjects had been sufficiently altruistic or compassionate towards the victims they would not have gone along with the experimenter's instructions. But then we have to conclude that a considerable number of ordinary people were not sufficiently altruistic or compassionate. To put it this way may mislead, if it suggests that the issue is one of *how much* altruism or compassion people have. The point is, rather, that these qualities are unlikely to be directed towards everyone equally. These experimental subjects may have been kind and considerate spouses and parents; they may even have felt they were showing altruism towards the experimenter by not messing up his experiment. Certainly, they had mixed motives in many cases (Milgram's book about the experiments devoted a good deal of attention to the question of their motivation).[5] To go against the experimenter's instructions would have been uncomfortable and embarrassing, and would have taken some courage. Besides, having agreed to take part in the experiment, most subjects will have felt some sense of obligation to go along with what the experimenter asked of them.

But if some of these people were acting out of a sense of obligation or duty towards the experimenter, does that not show that a sense of obligation can itself be dangerous? Certainly, it can be very dangerous if it amounts to obedience to authority or to tradition. But that is not the sort of motivation that I am talking about

or that Kant had in mind. In Kant's conception the moral motivation is informed by reason: it requires people to think for themselves about what is right and wrong, not to follow uncritically
what they are told by others. Guided by this motivation the experimental subjects, far from believing that they must go along with
the experimenter's instructions, would have said, or at least, would
have had the capacity to say, 'No. This is immoral. I will not do it.'
(Some people, but not many, did respond in this way.)

Suppose that one of the experimental subjects (who were mostly
male), perhaps a person of a normally benevolent and kindly disposition, was having an off day. Like the person in Kant's example, he
was depressed and fed up (maybe he was taking part in the experiment because he was bored, had nothing better to do and was getting paid for it). He had no particular fellow-feeling for the victim.
If anything, he felt bloody-minded: if he himself was in such a bad
state why shouldn't someone else suffer too? It seems to me that it is
in just such a case that the sense that there are certain things that
are morally beyond the pale, whatever one's own inclinations, could
operate; and that in this situation there might be no other kind of
motivation that could lead to the refusal to inflict the suffering.

The kind of motivation that I am talking about is one that, I
think, many readers will be able to recognize, but perhaps not
one that is very often explicitly addressed within education. To
the extent that it is not explicitly addressed within education, that
is one aspect of the tendency not to talk about morality as such,
to which I have already referred. Perhaps those who happened to
be writing the relevant documentation for the English National
Curriculum in the early 1990s were slightly more attuned to this
conception of moral motivation. A discussion document from the
then National Curriculum Council for England and Wales in
1993 put at the head of its list of the qualities to be developed in
moral education, 'The will to behave morally as a point of principle'.[6] That document was referring, I take it, to the capacity to
act, not out of one's immediate inclination or desire (even
though this might be thoroughly benevolent) but as a result of
recognizing that there is a way one *ought*, as a matter of principle,
to act. I cannot see that there is anything instinctive about this
kind of motivation; if we are capable of having it, it is because we
have acquired it. But there has been little in National Curriculum
documentation since that time, despite rather loose references to

understanding the difference between right and wrong, that would suggest that helping people to acquire that particular kind of motivation is part of the point of values education in schools.

We should care about justice too

The idea that there are things we ought to do 'as a matter of principle' brings us to the second kind of criticism of morality that I want to take up here: the idea that by seeing everything in terms of 'principle', moral thinking will, very often, miss what is distinctive to and important in the concrete circumstances. We saw in Chapter 6 that thinking in terms of general principles is characteristic of the kind of moral approach that Kohlberg argued for and that Gilligan, and others influenced by her, have criticized. We need to look further at what is at issue here.

As I mentioned, most teachers in my experience, faced with the scenario of the moles and the porcupine, will suggest a practical solution such as digging a bigger hole, rather than the porcupine being turned out because he has no right to be there. But it could well be that the setting of the story in an imaginary world makes it easier to give such a response. Suppose it is your own house, the schools and colleges have broken up for the winter holidays and your family is together for once, when a homeless person, who has been sleeping rough, knocks at the door asking for shelter. Would you be more inclined then to appeal to some general rights and principles? There is no doubt that, especially if we are settled in a relatively comfortable existence, we can use an appeal to our own rights to legitimate, in our eyes, a limitation to our cooperation and identification with the well-being of others. This is a criticism of the language of individual rights that goes back at least to Marx. But the trouble here is not the idea of rights as such, but the content we put into it. We could, after all, instead of appealing to our right to decide who can sleep in our own home, put more weight on everyone's right to adequate shelter.

The issue I want to pursue here is not who has which rights, but whether we do well to think at all in terms of rights, justice and general principles, when there are critics (some influenced by Gilligan) who think that we need only to attend to the circumstances of particular concrete situations. I would suggest that the

notion of justice is an important one to hang on to, precisely
because it does not let us concentrate purely on the immediate situation but leads us to make comparisons between the lot of persons in different situations.

The motivation of caring and concern in the concrete situation
is directed towards the particular others who impinge on us.
When the moles in the story take the porcupine into their home,
they are not thinking of his rights; rather they are responding
directly out of concern for the creature. The other side of this is
that there may be porcupines out there who do not get cared for
at all. We expect a teacher to have concern for the pupils he or she
is teaching. But we cannot expect that this concern will just happen to be equally distributed towards all pupils. Some pupils may
seem to elicit the teacher's concern more than others; sometimes
this will be for good reasons, but not necessarily. In addition to the
concern that the teacher is capable of feeling for individual
pupils, it may take a conscious sense of fairness or justice to see
that none of the pupils are favoured at the expense of others, that
no one gets passed over. The notion of entitlement clearly has a
place here.

While caring is important, we need to remember that it is, in
the first instance, caring for particular others. A community of caring persons would be one in which everyone acted in a caring way
towards particular others. But this would not, by itself, guarantee
that everyone was cared for, or that everyone's needs were met. To
ensure this, a more impartial view is also necessary. We need the
idea of justice, even though it may not come naturally to us (the
Scottish philosopher David Hume described justice as an artificial
rather than a natural virtue[7]). Our ideas of justice have been constructed in the course of human society; as with the idea of moral
obligation, we can only be motivated by the notion of justice
through having certain concepts, being able to use a certain kind
of language.

If we need justice, we also need people to care about justice.
Caring about justice is not the same thing as caring about particular persons; it is compatible with caring about particular persons,
but it is also the case that to do what is just sometimes means making particular persons, whom one cares about, worse off than they
would otherwise be. Rather than caring about particular others,
the guiding motivation here is caring about justice itself. (This

direction of someone's concern towards an idea, rather than towards specific persons, is part of what makes justice an artificial rather than a natural virtue.) To care about justice is an instance of what I have been calling moral motivation: it can call on people to act in a particular way, not because they are so inclined, not from their natural benevolence, but simply because this is what justice requires.

Justice will sometimes be necessary to correct too great an immersion in the concrete morality of a particular community.[8] We have too much experience of xenophobia and racism to suppose that the traditions, the respected ways of doing things, of a particular community can be relied on without some more universal sense of what is owed to all persons simply as persons. To illustrate this, imagine that in Milgram's experiment the experimental subject identifies with the experimenter as one of the same community, but identifies the victim as a member of a different group towards whom the subject is habitually prejudiced.

So far I have been suggesting that even when there are bonds of fellow-feeling within a community that will support altruistic behaviour, a principled sense of morality is still important. But there are many people in the modern world who do not feel part of a concrete community. While education should do what it can to promote a sense of membership of concrete communities, we must also provide a moral education for those who may not feel this sense of belonging – which could, in a society where there is great mobility both geographically and in relationships, turn out to be any of our children.

Even if there is no active hostility or prejudice to be overcome, a sense of justice and the existence of generally recognized rules can be important in providing some reliability and predictability in people's lives. You may well think it desirable that another person acts out of their sense of concern for particular others in the concrete situation; but if all you knew about how a person would act was that they would do what they thought best in the concrete situation, you could not be sure how they would act towards you when you are the particular other in the concrete situation. If, on the other hand, you know that the other person recognizes certain generally acknowledged principles or rules, you have some basis for relying on the person acting accordingly. In public and social contexts especially, this degree of reliability can be very important.[9]

While I have been speaking in this section mainly about the idea of justice, the points I have made could be generalized to apply to the idea of morality as such, or at least to the idea of morality in the narrow sense (see Chapter 4). I mean, the notion that in a given situation there is something I ought to do that (even if I have to think hard to identify it) does not depend on how I happen to react to the particular situation (notice that this is in effect one of the interpretations of objectivity that we looked at in Chapter 3). If I have no notion that there is something that would count as getting it right, or at least that some courses of action would be better than others for reasons that do not come down just to how I am affected (whether materially or in my feelings), then there will, in one important sense, be nothing to stop me doing whatever I like in the particular situation. This does not mean that I shall necessarily be selfish. It may very well be (if I am at all a caring person) that in a given situation I shall act partly on my feelings for other people involved in the situation, and these feelings may be altruistic. But if this is all that is motivating me, it may still be too easy for me to follow what are after all my inclinations, without sufficiently modifying them to take into account the point of view of others (including *their* perception, rather than mine, of what is good for them).

What I need here is a degree of objectivity in the way I look at the situation – objectivity in the third of the senses I picked out in Chapter 3. I need a degree of detachment. This does not mean not caring what happens but does mean seeing things in an unbiased way. One way of achieving this is simply to pursue the idea of objectivity in the first of the senses of Chapter 3: the idea that there is a right answer, or at least an answer that is better than some, that I am trying to discover. This does not mean that I have to apply some broad abstract generalization, such as 'don't tell a lie' or 'don't break a promise (whatever the circumstances)'. There can be no guarantee in advance that what I ought to do in the particular situation will involve nothing but the observance of simple rules of that kind.

Rather, I am suggesting that it is the very idea that there is something that would be 'the right thing to do' – or, if not that, then the idea that some things would be 'the wrong thing to do' – that makes a difference here. Even with all the difficulties that idea raises, we might be worse off if it were not a part of our repertoire of ideas.

This still leaves us with the question 'How do I go about establishing what would be the right thing to do?' To come to the remaining sense of objectivity that I mentioned in Chapter 3, is there a procedure, a specific way of thinking I could follow, that would help me to do this? I have already said enough (both in taking seriously some of the objections made by critics of morality, and in what I said about compromise in Chapter 5) to suggest that the right way of thinking will not be a matter of rigidly applying simplistically formulated rules. But it would be a start, at least, to ask oneself seriously, and even systematically, how the situation appears from the perspective of each of the other people involved. In other words (and you will probably find this quite a familiar idea) I ask myself what it would be like to be in their shoes. Having tried to answer that question (which again involves not the rigid application of rules but possibly a good deal of sensitivity and imagination) I ask myself whether I can still endorse what might at first sight have seemed the right thing to do.[10]

The importance of taking a view that is, in this way, objective but not oversimplified also casts light on the common idea that I noted towards the end of Chapter 6: that there is something suspect about passing moral judgement on others. There *is* something suspect about it if one's own judgements about others are liable to be made without a full knowledge of the circumstances of the case. There is also something impractical about treating social problems (which may need political and economic responses) as if they could be solved by the making of moral judgements. In such cases the pejorative word 'moralizing' may be appropriate. But this does not mean that it can never be right to have a view about the rights and wrongs of other people's conduct. If, in my own case, a consideration of how other people are affected by my actions can give me a reason for thinking that it would be wrong to do such-and-such, then in principle, if I know enough about the case, I could cite similar reasons for a provisional conclusion about what someone else is doing. And if I am in a position to be able to talk to the person concerned, then I can explain why I think his or her conduct would be wrong, and my reasons can be open to discussion in turn. This need involve no arrogation on my part of any spurious moral authority.

It is important to recognize – and this is perhaps of particular relevance to teachers – that in saying to someone that I think their conduct is wrong, and being prepared to give my reasons and discuss them, I am not necessarily condemning the person. I need not necessarily be saying that he or she is a bad person, and I certainly need not be, and should not be, getting annoyed or uttering insults. Indeed, since expressing a moral judgement about somebody's conduct – as opposed to keeping my thoughts to myself – is something I do, it is as much subject to moral appraisal as any other piece of conduct. There may be occasions when, even though I could amply defend my judgement about someone else's conduct, it would be better – morally better – to keep it to myself, perhaps because uttering it would do more harm than good. But by the same token, there may be occasions when I *ought* to tell another person that I think his or her conduct is wrong, perhaps because there is a third party whose interests would not otherwise be taken into account. All this, again, may be especially relevant to teachers. Though we shall not be discussing moral education as such until Chapters 11 and 12, it seems unlikely that teachers could get children into the habit of using moral ideas in their own thinking if the teachers themselves did not employ such ideas in their dealings with the children. It is worth remembering, of course, that we use moral ideas in praising others for doing what is right as well as in criticizing them for doing wrong. There would certainly be something suspect about passing moral judgement on others if the only judgements expressed were negative ones.

Morality without imposition

So far in this chapter I have suggested some reasons for thinking that human affairs will improve if people display – in addition to other sorts of motivation – the capacity to act out of a sense of general moral requirements, including those of justice. But it is still true that morality conceived in this way could be something imposed on people as a form of social control. Since teachers who want to educate rather than indoctrinate – in terms of the distinction mentioned in Chapter 2 – will not be happy about imposing something on pupils regardless of their capacity to think for themselves, we still need to reply to the criticism that morality is a form of alienation.

Our response needs to be, I think, straightforward in outline, though it requires care to fill in the details. It is that a sense of moral requirements properly understood does not have to be – or rather, cannot be – imposed from outside, but must be acknowledged through a person's own thinking. For moral philosophers this idea is, again, very much associated with Kant; but in developing it, Kant himself was drawing on an idea that was strong in the tradition of thought in which he was brought up (namely Lutheran Christianity). This is the idea that to be moral one has to be autonomous. To be following the dictates of others – whether of tradition, of one's society, or of the God one believes in – is not to be acting as a moral being at all.

We have to be careful with the notion of autonomy here, as it can easily be misleading. In many contexts, when we speak of people thinking for themselves, making their own decisions, we expect different people to come up with different answers – from which, in a moral context, some sort of subjectivism or lack of objectivity might seem to follow. But this modern association of autonomy with 'anything goes' must be put on one side if we are to understand the idea of morality as self-generated rather than imposed.[11] The comparison with mathematics, which I have already used in Chapter 3, may help. Any self-respecting teacher of maths will want pupils to work out answers for themselves – as opposed to, say, copying from someone else or from answers in the back of the book. But it does not at all follow from this that any answer is as good as any other. (I am thinking here of calculations within set parameters, rather than the kind of mathematical investigation where a pupil may indeed come up with an original way of going about the task. Even in the latter kind of task, some ways will work and others will not.) Thinking for oneself is not incompatible with the existence of a particular answer that, if one is doing the thinking properly, one will eventually discover.

We can adopt a similar position with regard to morality. It is not a field of free creativity; there are rational considerations. As a matter of rationality, there are moral claims we have to recognize. But *we* have to recognize them, rather than blindly following answers given by others.[12] If something like this is right, then the idea of imposing morality on others becomes a contradiction in terms. People will have to appreciate the force of moral thinking for themselves, and there will be a role for moral education, not in imposing anything, but rather in enabling people to see what in the end they will have to see for themselves.

All this leaves us, however, with a question that may seem much more problematic in the case of morality than in the case of mathematics: whether we can make morality intelligible to the people who have to do the thinking. I have said that morality is largely a matter of having and using, with a sense of its significance, a certain kind of language. But if we are trying to educate people to think for themselves, we must expect that they will cast a critical eye on the language we encourage them to use; that they will ask questions like 'What does it mean to say that something is wrong or that I morally ought to do something?' Do we have an answer?

I shall call this the problem of making sense of morality. It will be the topic of the next chapter, in which I shall look again at the question of the relationship between morality and religion, and between both of these and the idea of spirituality. The reason for raising those issues is that there will be little future for morality across much of the world if we cannot make sense of it outside a religious context, yet at the same time it is the lack of that context for many people – and in a sense for whole societies[13] – that raises the problem of making sense of morality in an acute form.

Before turning to that issue, I want to say a little more on the idea that there could be ways of thinking that people can follow for themselves which, if they are properly pursued, will lead to determinate answers. In my analogies with maths, I have assumed that the appropriate thought process is one that separate individuals can follow for themselves. We often make similar assumptions about morality, as indeed did Kant in his reference to a moral compass that the individual can use (the test of universalizability).[14] But in modern times the German social theorist Jurgen Habermas has suggested that the right kind of thinking (given, I would add, certain assumptions about the kind of issue in question) is one that can only be carried out in dialogue.

In Habermas's theory of 'communicative ethics'[15] the initial idea, very roughly, is that within a community where there are conflicting interests the way to resolve moral disputes is through dialogue. This by itself will not sound surprising, but it already moves away from the assumption that any individual by his or her own rational thinking can see the right thing to do. Habermas is saying that where the moral problem arises from a clash of interests, then dialogue, if it is unconstrained[16] can lead to a resolution that is in the interests of all. In that kind of situation, at least, we have a collective version of the idea that there is an objective procedure, the outcome of which will be what is right. In this case, what it means for something to be right is precisely that it is what would emerge from unconstrained dialogue in which everyone's voice has been heard.

I have mentioned that certain assumptions are involved because it would be difficult to fit all moral disputes, even in principle, under the idea of dialogue in which common interests can emerge.[17] For one thing, people do not necessarily see the moral stance they take on certain issues as being a matter of anyone's *interests*. This is true of a good deal of religiously based moral beliefs, and we shall see in Chapter 9 that it is also true of the positions that many people take on issues of abortion and the environment. Another consideration, as we shall also see in Chapter 9, is that communicative ethics seem not to take account of parties that cannot themselves be participants in a dialogue. Nevertheless, Habermas's arguments have been very fruitful. I shall mention them again in Chapter 12 in connection with the role of discussion in values education.

[1] Some of the issues about non-human altruism were famously popularized – but not necessarily clarified, as regards the use of the words 'altruistic' and 'selfish' – by Richard Dawkins (1976) in *The Selfish Gene.* Philosophers who have sorted through the issues about the biological bases for altruism and morality include Midgley (1979b) and Singer (1981). See also Ridley (2003).

[2] Kant (1948: 63–64) (first published 1785).

[3] Kant (1948: 64). (The language is, of course, that of one particular translation from the German.)

[4] No shocks were actually inflicted, and the 'victims' were actors. The set-up was explained to the real subjects of the experiment – the people who thought they were inflicting the shocks – afterwards. See Milgram (1974).

[5] Milgram (1974), Chapters 10–13.

[6] National Curriculum Council (1993: 5). I have said more about this idea of 'the will to behave morally as a point of principle' in Haydon (1999a).

[7] See Hume (1888), Book III, Part II, Section 1 (first published 1739, and frequently republished). Hume's account of the way in which justice remedies some of the defects of human nature bears some affinity to the Hobbesian account of morality that we looked at in Chapter 4.

[8] The notion of the ways of doing things in a particular community, in contrast with an abstract and universal sense of morality, is sometimes referred to by the German word *sittlichkeit*, used in this sense by Hegel.

[9] Kymlicka (2002: 398–420) makes this point well in the course of an illuminating discussion of the ethical perspectives of care and of justice. See also Haydon (1999b), Chapter 10.

[10] I shall come back to this idea in Chapter 12, where I shall also refer to the writings of Richard Hare for the more careful formulation that the idea needs. See also Haydon (2000a).

[11] Confusion with modern connotations of the term 'autonomy' has often contributed to misreadings of Kant. Secondary sources on Kantian ethics are not necessarily reliable. I am grateful to Lenval Callender for his forceful arguments about Kant and his modern interpreters.

[12] This ties in with the idea of morality as being universal in its form and content, in that it can be recognized by the exercise of the rationality that all normal human beings are capable of, independently of their cultural circumstances. For Kant, this is the basis of the requirement of 'respect for persons' – see Chapter 5.

[13] See the discussion in Chapter 10 of the idea of a secular society.

[14] Kant (1948: 69).

[15] Habermas (1990a), (1990b).

[16] In some of his writings Habermas has referred to an 'ideal speech situation' – a notion we shall encounter again in Chapter 10. See note 6 to that chapter.

[17] Habermas has acknowledged that, in terms of the justice/care distinction, he sees morality within the justice perspective. See Habermas (1990b: 171–188), and Benhabib (1992) on Kohlberg, Habermas, and feminist critiques.

Chapter 8

Making Sense of Morality – and Spirituality Too?

A parochial preamble

If there are any aspects of human experience that are potentially universal, rather than merely local or temporary phenomena, we might think that morality and spirituality would be good candidates. Yet where school curricula are concerned there is ample room for variation in how these aspects of human experience are approached – if they are approached at all. This chapter will say something about the possible relationships between morality, religion and spirituality. While most of the discussion would be applicable anywhere, this first section will briefly outline some relevant features of the school context that are specific to England.

Unlike the USA, where a separation of Church and state is enshrined in the constitution, England has an established Church. Had that not been the case, the *1944 Education Act* might not have made religious education a compulsory part of the school curriculum – at that time, indeed, the only legally compulsory part of the curriculum. For many years the compulsory presence of religion in the curriculum of schools in England made it easy for people to think that moral education could be safely left to the practitioners of religion and of religious education. Of course, the fact that many people do associate morality closely with religion is not a specifically English phenomenon. But in a country like the USA the question had to be faced much earlier of whether, and how, moral education could be taught in schools quite independently of religion.[1] In England, systematic attempts to develop a theory and practice of moral education quite independently of religion have appeared relatively late on the scene.

It may also have been a legacy of the institutionalization of religion within the school curriculum that even when there came to be a fairly widespread scepticism about the value of compulsory religious education, some people retained a sense schools had certain responsibilities, not unrelated to religion, that they could not shrug off. In the 1980s and 1990s these responsibilities were often put under the heading of 'spirituality'. In 1988 a concern with spirituality was written into the legislation governing the school curriculum. The *Education Reform Act* required every school to have a curriculum that would:

(a) promote the spiritual, moral, cultural, mental and physical development of pupils at the school and of society;
(b) prepare such pupils for the opportunities, responsibilities and experiences of adult life.

The reference to spiritual development has been retained in the more recent version of the aims of the National Curriculum, introduced in 2000, in which Aim 2 reads: 'The school curriculum should aim to promote pupils' spiritual, moral, social and cultural development and prepare all pupils for the opportunities, responsibilities and experiences of life.' It seems likely that the word 'spiritual' was originally put there, in 1988, to ensure that there would be, within the preamble of the Act, a legitimation of the role of religious education within the curriculum. Even the drafters of the legislation probably felt that in a liberal and plural society, they could not quite demand in law the *religious* development of pupils and of society. The word 'spiritual' offered a broader scope.

In the early 1990s, there were documents from the National Curriculum Council, its successor the School Curriculum and Assessment Authority, and from Ofsted, devoted to making sense of the notion of spiritual development and offering teachers some guidance in how to approach it. By the mid-1990s a consensus seemed to be emerging on at least two points: that spiritual development did not necessarily have to be tied to religion, and that spiritual and moral development were not the same thing, but were nevertheless difficult to disentangle. In those early years of the 1990s official concern with values in the curriculum seemed to be dominated by those twin notions of spirituality and morality. After 1997, as already noted in Chapter 1, attention turned more towards citizenship.

The task of the present chapter is not to try to untangle the intricacies of English educational policy at any particular time, but to try in more general terms to disentangle the three ideas of religion, morality and spirituality. The importance of doing that in the context of this book is that, as I said at the end of Chapter 7, we need to be able to make sense of morality. For many people, religion used to provide the way of making sense of morality, locating it within a wider framework of meaning. If we now have to make sense of morality independently of religion, could it still be that the notion of spirituality, or something like it, can be helpful?

I think it unlikely that the particular *word* 'spirituality' is indispensable, but I would not go so far as John White who in the mid-1990s said that he 'would advocate an absolute embargo on the use of the terms "spirituality" or "spiritual development" in all official documents on education, all conferences on education, all inservice courses for teachers, all inaugural lectures'.[2] Even if it is largely a matter of historical accident that the term 'spiritual development' features in English legislation about the curriculum, while the word is there teachers do need to make sense of it. And it may turn out that if we did not have that word, we would have to invent a different one to do the same job.

Morality and religion

I referred at the end of Chapter 7 to the conception of morality, which I associated in a quite unrigorous way with Kant, by which morality has to be autonomously endorsed by each individual. There is no doubt that morality, on that conception, is logically distinct from religion, since we are not acting as autonomous moral agents if we follow an alleged divine source. The word 'alleged' is important here, since there are many alleged divine sources, and their claims cannot be taken for granted. The idea that the claims of divine sources have to be assessed by human beings might seem difficult to accept if your standpoint is within one of the established religions. But if one stands back sufficiently to think of the many individuals through history who have claimed to be prophets or to have some sort of direct access to the divine will, it is not difficult to see that any religion needs some way of distinguishing between that which is genuine and that which is spurious. Logically the situation is the same, however firmly established a particular religion is. Kant was able to write, from a position firmly within Protestant Christianity, that 'even the

Holy One of the gospel must first be compared with our ideal of moral perfection before we can recognize him to be such'.[3]

Morality and religion, then, do not have to be linked in logic, and for very many people in the modern world they are not linked as a matter of experience. This is certainly something that schools have to recognize. The biggest danger in always linking morality with religion within schools is that if people reject religion they may reject morality along with it. At the same time, it remains true that if you have a strong religious belief, you will probably not see your morality and your religion as distinct. I have already stressed in earlier chapters that moral values may have for a religious believer a significance that they cannot have for a non-believer. Among the differences is that the problem of making sense of morality does not arise for the religious believer in the same way as it does for the non-believer.

I need to explain further what I mean by the problem of making sense of morality. There is a perspective – that of a sociologist or anthropologist, perhaps – that allows us to look at morality from the outside, and from that standpoint it certainly seems that we do not need to refer to religion to make sense of morality. We may see morality essentially in the Hobbesian way, as a social device by which, by and large, people benefit, because it restrains the exercise of human impulses that might otherwise be acted out in anti-social ways. We can also try to give biological and evolutionary explanations of morality, as sociobiologists and evolutionary psychologists are trying to do.[4]

These are valid, even if partial, ways of seeking to understand morality, and I see no reason why morality should not be studied in such ways within education. If we can detach ourselves a little from that traditional canon of subjects that we noted in Chapter 2, it may seem odd that whereas 'politics' or 'economics' or 'psychology' can be school subjects, at least at the upper levels of secondary education, 'morality' as a subject of study hardly figures in the school curriculum in England (unless it does so misleadingly, as a part of religious education). I suspect, though, that some people will object to the idea of morality being treated from the outside as a subject of study at school level, because they feel this will weaken whatever force it has from the inside. I do not think that need be so (any more than being a student of comparative religion is incompatible with being a believer within one faith). But it is true that the view from the outside is not the same as the view from the inside.

Essentially, the problem of making sense of morality is the problem of how it is to be seen from the inside. The question is roughly this: can I understand morality, not just as a system and a way of using language that I can observe (some) other people in society following, but as something that I can intelligibly see myself as part of, something that I am on the inside of and that has meaning and force for me? There is another question that is related to this one, namely, What's in it for me? Why should I take any notice of it? What will I get out of it? These questions have been debated at least since Plato had Socrates pose the question, 'Why should I be just?'[5] It is a question asked from the perspective of an individual who is interested only in his or her well-being (roughly the kind of individual Hobbes had in mind). The question can be given an answer of sorts within its own terms. It may well be that life will go better for you if you respect morality rather than ignore it when it seems inconvenient for you. It is not always easy to get away with behaving immorally.[6] But on the other hand, people do sometimes get away with it. So to reply to the question, 'Why should I be moral?' with the answer 'Because it will be in your best interests' is not very persuasive.

It may also seem beside the point as an answer. It does not just happen as a matter of fact that being moral sometimes means we cannot do what would serve our self-interest. It is a requirement built into morality (in the conception many of us have of it, and in the Kantian conception that I referred to in the last chapter) that we act for *reasons* that are not to do with our own interests, which sometimes means that we have to act in the face of these interests. There are occasions when, morally, we ought to be self-sacrificing. While it may be good for the interests of society as a whole that we have a set of ideas that makes such demands, it will not be at all plausible to say to an individual who is basically self-interested 'sacrificing your own interests is in your interests'. Sometimes, it simply is not: which is why there can still be a problem, from an individual's point of view, in making sense of morality.

A wider framework of meaning?

The first step towards resolving this problem (but only a first step) is to recognize that we do not make sense of things only by seeing that they are in our own interests. It is a common mistake, at least in Western thought, to suppose that this is the only way of doing it. Religion has not been immune to this mistake. When religion has said to people that they will reap the rewards of heaven if they are good and be damned to hell if they are bad, then it has been assuming that people can only make sense of morality in terms of their own self-interest, and trying to show them that, despite worldly appearance, it really is in their interest after all. Of course, once people give up any literal interpretation of the ideas of heaven and hell that appeal no longer has weight. Much religious teaching now does not make use of such an idea, partly because it is not credible to many people in modern society, and partly because much religious thinking would agree with Kant that if you are really only acting for the sake of your own interests, however long term, you are not being moral at all.

If the only way religion could offer to make sense of morality for the individual was by an appeal to self-interest, secular defenders of morality would have nothing to learn from it. But there is another way in which religion can, for its believers, help to make sense of morality, and it might be that this way has something to offer to people who have no religious faith. Religious belief can help to make sense of morality by enabling moral demands to be experienced within a wider framework of meaning, so that, while these demands can still be seen as independently valid, they are not isolated from other aspects of a person's life. It seems to be true of us as human beings that we can act in a certain way, not just because doing so serves some self-interested desires, or even because it serves non-self-interested desires related to particular others (in the way that advocates of an ethic of care often have in mind), but because it makes sense as part of a life that in turn is understood as part of something larger. Religion can provide a set of concepts and beliefs in which the 'something larger' can be expressed. It is worth asking whether there is some wider framework of meaning within which morality can be located that might be available to the non-believer.

Here it is interesting that some modern religious thinking has allowed traditional beliefs about God or the transcendent to be questioned, while retaining the traditional language; so that the language can still provide a framework of meaning even though it is not interpreted in the traditional way. For instance, one way of making sense of moral demands within a religious framework, without seeing them as arbitrary commands of God, is by *identifying* central moral values with the God that is worshipped. Some of the more radical versions of this move lead to an account that Marx would have recognized, by which God becomes (or rather, always was) a projection of human concerns. Thinkers who take this kind of line have been seeking to make sense of, or to retain a sense for, religious language and practice within a world, and an intellectual culture, in which for many people it has become hard to maintain wholeheartedly or with integrity all the older supernatural beliefs that went with such language and practice.[7]

Talking of God becomes, on such accounts, a way of talking about deep human concerns, about what we most care about, about what we recognize as most important in the world. What is most significant for the present argument is that, while God may be a projection of human values, this does not mean, for those who have developed this kind of account, that they have become atheists. The language and practice of religion that they are a part of still has meaning for them. Freeman (1993), for instance, who when he wrote his book was still a parish priest, claimed that giving up a belief in a literal, supernaturally existent personal God 'out there' did not leave a large hole in his life. It is the language, the practice, the whole 'mind-set' of religion that makes the difference, and this can continue, and can still even have much the same significance, after that belief in its literal truth has been abandoned.

The relevance of this to our question about making sense of morality is that it may be possible for moral language to make sense even if we consciously take a sceptical view about the reality of moral values. Let me spell out the analogy a little further. Some people want to go on using religious language although they cannot accept a literal reading of many scriptural claims, and in fact see religious ideas as a projection of human concerns (where these are not to be taken as confined to self-interested concerns). In a similar way, others may want to go on using moral language even though they are not at all sure that moral values have a reality independently of human concerns. Whatever the case with religion, we may all have good reason for hoping that people will go on using moral language, at least some of the time, even if we ourselves are not sure how to interpret it.

When we reflect on the way we attribute qualities of good and bad, right and wrong to people or to conduct, we may think (as some philosophers have, at least since Hume in the eighteenth century) that we do not observe real qualities that exist independently of our perception, but rather project these qualities on to the world. Such a view does not mean that we can simply invent and apply whatever moral labels we like: our moral conceptions will certainly reflect in some way underlying human concerns that are real aspects of human nature, of the human condition in the world or of rationality as a quality of which humans are capable. It may well be possible to argue that there are good reasons for holding to some particular conceptions of right and wrong and rejecting others. Thus it may be possible to establish a sense in which certain moral claims are objectively valid. But, as I noted in Chapter 3, it is hardly controversial that claims about objective rightness and wrongness cannot be resolved in anything like the same way that we might settle claims about things, like rocks and planets, that can exist independently of any human thought or action. So recognizing that the language we use for moral values does not pick out something existing independently of our thought need not stop us using the language for the same purposes as before, or experiencing the same effects in our feelings and motivations that this language has traditionally carried.[8]

There is a further important feature of the analogy. While some religious believers have begun, albeit gradually, to think of the language they use as a projection of human concerns, it is important that they have come to think in this way after starting from more traditional or orthodox religious interpretations. The religious language and practices already make sense to them, have a meaning for them; it is not so surprising that a change in intellectual interpretation need not destroy that meaning. What is much more doubtful is whether someone who had never held a religious belief on a more traditional interpretation could find any meaning in religious language and practice if, from the beginning, it were presented in an avowedly 'projectivist' way. There are in modern society (proportionally more in Britain than in the USA) many who do grow up without encountering religious language and practice in family or community contexts. For young people in this position, it does not seem very likely that the use of religious language, or a degree of institutionalized religious practice (as in school assemblies) within the context of schooling can supply what is not present in family and community. So while it may be true that for some people an early initiation into religious thinking has been a route into taking morality seriously, so that the commitment to morality survives after the religion has fallen away, this is not a route that can plausibly be advocated for young people growing up in a secular environment.

What remains from the analogy between religion and morality is that someone may be able to take the view that moral language is (merely) a projection of human concerns – that there is nothing other-worldly or transcendent about moral claims – and still find the same force in that language, *if* that person has already been on the inside of moral language and has become accustomed to using it in thinking about his or her own conduct and that of others. But if we were to present moral ideas for the first time to someone who had never encountered them, it is doubtful whether we could convert them to these ideas if we could only, in effect, represent the ideas as a sophisticated form of social control.

It is at this point that there may be an important role for educational institutions, a function to perform on a social rather than individual level: to ensure that moral language itself is kept alive by getting people used to using that language – because others around them are accustomed to use it – even before they begin to reflect on it critically. Only if the language is available will it be possible for someone to be motivated by the thought 'I ought not to do this' or 'I have an obligation to do that'. Only if that possibility is there is there any point in asking the next question: on what understanding of moral language is it possible for someone to be moved by it?

Individual (and spiritual?) understandings of morality

This is another instance when the long-standing question 'Why should I be moral?' is misleading. In the history of philosophy this question has often been conceived as addressed to a rational individual, as if it were a question that could be answered for an individual, in isolation from any consideration of membership in a community. Interpreted in that way, there is probably no satisfactory answer to it.

When someone has a tangible sense of membership in a community with particular others, and can see the importance that

moral values have for real people in a real community, then sceptical questions about morality may have no real weight – and in
any case a distinctively moral form of motivation may be less necessary. But this is a relatively straightforward example. What of
the person who is thoroughly alienated (or 'socially excluded' in
a current piece of political jargon), who has no sense of real community with anyone else, or who has a sense of community only
within a sub-community that is itself alienated from the wider
society? It is in such a case, if anywhere, that the force of morality
may be needed (as I suggested in Chapter 7) but also where it is
most difficult for morality to be experienced other than as an
alien imposition.

Think, perhaps, of what is needed if a teenager is to reject, on
moral grounds, peer group pressure to join in with some antisocial
behaviour. The only community they identify with is their immediate peer group; the wider community is not real to them in the
same way. Yet it could perhaps become sufficiently real to move the
person if they could ask themselves seriously a question like 'Could
I justify what I am doing to others in terms they couldn't reasonably
reject?' They may recognize that there is no way, in practice, that
they could persuade their associates to change their minds. Yet if
the person sees clearly enough that what they are proposing to do
is something that other people, from their own point of view (perhaps as victims), would have every reason to reject, this could be
enough to enable them to go against the peer group.

What is happening in such a case is that a distinctively moral
kind of motivation is operating: the desire to be able to justify
what one is doing.[9] This may on the face of it sound like a rather
thin and secondary kind of justification: it is not like acting out of
love for one's fellow creatures, and no doubt truly altruistic, caring
people would not go through life constantly asking themselves
whether they can justify what they are doing. Yet it is a form of
motivation that can operate quite strongly in human beings (it is
closely related to the caring about justice that I looked at in
Chapter 7), and one that it is possible to cultivate, and that is well
worth cultivating.[10]

To ask whether you could justify your actions – where this
means at least in principle justifying them *to others*, not just in
some abstract way – will involve seeing whether others (assuming
they were being reasonable) could approve of what you are doing.

To ask that will involve putting yourself in other people's shoes, in the way that I mentioned towards the end of Chapter 7. That is why imagination as well as reasoning is involved. Even if someone does not care about the particular individuals they encounter, it is conceivable that they could be moved by seeing themselves, in effect, as part of a notional community, of the community as it ought to be, even if to some degree members of their own actual community would reject what they are doing.[11]

What has all this to do with spirituality? Just that the notion of spirituality (assuming we can provide an interpretation that may be useful within education) will have to do with the sense of oneself within a wider framework of meaning.[12] By this I mean something not just cognitive, but involving a person's feelings as well. If we thought of someone as quite 'unspiritual' we might mean that the person is immersed wholly in the concerns of the immediate and mundane world. (Perhaps this is the condition of many people in the modern world, but by no means all, as popular interest in ideas of spirituality shows.) Spiritual development would have to do with achieving a sense – a *felt* sense, beyond mere verbal expression – of connection with, even perhaps membership of, some larger whole. For many people historically, that sense of belonging to something larger has been expressed in religious ways, but it need not be. There will be something of the spiritual, too, about identification with a wider human community, or, for some people, with a community wider than the human, involving all of life on earth, the biosphere.[13] For others, it may be a matter of seeing oneself as a part, an almost infinitesimally small part but nevertheless a part, of the universe.

Moral development, then, not necessarily in the sense of becoming more moral in one's behaviour, but in the sense of coming to have an awareness of a place in a moral scheme of things, can also be spiritual development.[14] Kant, whose conception of morality I do find in a way inspiring, though I can hardly claim to be following it, said that only two things filled him with awe: the starry heavens above and the moral law within. As we understand more and more about the 'starry heavens' through astronomy and cosmology, this cognitive understanding does not by itself make the vastness of the universe any less awesome. That can, importantly, be true both for those who see a divine purpose beyond the universe and for those who see it as the product of

132

blind physical forces. A moral sense, that links one, sometimes in spite of one's own inclinations and preferences, to other people and to a wider world, is also a remarkable thing, whether one sees it as a divine gift or as a 'social construction' and thereby a purely human achievement.

There is another analogy too. The universe is there, independently of the perceptions of it or reactions to it of human beings, but persons may react, or fail to react, to it in very different ways. Morality as a system of values may also have some content that is the same for everyone, but people may relate to it differently. In other words, the idea that there is something very personal and individual about moral development is not incompatible with the idea that there is a common core to morality. We might say, instead, that there is an area of spiritual development – one area among others – that involves each person's individual response to a common set of moral ideas. If, in the end, one sees those moral ideas as a purely human creation, that should not belittle them. Those who are inclined to see themselves as taking a modern, or indeed postmodern, view of things, may find it worth reflecting on the fact that it is possible to see moral ideas and ideals as a contingent human creation and still be moved by them. Given that it is possible, we can see it as one responsibility of education to help individuals to realize that possibility.

[1] See Kohlberg (1981), e.g., Chapter 8.
[2] White (1995: 16). Though we disagree about the use of the word, my argument towards the end of this chapter does have some affinity with White's.
[3] Kant (1948: 73).
[4] See, e.g., Ridley (2003). From a philosophical perspective Midgley (1979a) is still relevant.
[5] Plato (1995), *The Republic*, Book 1. It was Thrasymachus who pressed the question, while the rest of the dialogue concerns Socrates's attempt to answer it. See Foot (1978) for a modern discussion of the question.
[6] See Hare (1981), Chapter 11.
[7] Writers associated with this kind of move, within a Christian perspective, include Cupitt (1980, and many later works), Shaw (1987), Freeman (1993).
[8] Such a view has been explored and defended, under the headings of 'projectivism' and 'quasi-realism', by Blackburn, first in Blackburn

(1984), Part 2 (a book on the philosophy of language), and in more detail in Blackburn (1993) and Blackburn (1998).

[9] The argument is developed by Scanlon (1982, 1998). Scanlon's position is of the variety known as 'contractualism' (or sometimes 'contractarianism'): roughly the idea that morality functions as a kind of implicit or hypothetical social contract, so that I can test my moral positions by seeing whether they are ones that reasonable people would contract into (or, in Scanlon's argument, could not reasonably refuse to contract into) as a basis for shared life in society.

[10] Scanlon suggests that moral education is largely about cultivating the desire to be able to see one's conduct as justified, with an understanding of what kinds of consideration can count as justifications. (I am sure there are some aspects of moral education that Scanlon is overlooking here.)

[11] There is perhaps a link to be made here with Kant's notion (1947, Chapter 2), that we should live as if we were members of a kingdom of ends, by which he means (if it is possible to express it intelligibly in one sentence) that we should act in the way that we can conceive of all members of society acting, if every member of society were to treat every other member with the respect due to persons, and never to treat another purely as means to his or her own ends.

[12] This understanding of spirituality has been well discussed by Shirley Rowan, in her unpublished London University Ph.D. thesis. On spirituality see also Carr (1995) and Mott-Thornton (1998).

[13] See Clark (1993). Something like this sense of identification with a wider whole may underlie many people's strong moral concern for other animals and for the environment, when this is more than a utilitarian concern for the welfare of future human beings – see Chapter 9.

[14] I think I owe this point originally to Roger Straughan.

PART IV: CITIZENSHIP: SOME VALUE CONTROVERSIES

This book has been stressing the complexities of the issues about values that teachers need to understand and to handle. Teachers face controversial issues that concern values both within their teaching and in their thinking about questions of educational provision and organization. This part illustrates these points by discussing just two sets of issues. What links the two sets of issues – chosen out of many possible topics – is their relationship to citizenship.

1. In any society in which there is diversity of values and a multiplicity of views, there will be issues that are controversial among citizens. Education for citizenship, of course, rests on the hope that citizens who are well informed and have developed skills of political participation will be able to find ways of resolving their disputes peacefully – or if not resolving them, then being able to live with them. But there are always likely to be some issues that weigh so strongly with some citizens, that these citizens will not be content to pursue their cause through peaceful means. Among the issues on which some people have turned to violence to press their case are abortion, the environment and the treatment of animals. Chapter 9 (using the treatment of animals as an extended example) will show that one thing these issues have in common is the importance of recognizing different *kinds* of values.

2. The fact that some controversial topics will be discussed in citizenship classes is not the only link between citizenship and schools. The kinds of schools we have; how these schools are funded and governed; whether there are private schools; whether pupils are selected by ability – issues of this kind affect the kind of society in which we live. They are issues, then, on which any citizen may have a view, while of course they also have special relevance to people who spend their working life in schools. Chapter 10 focuses on one issue of this kind, one which connects with points already made about how values can be different both in their content and

in their significance, from within or from outside of a religious position: should all schools in a multifaith society be secular, or is it acceptable, or desirable, that there should be schools committed to particular faiths?

Chapter 9

Fighting for a Cause: Violence, Persuasion and Education

Non-violence and education

The National Curriculum Statement of Values includes (under 'Relationships'): 'we should resolve disputes peacefully'. This echoes a view that most people would agree with, at least so long as they are not pressed too hard in relation to issues they feel strongly about. For in fact some people do resort to violence in cases of conflict, and it is not always for the sake of their own interests, let alone for the sake of the violence itself. If someone resorts to violence for the sake of it, as may happen in bullying, they are more likely to be creating a conflict than trying to resolve one. Yet sometimes people resort to violence for the sake of others or for the sake of what they see as a matter of rights or principle. Think of the recent history of South Africa and of Northern Ireland; think of protest and direct action in Britain and North America over abortion, animal rights or the destruction of the environment.

Clearly there are a number of ways in which schools might try to promote a readiness to resolve disputes peacefully: through their ethos, their rules (which will not necessarily be made and imposed from above), by teachers' example, and perhaps through techniques of conflict resolution and mediation that can be taught.[1] But why should schools have any special concern with this value among others? I would suggest that to be concerned with peaceful resolution of conflict is not an optional extra. Nor is it only a practical concern which is necessary to make the work of the school run smoothly. Anyone has reason to value the non-violent resolution of conflict if they recognize values that have more traditionally be seen as the concern of education, such as rationality and autonomy. These are not just values that have been popular in liberal philosophy of education. It is doubtful whether anyone would deny that there are some circumstances in which it is better for people to be rational rather than irrational, to think for themselves rather than merely follow what others tell them (there is, of course, no guarantee, especially in a plural society, that the others in question will be 'proper authorities'). The resort to violence is, in a sense, the direct negation of these values. To pursue a dispute by violence is not to settle it by reason, and does nothing to ensure that the conflict will be resolved in the way that might be most reasonable, all things considered. And to use violence against persons is generally to interfere with their pursuit of their own goals, plans and hopes, and is thus an interference with their autonomy.

However, it does not follow from that argument that violence, or indeed an interference with people's autonomy, is always wrong. There may be cases in which the settlement of a conflict by rational discussion is not possible or has been tried and has failed, and where the readiness to use violence at the expense of someone's autonomy may be justified in defence of others. If one believes that a resort to violence can never be justified, one has to be not merely a pacifist so far as war is concerned but also an opponent of any use of constraint by police or prison officers. In effect, one has to be an anarchist, and trust that there will be less violence without the state than with it. That is another illustration of how difficult it is to hold absolutist positions, without at least the willingness to make careful and sometimes complex distinctions.

But it clearly should be possible for schools to promote the readiness and capacity to resolve disputes non-violently without taking a stand for an ethic of non-violence in all circumstances. At the same time, though, and as one instance of a general concern for independence of thought, a school needs to develop in its pupils the ability to think for themselves about whether violence is ever justified, and if so, when. That question may very well come up explicitly for discussion in schools, in general terms or in one of its specific applications. I want to say more here, then, about the reasons that may lead people to use violence in a cause that they see as moral. This will also give me the opportunity to bring out an important distinction between different kinds of value, or between consequentialist and other kinds of argument about the value of life and of the environment.

Abortion, animals and the environment

At the end of the discussion of compromise in Chapter 5 I referred to the kind of informal negotiation over values that can go on between groups within a plural society. Consistency with democratic principles in a plural society requires, not just that questions of values should be publicly discussed and negotiated, but that no one's voice should be excluded from the discussion for reasons of gender, ethnic identification, religion, disabilities, age, sexual orientation or any other differentiating factor. This principle will be relevant again in our discussion of the secular society in the next chapter, and in relation to equal opportunities in the final chapter. This principle does not say that everyone's view is equally valid or that no one should express disagreement with or disapproval of another's point of view; it emphasizes that everyone has a right to be heard. (In the case of persons born and living with disabilities, however severe, we should, if at all possible, acknowledge that they can have their own voice in the discussion – rather than having to be spoken for by someone else – and that the onus is on everyone else to find ways of listening to it.)

However, some of the most deeply held values encountered in our society concern parties (or objects) who (or which) cannot themselves join the discussion, such as unborn babies, people in a persistent vegetative state, non-human animals, and aspects of the natural environment (trees, forests, mountains and so on). The discussion that goes on about, for instance, the morality of abortion or the treatment of animals does not, and cannot in any literal sense, include the very parties that the discussion is about. The conflict that can arise over these issues is not conflict with the unborn child or (with occasional exceptions, as when wild animals are directly dangerous to human beings or are carrying infectious diseases) conflict with the animals. This fact itself may increase the danger of conflict breaking out between persons, and make compromise more difficult between those persons who hold different moral positions on the issues.

Some of the issues over which people get into conflict are issues concerning the interests or rights of those same people (or objects). When people are in conflict over an issue of this sort (say, over the distribution of resources to which both sides have a claim), each side at least has the possibility of shifting ground, of making some concession on their own behalf. This opens the possibility of a compromise, which would in the most direct sense be a compromise between the parties concerned. The situation cannot be quite the same when people see themselves as defending those who cannot defend themselves: as when they are speaking for unborn children or non-human animals. The unborn or animals cannot enter into a compromise; and their self-appointed defenders may feel that they cannot compromise with the interests or rights of those who cannot compromise for themselves. (I am here, in effect, expanding on the point I made in Chapter 4, that many things perceived as moral wrongs are perceived as actions having victims.) Perhaps this goes some way to explaining why, in recent years in Western societies, people have been willing to turn to violence over issues of this sort. Violence on behalf of those who cannot defend themselves may, because it is clearly not selfish, seem more defensible than violence on one's own behalf, even if those fighting on their own behalf can claim that they have justice on their side (as many oppressed minorities fighting against their oppressors have been able to claim).

The case of defending the natural environment raises some issues that are similar, and others that are quite different. There are, roughly speaking, two quite different kinds of concern about the environment. First, people can be concerned about the effects that action on the environment has for other people and animals. This category can be subdivided:

1. Someone may be concerned about the effects of a policy on themselves, as when people protest about a new road being built too close to their own house. Their protest may be justified, but it will not be a case of protest in defence of others.
2. Someone may protest about the effects of a policy on other people, and these may be people who are not able to speak for themselves because they do not yet exist. Into this class come protests about the storing of nuclear waste, on the grounds that it could create a dangerous environment for future generations.
3. Someone may protest about the effects of a policy on animals – again, it could be the effects on existing animals, or the effects on future animals which might, for instance, have a harder struggle to survive because of changes in their habitat.

All the subdivisions in this first category have something important in common: the reason for objecting to a course of action is its effect on sentient beings, whether persons or animals, that have feelings and interests, can suffer pain, and therefore can be harmed or benefitted. In terms I introduced in Chapter 5, the reasons are consequentialist, because they are concerned about consequences, and utilitarian, in that they assess the consequences in terms of the interests or welfare of sentient beings. Only *sentient* beings can have interests or welfare (in the sense in which I am using the terms here, which seems to be a quite normal sense) because only beings that can experience something can suffer pain and misery (and sometimes feel pleasure and happiness too). So there can be reasons for objecting to, say, fox-hunting (sheer pain and probably terror too) that cannot apply to cutting down trees (assuming that people's education in biology has left them with no reason for attributing feelings to plants).

It does not follow from this that morally we can do what we like to trees, but it is true that reasons for not doing what we like to trees must be of a different kind. This brings us to the second kind of concern about the environment: many people treat the destruction of the natural environment (or particular parts of it) itself, quite apart from any consequences for people or That is because they see the natural environment as bein in its own right, not just good for sentient beings that may benefit from it or depend on it. (You can see for yourself that reasons of both kinds may be put forward for saving rainforests.)

Similarly, there are two different kinds of reason for objecting to the destruction of a beautiful landscape. One is that people in future will no longer be able to enjoy its beauty. That is another utilitarian reason. That will perhaps sound surprising, given the everyday use of the term 'utilitarian' to indicate that something is being valued only for what we can get out of it in monetary or material terms. But the stricter philosophical meaning of the term (see note 5 to Chapter 5) refers to the value of anything being assessed in terms of its consequences, where the consequences are themselves assessed in terms of pleasure or well-being. So people who appreciate the landscape for its sheer beauty are not themselves thinking as utilitarians. But if someone else says that the landscape should be preserved so that people can continue to appreciate its beauty (i.e. experience pleasure of some kind in looking at it), *that* is a utilitarian reason for preserving it. So it is different from another kind of reason that says that the landscape, or the beauty of the landscape, is important in itself, quite apart from whether anyone gets pleasure from seeing it.

Though it may be far from obvious, there is a similar difference in people's thinking about the value of life. This difference lies behind some of the controversy, and some of the misunderstanding, over issues such as abortion and euthanasia. To some people, the only value a human life can have is its value *to persons*, including its value to the person whose life it is. When human beings are in a persistent (and irreversible) vegetative state their life has no meaning and no value *to them*; if they have no consciousness, no experience, then it makes no difference *to them* whether they live or die. Of course, there may be other people who will be upset if they die. But if that happens not to be the case, then in terms of the value of a human life *to persons*, we would have to say that a life in such circumstances has no value. But many people think that the life of a human being, even in such circumstances, still has value. Then they are saying that the life has value *in itself*.

Similarly for a foetus, at least in the early weeks of gestation, it makes no difference *to the foetus at that time* whether it lives or dies. Of course, a normal foetus in normal circumstances will develop into a person who will consciously live his or her life. If we say that it would be wrong to abort a foetus because, if it lives, it will probably have a good life, that is thinking in terms of consequences. By the same token we could say that it would be right to abort the foetus (perhaps even wrong to let it go on living) if we think it will probably have an unhappy life. Neither argument is saying that there is anything wrong *in itself* in destroying a foetus, independently of the consequences. Nevertheless, many people do think that, because they think a human life has value in itself.

In addition to the idea that human life is valuable in itself, some people consider human life to be the most valuable thing there is. These ideas are at least part of what is meant by the idea of the sanctity of life. We can find further meaning in that idea, and perhaps have a further reason for holding it, if we believe that any human life is the creation of God. But the notion of sanctity of life is not confined to theists.[2]

It is not my purpose here to argue for a specific conclusion on issues about environmental ethics or the morality of abortion. The distinction between consequentialist reasons and the valuing of things or states of affairs in their own right is, however, an important one, and neglecting it could well lead to confusion in discussion, or to some points of view not being taken seriously. The same distinction comes up in relation to animals as well. When people campaign to save a species of whale, it is usually the survival of a species as such that they are concerned about. A species does not have feelings, although the individual members of it may. People may also, of course, be concerned about the suffering of whales that get harpooned or about the welfare of the young that get left alone. But suppose there were a painless way of killing all the surviving members of a species at once. There could be no objection to that on grounds of the suffering of individual animals; but there certainly would still be objections, because the existence of the species itself is valued.

In what follows, returning to the issues about whether violence can be justified in defence of beings that cannot defend themselves, I shall take the treatment of animals as an extended example, but confine the discussion to reasons that come down to the welfare of animals. I shall not here speak of 'animal rights' because the language of 'rights', as noted in Chapter 3, is another piece of terminology that can cause difficulties. Some people would argue that you can only have rights if you are capable of rational thought and of making claims on your own behalf. That is a controversial position, but for present purposes the important point is that for serious issues to arise about how animals should be treated it is not essential to claim that animals have rights. It is sufficient to recognize that the fact that a way of treating an animal causes it to suffer is a moral reason – not necessarily a conclusive reason, but still one that counts – for not treating it that way.

Animals, violence and education

One observation about the dispute over the use of animals (especially, but not exclusively, their use in scientific research) is that, on one side at least, it is likely to be motivated largely by moral considerations (in the sense in which moral considerations are contrasted with considerations of self-interest). Most people would not have reasons of self-interest for campaigning for an end to cruel treatment of animals (though it is possible that someone may seek to advance their own position through the role they play in a protest movement). Even when a concern for animal welfare has led some campaigners to use violent methods, it is still plausible to see their motivation as predominantly moral, though others may judge it to be misguided.

It is less easy to generalize about motivation on the other side, or even about who is to be included in 'the other side'. Different people, out of a concern for animal welfare, will include a variety of categories in 'the other side': hunters and shooters of wild animals; suppliers of fur; animal experimenters; arguably all those who simply eat meat without qualms. But there are certainly moral views and moral motivations among at least some of those categories. Some simply see nothing wrong in using animals in whatever way suits human purposes: that is a moral view, but one that does not usually involve a specifically moral motivation for one kind of action or another. In the case of animal experimentation for medical purposes, some argue not just that this is justified for the sake of human good but that it would be unjustified not to use animals for that end. There are other disputes again that are relevant to relations between cultural groups in a multifaith society, in which Islamic and Jewish methods of slaughtering animals have at times been a point of controversy.

It is not my purpose here to take sides in these disputes, though I should perhaps indicate what my own approach would be. The issues are ones, I think, that need to be worked through primarily in terms of consequences rather than by appeals to rights. Appealing just to consequences and not at all to rights, there is already a strong consequentialist argument for vegetarianism.[3] In fact, the case against eating animals is much stronger than the case against the use of animals in at least some medical research, simply because in the case of research it is plausible – though controversial – to claim that important human interests are protected and promoted through research on animals, so that there is a serious weighing of consequences to be done. There are no human interests of comparable importance that are protected or promoted through the eating of animals. One might well conclude even from this much that anyone who is serious about defending research on animals on ethical grounds ought to be willing to demonstrate their sincerity by being a vegetarian.

I shall not pursue the point further here since my purpose is not to argue through the ethical issues in the human treatment of animals, but more specifically to ask about the ethics of resort to violence by campaigners who sincerely believe that they are defending the interest of animals.

Are there, then, any reasons that should persuade campaigners for animal welfare that they ought not to resort to violence, even when they feel that the odds are stacked against the innocent victims they are fighting for? I want to suggest that the reasons for compromise and negotiation still have weight on questions of animal welfare, even though the intended beneficiaries of the campaigns cannot be party to the compromise. Precisely because animals cannot speak for themselves, how they are treated depends on the moral values of people in society. It will only be through changes in the prevailing moral climate of society that significant changes will come about in the treatment of animals. It is, then, appropriate and inevitable that it is between the conflicting moral positions of persons that the issue is played out.

To try to arrive at a moral consensus or a basis for legislation that will improve animal welfare *is* to work for the defence of animals, even if someone has to compromise and retreat, at least temporarily, from their own stronger position. This does not mean, of course, that there are not moves that an individual can make, and may feel morally obliged to make, independently of whether they are having any effect in shifting a broader social consensus. The person concerned could become a vegetarian, avoid products tested on animals, or join peaceful demonstrations, independently of how many other people are doing the same. It does not follow that the same person would be justified in resorting to violence against other persons who disagree or who take no action. The reason for the difference is that in the case of individual non-violent action there are no strong countervailing moral values that have to be set against the defence of animals. In deciding, say, to be a vegetarian, a person may not be compromising at all between different moral values. If such a person is consciously making some sort of compromise, it is likely to be that in giving some weight to reasons such as their own convenience or lack of social embarrassment – which they might acknowledge are not really moral reasons – the person is not going as far as they might, perhaps only becoming vegetarian rather than vegan.

As an aside, and bearing on the general theme of compromise between values, it is worth adding that compromise of this sort arguably does not merit the opprobrium sometimes, perhaps disingenuously, laid on it. The argument often heard, that if one does not eschew absolutely all human benefit from animals one has no business taking any steps in the direction of doing less harm to animals, collapses in the face of the argument that if it is the welfare of the victims one is concerned with (rather than one's own moral virtue) something can be a great deal better than nothing. The same would go for the argument that one has no ground for criticizing or trying to avoid violence unless one is prepared to be a complete pacifist. For the victims or potential victims of violence, less violence is almost always better than more.

Think, then, of a person who is inclined towards using violence against other persons, or endangering other persons, in order to promote the cause of animal welfare, but who does stop to reflect. At the risk of gender stereotyping, I shall assume this person is male, and call him the activist. What values should weigh with him, in addition to those that led him to protest in the first place? The values that weigh in favour of campaigning on behalf of animals are still in place; but on the other side there is the value of non-violence against persons. For anyone to whom that value is an absolute, the case against violence is clear-cut. However, it may be that an absolutist stance towards non-violence is itself too uncompromising. In the present case I would have to say that the activist may rightly recognize that there are values having some weight on each side of this decision, both for and against the use of violence, so that whatever the activist decides will be a compromise: if he does not use all possible means at his disposal in pursuing his concern with animal welfare, he will be compromising to some degree on that concern.

But if the activist is not appealing on either side of the case to an absolute principle, it will be quite appropriate for him to give considerable weight to the question of whether his proposed methods are likely to promote his cause. He must therefore look at the broader social context, asking seriously whether violent methods are actually more likely than any others to achieve what he wants to see, given that such methods are also certain to antagonize many of those whom he would presumably wish to win over. Since there is no good reason to think that the non-violent methods available to campaigners for animals have been exhausted, any case for violence becomes very weak at this point.

How far might the available non-violent methods themselves be educational? Any such methods will, of course, be indirect from the point of view of animal welfare, since they will be seeking to influence human behaviour towards animals in the longer term, rather than seeking directly to change the conditions of animals living here and now. From a consequentialist point of view, however, indirect and long-term methods will sometimes do more good in the long run than direct ones. So campaigners for animal welfare may well wish to take their message into schools.

The question then arises whether this kind of campaigning is something that can legitimately be done in schools. I suggested in Chapter 2 that the kinds of aims people may try to pursue through schools are many and varied. But in practice the pursuit of any aim needs some degree of consensus, and there would not, in the face of many competing aims, be widespread consensus on pursuing the case of animal welfare though schooling. (If there were, in some society, a much greater consensus on the ethics of the treatment of animals, it might seem natural in that society that the values concerned would be among those 'transmitted' by schools.) Even if schools are not always committed to educational aims and values (where 'educational' has connotations of independence of thought and rationality), the pursuit of such aims is likely to be less controversial. We can ask, then, whether the promotion of animal welfare in schools is compatible with educational values. The kinds of consideration that are relevant here will be relevant also to many other issues on which we might wonder whether controversial positions can reasonably be promoted in schools. What role, if any, should groups and organizations that have a particular ethical or political agenda have inside schools? Should they, for instance, be invited into schools as part of citizenship education?

Someone might think that the promotion of animal welfare is not compatible with educational goals simply because the goal of the campaigners for animal welfare is not itself an educational goal. But from the fact that people are pursuing aims that can be characterized quite independently of education, it does not follow that they cannot use genuinely educational means towards their aims. Indeed, if they believe that evidence and reasoned argument supports their case, and that other people, if unbiased, will see this, then they have every reason to use educational means. Campaigners for animal welfare might make a judicious calculation that people who are encouraged, in an openly educational way, to think about the treatment of animals are on the whole likely to end up taking a position opposed to a great deal of current treatment of animals. They cannot be confident that this will be so in every individual case: an individual who thinks critically about these issues may end up supporting the eating of meat and experimentation on animals. But all that the campaigners need, to be able to use educational means in pursuit of their cause, is a degree of confidence that, by and large, educated and informed people who think about animal welfare are likely to support some changes from the status quo in favour of animals.

So people who have a liberal concern for educational values need to ask campaigning groups – and for that matter, sponsors who wish to put money into the funding of schools – not whether they have a disinterested concern for education for its own sake but whether the methods they would use or support are themselves educational. A distinction will still have to be made between education and propaganda. Campaigners might, for instance, be coming close to pure propaganda if they did little more than present harrowing pictures of laboratory experiments. If instead they engage pupils in discussion, accept criticism, are willing to admit that there might be difficulties and grey areas in their case, what they are doing will be educational. While the distinction may be far from clear-cut in practice, I would suggest that it is important for the campaigners themselves to try to keep it in mind (if only for the reasons that if they do not, they will have little cause for complaint against campaigners on the other side waging their own propaganda drive).

What of the issue of *halal* meat, which might be seen as something of a test case for the values of toleration and compromise in a multifaith society? If a new religion were to spring up that advocated child sacrifice, there would be very few outsiders who would advocate toleration of its practices; most people would feel the issue so clear-cut that it would hardly constitute a test case. Why should liberal defenders of animal welfare (let me in this context call them simply 'liberals' for short) be any more tolerant of Islamic methods of slaughtering animals? Of course, liberals may believe, or at least hope, that liberal education and reasoned argument will have their own influence in the end; but what should be their attitude in the meantime? Let me give at least some indication of how that question might be answered. Any compulsory restriction of Islamic slaughter would be perceived as an imposition of the values of the 'host culture' on a minority. In fact, this would be a correct perception (since the law generally is a matter of imposition, not persuasion), even though the majority culture would be making this imposition on moral grounds, not just to demonstrate its dominance. The question is whether, in this case, the imposition would be justified (as it surely would be in the case of child sacrifice).

Liberals would first have to be quite sure (and not just assume in advance) that the Islamic method of slaughter is less humane than ordinary non-Islamic practices. Then they must be aware of the broader context in which this particular question arises. If liberals could be sure that there are few other ways in which Muslims (in common with members of other minorities) are discriminated against, they might have better ground for confidence in justifying this particular imposition. Then, liberals have to consider whether the value of protecting animals outweighs the value of respecting other cultures, especially those aspects of other cultures that are tied up with religion, and whether alternative approaches are available. If Muslims in Britain have to compromise in some ways with the dominant culture, then liberals may also have to make compromises.

Liberals also have to look at their own record and practices. The liberal tradition has by no means been free of the attitude that animals, with the rest of the natural environment, are so much material to be exploited for human purposes, including the satisfaction of scientific curiosity. (Perhaps it had better be said, though it should not be necessary, that to think that not all scientific use of animals is justified is by no means to take a general 'anti-science' stance.) In a predominantly secular society there are many millions who, with no justification from any particular moral or religious tradition, and with no sense that *they* have to defend a culture that is seriously under threat, continue to eat animals whose slaughter, whether human or not, is actually unnecessary, since eating meat at all is unnecessary.

If we could suppose some sort of society-wide negotiation over the treatment of animals, in which all points of view could be put forward, criticized and, if possible, defended, I suspect that the outcome would be an improvement in the overall lot of animals, and that the greater part of the improvement would come about through changes in the largely taken for granted practices of the dominant, more-or-less secular, more-or-less liberal community.

[1] To teach such techniques was part of the point of the Peace Education referred to in Chapter 2.

[2] Two very different views of the idea of the sanctity of life, both argued in non-theistic terms, are in Dworkin (1993) and Singer (1996).

[3] The argument (without the qualifications that would be needed to make it watertight) can be set out as follows:

1. We ought to avoid suffering if we can do so at little cost to ourselves (this is plausibly a minimal moral principle that it would be difficult to reject if any moral principles are recognized at all).
2. By not eating meat we can avoid (some of) the suffering that is inevitably caused by the large-scale rearing and killing of animals for food, and we can do this at little cost to ourselves, since we do not need to eat meat.
3. Therefore we ought not to eat meat.

See Singer (1976) for an argument of this kind, with supporting evidence. It should be said that philosophers are no more unanimous on this issue than on any other.

Chapter 10

Secular Society, Citizenship and Faith Schools

Should all schools in a modern society be secular? Or, if that would be too illiberal, should all state-supported schools be secular? The issue arises because many parents within religious traditions feel, not just that they want their children to be taught their faith (which might be possible outside school) but that the values that secular schools are promoting are incompatible with the values of their tradition.

We may think of this as an issue arising within a plural society. That is a correct perception, but *not* because a plural society is a multicultural and multifaith one, still less because it is a multiracial one.[1] For a plural society is not necessarily any of these things. Too often the idea of diversity in beliefs and values is associated with the existence in a society of many different cultural, religious and ethnic groups. It is worth remembering that England was a plural society in terms of religious belief long before the large-scale immigration of the third quarter of the twentieth century. Even if it had not been plural in this respect, if there had been only one denomination of one religion in England, there could still have been both belief and unbelief, and the differences in interpretation and significance of moral values which that difference can bring in its train. There are multiple influences on people's values in the early twenty-first century, quite apart from large-scale movements of people. If we could identify one country as monocultural, we might still find within its culture sufficient plurality to fuel controversy on issues such as abortion, the treatment of animals, sexual orientation – and our present issue of secular or non-secular schooling. This issue is one on which different views will cut across different religious outlooks, but the most significant divide seems to be between those for whom any adequate upbringing and education independently of a religious framework is inconceivable, and those for whom that is not so.

The issue is a worrying one for people with liberal values, particularly if their own outlook is thoroughly secular (there are, of course, many people with religious beliefs who are also liberals). Liberals who have a secular outlook are well aware that there are many people who differ in this respect and, of course, being liberals, they would defend the right of people in a liberal society to hold and practise their religious beliefs. Thus, it would seem illiberal to suggest that parents should not be allowed to bring up their children within their faith. But liberals are also often uneasy about the existence of schools that are committed to a non-secular education, or uneasy at least about state support for such schools (though in Britain perhaps the climate of opinion has been swinging towards faith schools in recent years). They may be worried that such schools will inculcate in pupils views that the pupils would not have chosen for themselves or that tend to be divisive in society. Or, more positively, they may be impressed by the thought that the citizens of a plural society are more likely to live harmoniously together if they have shared a common schooling together.

There are many ways in which the discussion of these issues could be approached: through the notion of parental rights in the upbringing of children; the dangers of indoctrination; the meaning and value of autonomy, and so on. These issues have been much discussed in an educational context. Somewhat less often examined is the idea of a secular school: what does it mean to say that a school is secular, and is it desirable that schools should be so?

Secular society

In some respects a school, while artificially hived off from the rest of society, may still be a microcosm of the wider society. That is one reason for looking first at what makes a society secular. Another reason is that, if the surrounding society is secular, then schools, whether they are themselves secular or not, have to prepare their pupils for life in a secular society.

Whether a society is secular is a matter of degree: we can speak of the secularization of society as a gradual process, and there will hardly be an identifiable point at which a society becomes secular.[2] Secularization involves various changes, but I take it, as does

Hirst,[3] that they are linked by 'a decay in the use of religious concepts and beliefs'. But the degree to which a society is secular is not simply a quantitative matter of the extent to which religious concepts are used; it has to do also with the relative position within the society of religious and non-religious thinking.

A lot of thinking goes on in our society which is thoroughly secular, in the sense that it involves no distinctively religious concepts or beliefs at all. This will be true, for instance, of the thinking of the great majority of mathematicians, scientists and engineers *within their professional role*, and it will be true also of much of the everyday thinking of many people within a society like Britain. In this sense much of the thinking of many people in modern societies is secular, whether or not those persons have religious beliefs. Take a scientist who is a Christian. This person's thinking as a scientist, in doing experiments, writing up the results, reading articles and (if they are an academic) teaching, may be qualitatively indistinguishable from that of an atheist. However, there will be other contexts – during church services, for instance – in which their thinking is radically different from the atheist's. There may, then, be a degree of compartmentalization in their life. An important feature of a secular society is that it allows and facilitates this kind of compartmentalization.

It is also the case, though, that the boundaries between compartments are not the same for everyone. There are many contexts which for some people call for the use of religious concepts while for others they do not. Among such contexts could be (in contemporary Britain) celebrating Christmas; discussing some public moral issue; consoling a dying relative, and everyday domestic conversation. Perhaps, then, the degree of secularization of a society is a matter not only of the extent to which it allows compartmentalization but also of the relative prominence of three sorts of context: those (such as doing maths or shopping at the supermarket) which would be generally acknowledged to call for no religious thinking; those, such as religious worship, which would be widely acknowledged, even by those who do not participate, to call for such thinking; and those that are viewed in different ways by different people.

A related difference is in the extent to which different contexts are seen as part of the public life of the society or as part of the private life of individuals. The proportion of the population using religious concepts and holding religious beliefs is itself a far less important measure of secularization than the extent to which such beliefs enter into the public life of the society. At a theoretical extreme, we could imagine a society in which everyone holds religious beliefs, but that all of these are kept private – they do not enter into interpersonal discourse at all. (We would have to imagine some way in which people acquire these beliefs: perhaps parents initiate children into them, but apart from that it is simply not done to mention them.) In such a society there could be, quantitatively, a good deal of religious thinking; but in an important sense the society would be secular, because social discourse would be secular.

Clearly that example rests on a most impoverished view of religion. Sharing one's faith with others, coming together to celebrate and to worship, is a central element of most if not all religions. But there is a sense in which, even given this, religion can still be a private matter. It is possible to know someone, a work colleague for instance, without ever knowing whether that person has a religious faith or not: for if he or she does, it may be practised, not strictly in private, but with like-minded others at the appropriate times. One aspect of secularization, then, is that the expression of religious beliefs, both in speech and in ritual, can become marginalized from the mainstream life of the society. Another aspect related to this is that there are many people, whose own thought is predominantly secular, who assume unless there is evidence to the contrary that the same goes for everyone they encounter.

There are many of us – this again being part of what it is for a society to be secular – who are comfortable with this situation. In academic discussions about education it is often the case either that religious claims do not appear, or that if they do they are treated hypothetically only. It may happen in some educational institutions that after a whole series of seminars in which religious claims have been simply bracketed out, apparently by common consent, it becomes apparent that there is at least one member of the group whose own thinking is by no means thoroughly secular, for whom his or her belief is relevant to the issues discussed, but who has – in effect, albeit unintentionally – not been allowed to bring this belief into the discussion. Of course, this would not be true of all institutions: there may be others in which the reverse is nearer the truth. It is significant that in a secular society institutions of both kinds can exist.

So far I have said nothing about law and politics in a secular society. A country like Britain which has a constitutional, though largely symbolic, link between Church and State can still be a secular society, but this could hardly be the case if it had a law enforcing church attendance. There were arguments towards the end of the twentieth century about whether there should be restrictions on the opening of shops and public houses on Sundays.[4] Such arguments were partly (but only partly) about whether the law was out of step with the secularization of society. There were similar arguments about whether there should be compulsory religious assemblies in schools. But a more central issue is whether law and national policy are made on secular *grounds* or not. In a democratic society government policy and law will be responsive to popular thinking (though not necessarily determined by it). So if people's thinking about the issues of the day goes on largely in non-religious terms, we should expect that the reasons that influence government thinking and politicians' voting will be largely non-religious too. But at the same time there are substantial numbers of people whose thinking is religiously based, especially on moral questions, as we have seen. For them it would be natural that questions of the law on capital punishment, abortion, the age of consent for homosexual intercourse, and many other issues should be influenced by or even based on considerations that are central to their religious beliefs.

Should such considerations come into law and policy, or not? There is one school of thought which argues that in a liberal and democratic society the only considerations that should influence public policy and law are those that any citizen could recognize the force of – and that means non-religious considerations.[5] For instance, in debates about whether there should be any restrictions in businesses trading on Sundays as on other days, arguments about the possible exploitation of workers are secular arguments. Any citizen, whether Christian, of another faith or of no faith, can understand such arguments. While Christians may also have quite different reasons for wishing to restrict trading on Sundays, for the school of thought in question it should be only the arguments accessible to all that come into the public debate.

In a democracy, though, it is hard to see why any kind of argument should be ruled out in advance, or indeed how that could be done in practice. If an argument is irrelevant or inconsistent or unpersuasive, this will, ideally, emerge in the course of the debate. I say 'ideally' because there is an ideal at work here: the ideal of free and open discussion in which all voices are heard.[6] In practice there are many constraints on open discussion. For instance, people whose own thinking is entirely secular may, without repressing non-secular points of view, not really listen to them. This may be simply a matter of settled habits of thought or a lack of understanding, but it can also show a lack of respect and neglect of equal opportunities for the people whose voices do not get heard on matters that may be of central importance to them. In some cases, where links are made in the listener's mind between a person's religion and their ethnicity, it can amount to a form of racism.

So long as religious positions on issues with moral import can be heard in public debate, it is at least possible that their entry will modify the outcome. The outcome in any case is not, in the real world, likely to be a consensus on one view of what is good or right. What may, however, be achievable is an agreement for practical purposes about what ought to be done.[7] In the process of reaching that pragmatic agreement, there is no reason to assume that religious points of view must entirely give way to secular ones. The entry of non-secular views into the debate does at least make it more possible for secular thinkers to appreciate the force that the other points of view have for those who adhere to them. Secular thinkers may pragmatically be willing to make some accommodation to the views of religious thinkers; movement need not be all one way (as it would be, by default, if religious viewpoints were to remain only in the private realm). The suggestion is not that secular and religious thinkers will meet halfway on the truth of their respective worldviews, but that they may indeed meet halfway on practical proposals. Though there is not space here to spell out the detail of the possibilities – on issues such as abortion law, or the limitations of free speech and the legal recognition of blasphemy – there is, as I suggested in discussing compromise, nothing incoherent in the idea of a practical accommodation.

The secular school

What makes a school secular? There are different political traditions that would answer this question in quite different ways. The tradition of *laïcité* in France has been interpreted to mean that a school is not fully secular unless there is a complete absence within it of any observable manifestation of religious belief: hence legal rulings in recent years that clothing and symbols expressing a religious affiliation are not to be worn in state schools. In this way of thinking, an institution is not secular unless it *excludes* religion altogether. The discussion above of secular society shows that a different, *inclusive*, interpretation of secularity is possible, by which an institution is secular, not by excluding religion, but by not being biased in its favour.[8] Within a school that is secular on an inclusive interpretation, religion may be declared, studied and talked about, and the school can aim to promote understanding of religious as well as of non-religious viewpoints (though not to promote adherence to any religious belief).

As in the wider society, secularity may be seen as a matter of degree. The relevant differences between schools will not be primarily a matter of what kind of religious education, if any, goes on in the school. It is conceivable that the timetable of two schools could be identical except that in one a couple of periods a week are devoted to comparative religion and in another the same time is set aside for the teaching of the Bible or the Qur'an. But it is unlikely in practice that there would be only this difference. If we assume that the first school is secular and the second not, we would expect to find other differences. I suggest it is in the other differences, rather than in the content and approach adopted in particular parts of the curriculum, that we need to look for the distinction between the secular and the non-secular. It should be possible to apply here the ideas about thinking and about policy-making that came up in the discussion of what makes a society secular.

We can look, then, at the extent to which the life of the school is compartmentalized into areas in which any use of religious concepts and beliefs, perhaps even any mention of them, would be thought inappropriate, and areas in which it will be expected. We may find that in many schools religious concepts will be mentioned in religious education lessons, and sometimes (but by no means always) in assemblies, but otherwise hardly at all. In some other schools, by contrast, religious language and assumptions might be constantly coming up in the life of the school, if not always in the content of lessons then outside of lessons, in the interaction between pupils and pupils, staff and staff, staff and pupils, staff and parents. So the extent to which a school is secular will have a lot to do with the extent to which religious concepts are used right across the life of the school, and the attitudes adopted regarding their use. As with the wider society, the proportion of pupils or staff holding religious beliefs is not in itself the major factor, for such beliefs may to a greater or lesser extent be treated as private and so, for practical purposes, marginalized.

The issues about the debate and policy-making in the wider society can also be raised in relation to decision-making in the school. We can imagine all the gradations along a spectrum that at one end would have important decisions being made exclusively by a headteacher who claims to be following divine guidance, and at the other end a convention by which any distinctively religious claims would be disqualified from entering into decision-making within the school (so that, for instance, Jewish objections to plans for a special event on a Saturday would have to be couched in some ostensibly secular language). If the wider society is secular that does not directly determine the secularity of schools: both secular and non-secular schools are possible within the same society. So we can move to asking how far and in what ways it is desirable that schools should be secular.

One argument is the often-heard appeal to the importance of tolerance and hence of understanding: that a democratic polity requires tolerance of different points of view and lifestyles, and that tolerance in turn can rest most firmly on understanding. This is a strong argument for teaching everyone – whatever kind of school they are in – about the variety of religions within their own society. This argument needs to be made not only as a matter of interpersonal morality but also as a matter of the preparation of citizens to take part in democratic decision-making. If, as I have suggested, this decision-making should not be confined to purely secular considerations, then an important element of education for citizenship will be to ensure that all can understand the arguments that their fellow-citizens are making.

For the majority of students in secular schools, assuming that their general education is adequate, understanding the terms of *secular* discussion should present no special problem. Almost the whole of their education will have been conducted in secular terms. This will apply to them whether they are themselves from a religious or from a non-religious background. It follows that those who are themselves from religious backgrounds, and who attend secular schools, will have experience of both religious and non-religious discourse. On the other hand, pupils from non-religious backgrounds may not have the basis on which to understand contributions to discussion that are expressed in religious terms, or which depend on religious assumptions. This lack of understanding on the part of some may create an imbalance in discussion – including discussion of any of the public issues that may come up within citizenship education – between religious and non-religious points of view, the effect of which may be that the secular will be privileged and the religious marginalized. A certain sort of religious education, then, can be defended as part of citizenship education, even apart from any other grounds.

There are implications here for the whole ethos and organization of a school. If pupils are being prepared for citizenship in a society that, while secular, is also plural and multifaith, then in any context of school life, and not only in religious education, contributions that have a religious dimension will need to be taken seriously rather than dismissed as irrelevant. What this means in practice will be different for different areas of school organization and curriculum. It may mean one thing in the context of actual decision-making in the school, another thing in curricular areas where the relevance of religious beliefs would be quite widely recognized, such as Personal Social and Health Education; and something else again in subjects such as science where the making of a point on religious grounds will be at least unconventional.[9] But in general we should remember that to argue with a view, if that can be done with understanding and without being patronizing, is to accord greater respect to the holder of the view than simply ignoring it. The point, though, will be not only to accord respect to religious beliefs but also to prepare pupils whose own thinking may be thoroughly secular for their participation in a public life that will not be *exclusively* secular.

Should there be separate religious schools?

So far I have been talking about ways in which a school that is not dedicated to one faith, or to any, should nevertheless not be *completely* secular. But how do these considerations bear on the debate about whether separate schools, dedicated to one faith, should be supported and funded by the state within a predominantly secular society?

If any school can do the job of preparing people to participate as citizens in a democratic, plural and not exclusively secular society, it will to that extent be fulfilling an important role. In this respect, religious schools may be *better* placed to carry out such a preparation than the average secular school. For no school that covers a broad spectrum of forms of enquiry including, for instance, science and mathematics (as required, of course, in all schools subject to the National Curriculum in England and Wales), can fail to expose its pupils to a good deal of secular thinking. So far as the secular/non-secular dimension is concerned, it is only the secular school that can expose its pupils to one sort of thinking only. The possibility of this should be seen as a risk rather than a merit of such schools. On the other hand, there is the question of the actual range of substantive positions that are taken across the whole spectrum of religious and non-religious thinking. While a non-secular school cannot avoid exposing its pupils to some secular thinking, it can, whether deliberately or inadvertently, avoid exposing them to some of the particular moral views, say on homosexuality or on abortion, that are taken by many people within a secular worldview; or if it does not avoid exposure to those views, it may by looking at them from its particular perspective restrict pupils' understanding of them. In this direction lies the major danger of the non-secular school within a plural society.

There remains force too in the familiar arguments for the benefits of educating children from different backgrounds together, if they are to become citizens who can share in the public life of a society into which all citizens can enter on equal terms, regardless of differences in religion, race, gender, class and other categorizations. In arguing that separate religious schools may nevertheless be justified, McLaughlin[10] has stressed that his arguments support a particular kind of religious school, namely one that is promoting autonomy through upbringing in a particular religion. It is also the case that a particular kind of liberal argument for mixed schools will only support a particular kind of mixed school. If the reason for keeping schools as far as possible mixed – in religion or lack of it, as well as in other respects – is to promote tolerance and cohesion between different groups, this argument will support mixed schools that prepare their pupils to participate in a democratic society in which public discussion is not exclusively secular. It may be that the more the ordinary state school is successful in taking non-secular thinking seriously, the less reluctance there will be on the part of many religious believers to send their children there.

If a secular school were taken to be a school that excluded any mention of religious conceptions and beliefs both from its curriculum and from its extracurricular talk and activities, I would argue, on the basis of the requirements of a good education for citizenship, that *no* state school ought to be secular. Of course, the notion of a secular school is not usually, and ought not to be, understood in such an exclusive sense. Most proponents of secular schools intend rather that state schools should not be committed to bringing up children within one faith, nor to maintaining the superiority of a religious over a non-religious worldview. I would agree that most schools in a predominantly secular society should be secular in this thinner sense, though I would also maintain that such schools should not privilege the secular to the extent of marginalizing in advance the voice of the non-secular within public debate. Whether all schools funded by the state should be secular in this thinner sense seems to me to be an open question that still needs further debate (debate that could not, without prejudicing its outcome, exclude religious considerations from the start). There are many practical issues to be considered, but so far as the principle goes, if proponents of religious schools could show that such schools can achieve all that secular schools achieve and more, the onus would be on those who argue that there should only be secular schools within the state system to show why.

---

[1] For the sake of clarity it is worth making a distinction between 'plural' and 'pluralist'. Whether a society is plural – meaning that it contains a diversity of values, beliefs, etc. – is a matter of sociological fact. To say a society is pluralist is to say that it has adopted – perhaps in practice, perhaps officially, perhaps only as an ideal – the position that different cultures and traditions have a right to exist alongside one another without discrimination. It is possible for a society to be plural without having adopted pluralism: South Africa under apartheid was a clear case.

[2] This is a claim about *society*, not about legal and political systems. A change in the constitution of a country could change the official character of a political system from non-secular to secular overnight.

[3] Hirst (1974: 1).

[4] In 2006 there were special restrictions regarding one Sunday in the year – Easter Sunday.

[5] John Rawls' idea of 'public reason' has been influential here: Rawls (1999).

[6] In theoretical discourse this ideal has been articulated in Habermas's notion of an ideal speech situation. See Haydon (1994) for more on Habermas in the context of the present argument, and McCarthy (1978: 291–310) for an accessible treatment of the ideal speech situation.

[7] See Chapter 5; and Benhabib (1992: 9).

[8] The difference is reflected in the fact that in Britain, while there have been disputes over what kind of Islamic costume girls may wear to school, the disputes have been interpreted more in terms of the school's authority to enforce rules about uniform than in terms of whether the secularity of the school is being maintained.

[9] What view should teachers in a secular school take if a pupil in a science lesson raises an objection, from the perspective of creationism or intelligent design theory, to an orthodox evolutionary perspective? An appropriate practical response is something that would need to take the circumstances of a particular school into account. But a good case can be made for two guiding principles: 1) that perspectives that do not count as science, as that is generally understood, do not have to be entertained in science lessons; but also 2) that perspectives that are not obviously irrelevant to an issue should not be dismissed altogether. While it is not part of science (as generally understood now) to mention God as part of an account of the origins of the universe or of life, it is not obviously illogical to do so, and therefore not irrelevant from a broader educational perspective. Consistently with the arguments of this chapter, schools should make it possible somewhere in their curriculum for pupils to consider and discuss religious perspectives on any issue, both as part of their general education and as part of education for citizenship.

[10] McLaughlin (1987, 1992).

PART V: VALUES EDUCATION

Only after seeing something of the variety and complexity of values can we come back to thinking about moral education or values education as specific aims within education.

The usage of the terms 'moral education' and 'values education' is not very consistent. Perhaps there is some tendency for 'values education' to be the broader notion, as would seem logical given that not all values can be construed as moral values. The broad notion of values education will recognize the variety of ways in which values are involved in issues of, say, personal lifestyle, health, religion, citizenship and the environment. There will be, then, large areas of overlap between values education and such curricular concerns as (in England and Wales) Personal Social and Health Education (PSHE) and citizenship education. These same areas will not, of course, be exhausted by values: they will contain bodies of knowledge and skills that are specific to each of them: knowledge for instance about the effects of drugs and about political systems, and skills in handling personal pressures and in political participation. But it is arguable that values, and more specifically moral values, are at the heart of such areas of the curriculum. It is also worth noting that while there is more to values than morality, 'values education' is not usually understood to include education relating to aesthetic values (which explains why I can discuss values education here though I have barely touched on aesthetics in this book).

The term 'moral education' is probably sometimes used as equivalent to 'values education' and sometimes used more narrowly. It would certainly make sense to use it more narrowly. If we accept that morality is only a part of the whole field of values, then we could understand 'moral education' as education in morality, which will only be a part of education in values. However, this understanding of morality as what I have called, earlier in this book, 'morality in the narrow sense' is not shared by everyone. Besides, as noted in Chapter 6, some people are suspicious of the idea of morality and therefore likely to be suspicious of the idea of moral education. While I certainly think that one aspect of values education ought to be to encourage and enable pupils to take the notion of morality (in the narrow sense) seriously, it may be better not to prejudge the place of morality within the wider field. I shall therefore in this Part mainly use the terminology of 'values education'.

The burden of Part V is that values education is by no means equivalent to 'the transmission of values'. In Chapter 11 I show some of the problems with the idea of transmitting values, and, recalling the questions about aims of education that I raised at the end of Part I, I ask those same questions about possible aims of values education. I suggest that the major and distinctive contribution of schools as regards to values will be, not in 'transmission', but in promoting cognitive aims of knowledge, understanding and engagement in discussion. In Chapter 12 I argue that such a contribution where values are concerned is a large one, and very much needed.

Chapter 11

Values Education: Teachers as Transmitters of Values?

The transmission of values

It is a commonplace idea that education transmits values. This is not so much a particular approach to values education – since it says nothing specific about what processes might be involved – as merely one way of talking about it, and one that turns out to be fairly unhelpful. The notion of transmission suggests a rather passive picture of what is going on. A transmitter, after all, does not originate anything itself: it has information fed into it in some form, which it then sends out to be picked up by a receiver – which is equally passive. Perhaps that metaphor from radio and television is not what is intended by the language of transmission. There are other possible metaphors – for instance, the transmission of diseases – but they are also unlikely to be very helpful for teachers considering their role as regards values.

One reason why teachers might not like the idea of transmitting values is that, with its associations of passivity on the part of the receiver, it could suggest indoctrination. I want to look only briefly at this idea before moving on, because a possible association with indoctrination is not the main reason why the idea of transmission of values is unsatisfactory. The notion of indoctrination (mentioned briefly above in Chapter 2) has been examined often within the literature of philosophy of education, without agreement on any particular way of analysing it.[1] It will be sufficient to say here that by 'indoctrination' I am referring to any process that leaves people accepting certain ideas that they are incapable of subjecting to rational assessment. I shall assume that you agree that indoctrinating people is a bad thing to do. (If you do agree, it will be because of certain values you accept, perhaps values to do with rationality and independence of mind. Not everyone, however, will necessarily acknowledge these values, while some people may think that the indoctrination of *certain* ideas is both good and necessary.)

I would suggest that the likelihood of teachers indoctrinating pupils in moral ideas is actually quite low. This is because the extent of teachers' influence over their pupils is limited, and will have to compete with other influences in the young people's lives. Of course, teachers who want to promote their pupils' ability to think for themselves and to think rationally will avoid indoctrination more effectively by encouraging their pupils to ask questions and to consider whatever values the teacher may be hoping to get across.

In general, transmitting some content through teaching does not necessarily constitute indoctrination. Talk of transmission need imply only that the teacher is initially in possession of some content that the pupil does not have, and that it comes about through the teacher's activity that the pupil comes to possess that content too. If you tell someone who does not already know it that an atomic bomb was dropped on Hiroshima in 1945, and the person takes this in, then you have transmitted that item of information. There need be no indoctrination here. The content that teachers are transmitting will often be more complex than an individual statement of fact, and teachers may, of course, have other aims besides wanting their pupils to be able to reproduce statements of fact. They may consider that they have not succeeded in their task unless the pupils are not only able to repeat the information but are able to demonstrate understanding of it, back it up with evidence, argue a case for it, and so on. Such activities may build on information that, to begin with, has indeed been transmitted. In many parts of the school curriculum transmission is an important and legitimate *part* of what a teacher does.

So if there is a problem about the transmission of *values*, it must be something about values that creates the problem. In fact there are several possible problems: that what would count as transmitting values, if the idea makes sense at all, must be quite a complex matter; that the precise content to be transmitted may be indeterminate; and that the values of a society cannot be transmitted as a whole if there are inconsistent values within the society. Think of a teacher who holds certain beliefs about the importance of, say, telling the truth and who always tells the truth herself or, if she does not, tends to feel guilty about not doing so. (Remember that in Chapter 3 we treated people's values in terms of what they care about or what they consider is important.) I suppose we can say, as a first step, that she will have transmitted this value to her pupils if they develop the same, or a similar, attitude towards truth-telling.[2] Again, there need be no indoctrination here: it may well be the case afterwards that while the students have adopted truthfulness as a value of their own, they are at the same time able to defend it with reasons and think about its limits. Such an outcome would hardly amount to indoctrination.

It is still not easy to see, in the case of values, what process would count as transmission. In the case of items of knowledge that we can identify as 'facts', we do know that, whatever its short-comings, simply telling people something *can* work as one method of transmission. It *is* possible to tell people the chemical formula of water, or the date of the Battle of Hastings, and simply telling *can* turn out to be successful transmission. When it comes to values, the picture is much less clear. Even apart from moral values, can a love of science or enthusiasm for history be transmitted? Possibly, but certainly not just by telling people that science and history are good (interesting, exciting, important) things. Almost certainly, the teacher's example will have more to do with what is transmitted than the fact of simple telling. But once we begin to talk about the teacher's example we are speaking of something that will by no means have the same, or any, predictable effect on each pupil. For this reason too, the terminology of transmission begins to look out of place.

Perhaps a more important difference between the transmission of information and the transmission of values is that the first can be much more clear-cut. In the case of a chemical formula, for instance, you may know *exactly* what it is you are trying to get across. Values are certainly not like that. The fact that values are not at all clear-cut (they have a degree of indeterminacy) is one reason why the transmission model is a difficult one to work with.

Another reason why the transmission model of values education is at least inadequate is the fact of the diversity of values in a plural society. This does not mean that transmission of values, as such, is impossible; what it does show, however, is that there cannot be a common values education that consists of the transmission of something like a complete set of the values of the society (unless we are content to recognize that some of the values transmitted will be inconsistent with others). If we wish to use the idea of transmission of values as a model for a common values education within a plural society, we have to acknowledge that out of all the values held in the society, there has to be some selection of the values to be transmitted. The idea of transmission as such tells us nothing about how that selection is to be done.

The suggestion is sometimes made that people should get together to discover which values they do in fact share, and that whatever values they are agreed on are the ones that should be transmitted. The idea is that a common core of values would then emerge. This might well be so, providing the values in question are characterized rather broadly, and in terms of their content, rather than any agreed sense of their underlying interpretation or the grounds for them. In fact, this is just what happened in England and Wales with the setting up of the National Forum on Values in Education and the Community, that led to the Statement of Values introduced here in Chapter 1: except that the Forum stopped short of actually recommending that the agreed values should be *transmitted*.[3] The Preamble to the Statement of Values explicitly acknowledges that in a plural society there will not be agreement on the sources of the values selected or on their detailed interpretation.

But suppose that in fact one generation within a society had sufficient agreement, not merely on a set of labels for values but on a determinate interpretation of certain values. At that point another problem arises: I would argue that to transmit certain values as fixed – when those values may be open to a variety of interpretations – is to be undemocratic.[4] Democracy is partly to do with people working out for themselves and amongst themselves the values they are to live by. For one generation to try to fix the values that the next generation will live by has at least some analogies with a colonial power trying to determine the values that the indigenous inhabitants of another part of the world are to follow (perhaps we could label the phenomenon 'generational imperialism').

To sum up, if the content of a set of values is too indeterminate, there will be nothing definite to transmit; on the other hand, if the content is tightened up too much, this will put constraints on the next generation that can hardly be justified within the terms of the very values that a democratic and plural society has to subscribe to. So there appear to be a number of problems with the notion of values education as the transmission of values. But it may be that these problems only appear because in this discussion so far we have no details of what the transmission of values actually consists in: the whole way of talking is just too abstract. Recently, many writers on values education have been attracted by an idea that might provide one concrete interpretation of the transmission of values: that idea is the development of virtues.

Developing virtues

In Chapter 6 I referred to two different conceptions of virtues, distinguished primarily by the interpretation of the motivation underlying the possession of a given virtue. In one conception (which we could associate with the Kantian understanding of morality) having a virtue is largely a matter of being able to control one's amoral or immoral inclinations by deliberately following a moral imperative. On the other conception (associated particularly with Aristotle by many recent writers) having a certain virtue involves having appropriate inclinations in the first place (or rather, as second nature, because they have to be acquired), so that one does not have to make a deliberate moral effort to overcome counter-inclinations.[5] It is a more Aristotelian conception that many recent writers have had in mind when they have spoken of the development of virtues as an educational aim. It may be that the major reason for following this approach has been the sense that moral education, whatever else it does, should make a difference to how people behave, to how they live, even to what kind of people they are. Talk of virtue does capture this sense of the difference that values education should be able to make.

A virtue (following roughly Aristotle's conception) is a complex state involving desire, feelings and even perception. The compassionate person, for instance, is likely to notice when someone is suffering (though this could also be true of the sadistic person); but the compassionate person will be distressed by other people's suffering, will want to help, and will in fact do so. I shall not go into more detail here about the nature of the virtues, because other treatments of the topic within an educational context are available.[6] The idea of virtues is an important one, and the concept of the development of virtues might provide a way of interpreting what it is to transmit a value. But before we conclude that the development of virtues gives us a complete and satisfactory notion of values education, I want (swimming somewhat against the tide of recent discussions, at least among philosophers of education) to raise some awkward questions about the idea.

First, despite the recent attention given to the development of virtues as an educational aim, it is by no means clear how the aim is to be pursued or how far it can be achieved. Too often there are only rather vague references to the ethos of the school, the example set by teachers, and the good character of teachers themselves. But these may be relatively small influences among all the influences in a child's life. Since in speaking of the development of virtues, we are speaking of a person developing a certain 'mindset' that is more than just cognitive, that also involves some of a person's deepest desires and feelings, we have to wonder how much teachers can do. In fact, the Aristotelian account of the development of virtues has it that initially the main consideration is that people are brought up in the right habits of action. Here again, the influence of a school is limited compared with all the rest of a child's familial and social environment.

Still, it may be possible that schools can do something significant towards the development of virtues (see the writers already mentioned). In any case, even a modest influence in a desirable direction may be a lot better than none, and we would hardly embark on any approach to values education if we had to have a guarantee that the results aimed at would be achieved in every case.

My second query is rather different. By its nature, the possession of a virtue runs fairly deep within a person. The advocates of virtues, as compared with more rationalistic approaches to values education, see this as a great advantage: too much theorizing about moral education, they tell us, has been concerned only with the question 'What should I do?', whereas the important question is 'What *kind of person* should I be?' But it is possible to turn this point around and wonder what authority schools (that is, state-run publicly financed schools) have to try to turn children into certain kinds of people.[7] I shall say nothing here about the influences of families or other communities: perhaps it is appropriate for parents to do all they can to bring up their children as the kind of people they (the parents) want them to be, or perhaps not. I am only raising here the question of whether *schools* should be doing this.

That brings us to the question of selection of values, which is really the same question already raised about the transmission model. The deeper our influence over people is, the more important it surely is to see that this influence is desirable. Modern virtue theorists like to refer to Aristotle on the general nature of virtues, but they do not usually follow him all the way on his particular list of the virtues that are to be cultivated. Different qualities are treated as virtues in different traditions.[8] For Aristotle, for instance, a certain kind of pride was a major virtue, and humility was not on his list at all. For Jesus of Nazareth, about three centuries later in a world that was subject to Greek cultural influences among others, it was almost the reverse. Within a modern plural society there will be at least some differences in the virtues that are favoured within various cultures, either because there will be quite different items on different people's lists, or because different weightings are put on the same virtue, or different interpretations given to what is nominally the same virtue.

But suppose the problem of selection can be solved. It is also true that however successfully the development of virtues could be carried out, it would not do the whole of the task that a modern society can call on education to perform where values are concerned. For society's concern is not only with the motivation and behaviour of individuals; a modern society also faces moral issues that somehow have to be tackled on behalf of the society as a whole (issues such as freedom of speech, censorship, abortion, treatment of animals, genetic engineering, capital punishment and many others). However virtuous people may be, they still have to think about questions of this sort, and the possession of virtues does not guarantee an agreed answer (or any answer) to them.

If the development of virtues is to be a viable model even for some aspects of values education in a heterogeneous society, I think the virtues in question have to be interpreted in a way that is conceptually quite rich. Let me illustrate what I mean by first contrasting two different virtues without initially making any assumptions about the cultural setting in which they might be exercised. Compassion, or at least something like it, is a quality that we could imagine being displayed by a creature without language or self-consciousness: for all we can tell, the feelings and motivation to help that are involved in human compassion may at bottom be the same as, or share something in common with, those experienced by one ape or elephant towards another. But contrast this with justice (the quality of the just person, which was one of Aristotle's major virtues, one of the cardinal virtues in the Western tradition, and for Hume, as we saw in Chapter 7, an artificial rather than natural virtue). To be a just person one has to be aware of the claims of others, to be able to make comparisons between different claims and to be able on occasion to adjudicate between them. One cannot be just without having and using a conception of justice. There is no way, then, in which someone could be unthinkingly just.

I would suggest that the more complex the cultural setting, the less possible or desirable it is for any virtue to be possessed in an unreflective way. Compassion, for instance, might be unproblematically a virtue within an isolated group, where its exercise would always be a matter of immediate face-to-face response to another. But in the modern world we can be aware of the sufferings of people thousands of miles from us. Are we then moved in the same way? The unreflectively compassionate person would probably not be moved by the mere knowledge that other people were suffering, but might be moved by the sight of their suffering, perhaps on television. But is it reasonable to be moved only by suffering directly seen; is it even just (for compassion and justice do not always coincide)? In the modern world, the compassionate person needs to *think* about what to do. (This is, in effect, a restatement in terms of virtues of points already made about caring and justice.)

A number of writers who have discussed the role of public education in a liberal society have emphasized the importance of certain virtues, including qualities such as a sense of justice, tolerance, respect for the opinions of others, and so on.[9] These are clearly qualities that require a good deal of thought for their exercise. The interesting upshot is that when we are thinking about the values education that schools should be responsible for in a modern, plural society, it may be that seeking to develop virtues in people, and enabling and encouraging them to think in certain ways about moral issues, may not be so far apart after all. While it may be that an approach that emphasizes the cognitive side has too little influence on motivation (one of the complaints that advocates of the virtues approach have made against more rationalistic approaches), it is also the case that concentrating on the idea of virtues does not allow us to neglect the cognitive side.

Should liberal teachers transmit liberal values?

The point has been made before that many people in teaching, or thinking of going into teaching, are liberal-minded people: they are for diversity of thought, tolerance and individual freedom of choice; and they are against imposing their values on others. They hold liberal values, and they may hope that their pupils will come to hold equally liberal values. So they have some reason to try to transmit these liberal values. But should they be worried that in doing this they might be illegitimately imposing their own values? If they are worried about that, does this mean that they should scrupulously try to be neutral on matters of values? The question is more than a quibble. The difficulties, for instance, that we looked at in Chapter 10 relating to secular and non-secular schools arise partly because there are many parents who feel that secular schools are going too far in transmitting distinctively liberal values, which are not the values that they, the parents, wish their children to hold.

Let me pose the question again, then, and follow it up with particular reference to the notion of tolerance that we have already looked at in Chapter 5. Because they hold values such as autonomy of thought and freedom of choice, liberal teachers will not wish to inculcate specific points of view. At the same time, because they are liberals, they must hope to see the continuation of the kind of society in which it is possible for their values to be realized. That will be a society which at the very least does not discourage people from thinking for themselves: in other words, it must be a tolerant society. But it cannot be a tolerant society if enough of its individual members are not themselves, to a sufficient degree, tolerant of diversity. So liberal teachers will want to promote the value of tolerance, and in doing so, of course, they cannot be neutral between tolerance and intolerance (just as they will not be neutral between reasoned argument and resort to force, and so on).

At this point, however, liberal-minded teachers may be challenged. If they think (as many teachers do) that they ought not to promote allegiance to specific moral positions or particular lifestyles – that it is not for them to try to turn their pupils into, say, vegetarians or believers in women's right to choose abortion – then should they also think that they ought *not* to try to turn pupils into people who will value tolerance? For that is just as much a moral value, and one not shared by everyone; indeed, it may be more far-reaching in its effects on people's lives just because it is more general. If education seems to be preaching tolerance as one of the highest of virtues in its own right, it could well be charged with being, politically and religiously, sectarian.

What liberal educators must do in response to such a challenge is to distinguish between encouraging people to show tolerance towards diversity and persuading people that tolerance is an ideal in its own right. It may be quite enough that people appreciate the more pragmatic reasons for tolerance. More generally, liberal educators need to distinguish between the liberal values that are necessary to maintaining a plural society (not because a plural society is necessarily the ideal, but because it is inescapably the kind of society we are in) and the values that are themselves marks of a specifically liberal response to moral issues.

We can distinguish between a liberal society and a liberal morality.[10] A liberal society leaves people free to hold different moral outlooks and different sets of beliefs, and within some limits to practise different ways of life (the limits are set by the need to constrain people from causing harm to others). If there is a sense, then, in which being a liberal is itself to have a particular moral outlook, this liberal outlook will be only one among those that a liberal society must accommodate. It is not too difficult to recognize the sense in which a liberal outlook can amount to having a particular set of moral views. The liberal-minded person characteristically puts considerable weight on individuals' freedom to choose their own lifestyle and to come to their own beliefs; considerable weight, that is, on individual autonomy. The liberal sets store by the kind of life in which individuals choose their own goals and their own route towards them ('I Did it My Way' could be their anthem). This underlying value characteristically leads to the liberal holding certain moral and political positions rather than others: so that we know roughly what is meant by a 'liberal' position on the morality of, say, abortion or homosexual activity. In education the liberal puts relatively more weight on the importance of enabling people to think for themselves and choose their own way of life, rather than on inculcating a particular set of values or a traditional lifestyle. In this sense, then, to be a liberal is itself to have a certain sort of moral outlook.

It is vital to say now that being a liberal, in this sense, is not a requirement for being a member of a liberal society. Indeed, a society that tried to exclude anyone who was not a liberal in their moral outlook would be a markedly *illiberal* society. It would have no place for those who believe that abortion is murder or that homosexual activity is sinful, or for those who see education simply as a matter of transmitting a traditional way of thinking and living. A liberal society, then, has to be one in which liberals and non-liberals can live together. It will hardly be surprising if this requirement generates problems, if not paradoxes. The liberal educator has to promote the values that are necessary to living in a liberal society, but stop short of promoting a liberal set of moral beliefs or a specific kind of lifestyle.

Take, for instance, the value of compromise which we looked at in Chapter 5. Should schools try to foster a willingness to compromise? Yes, but they should not foster it as an absolute value (it would perhaps be rather paradoxical to hold an uncompromising position that refusal to compromise is always wrong). I suggest that in a plural society it is not the business of publicly supported schools to inculcate (even if such inculcation were possible, which is doubtful) either the idea that certain specific values must never be compromised, or the idea that compromise must always be the best outcome. But what schools can try to do is to help pupils realize the extent to which individual decisions often involve a compromise between values; to ensure that pupils are aware of the different attitudes towards compromise that exist within their society, depending on the significance people's values have for them; and to encourage pupils to explore these different attitudes, enabling them to make the distinctions (such as the distinction, vital in a liberal society, between law and morality) that enable them to avoid an oversimple view of the ways in which compromise is or is not acceptable.

Consider too the value on which we concentrated in Chapter 9: the readiness to resolve conflict without resort to violence. I said then that there are ways in which schools can and should promote the skills of non-violent conflict resolution and the willingness to use them. But I did not say that schools should, even if they could, commit themselves to promoting the belief that violence must never be used. For that itself would be a highly controversial position, implying that the absence of violence is such an overriding value that it must never be jeopardized for the sake of any other value. (Peace and the avoidance of violence are high on my own scale of values, but not absolutes.[11]) Not only would it be controversial, it would also mean adopting a non-neutral position between different cultural and religious traditions: an ethic of non-violence is far stronger in some traditions, such as Buddhism, than in others. For the liberal thinker, the chances are that even a commitment to peace will not be held in an uncompromising way.

It is partly because values such as tolerance and willingness to compromise are not ones that can be applied unthinkingly (because people need to be able to think for themselves so as to be able to decide when they should not compromise, and where they should draw limits to their tolerance) that liberal educators are committed to enabling people to think for themselves. But if educators leave people with the conviction that the only worthwhile kind of life is one in which the individual establishes all his or her goals and standards, taking nothing as given, and works out a particular route to achieving them – in effect, treating life almost as something to be rationally designed – then the educators have gone too far towards promoting a rather partisan view of how best to live one's life. Just where the line is to be drawn between the responsibilities for their pupils' values that educators in a plural society must accept, and the partisan commitments they must hold back from promoting, will probably be a matter for continual debate and modification in such a society.

What can schools do best?

At the end of Chapter 2 I proposed a number of questions that we can ask about any aims proposed for education. It is time to raise these questions again, with reference now to the idea of transmission of values, and with a view to possible alternative approaches to values education.

1. Is the aim for something of positive value?

We cannot say that the transmission of values from one generation to the next will always be of positive value, since it must make a difference which values are being transmitted. If a whole society were imbued with racist values it would be better if these values were not transmitted, so that the whole society could, if this were possible, make something like a fresh start.[12] But if we can assume that the values in question are positive in themselves, then the transmission of them will itself be of value.

2. Is the aim for something that can feasibly be realized or at least promoted through formal education?

After the arguments of this chapter, we have to be cautious here. No doubt *to some degree* values can be transmitted, and are transmitted, through formal education. It does not follow, however, that the values actually transmitted through schooling are the ones that we would wish to see transmitted. Deschoolers and other critics of schools have long argued that values such as docility and reliance on the authority of others are actually transmitted in schools, regardless of the stated intentions of the staff. If values education had to be a matter of a school deciding which values it wished to transmit and deliberately setting about this, then, given all the other influences on young persons within society, I do not think we could be very confident of success.

3. Is what is aimed at something that can be seen as both good for individuals and good for society, or at least as not merely benefitting the few at the expense of many others, or the majority at severe cost to a few?

Here again it makes a lot of difference which values are being transmitted. The example of racist values given earlier shows that certain values can hold sway in a society at the expense of part of the population. There may be quite other examples: some critics of educational selection, for instance, would argue that the values associated with academic excellence benefit a minority at the expense of a majority. Perhaps it should be, above all, the values associated with ideas of justice and equality that should be to the benefit of all, at the expense of none. But we can hardly aim merely at the transmission of these values, because to a considerable degree our society (any modern plural society) still has to work out what the demands of justice and equality entail in practice.

4. Is the aim of broad relevance rather then narrowly specific?

Here we should remember the problem mentioned in the first section of this chapter: trying to transmit too determinate a version of certain values. Can we say in detail what values will be of most importance in, say, the mid twenty-first century? The aim of broader relevance would be to enable each generation to think through and, if necessary, rethink its values.

5. Is what is aimed at something that teachers and schools are particularly well placed to promote? Or is it perhaps something that would come about anyway, independently of formal education?

We need to be cautious here, too. If, suddenly, we did not have schools for, say, a decade, would society fall apart morally? Would nothing of the moral values of society be transmitted? I doubt it. On the other hand, we can probably say that if we were to set out with a clean slate to devise the best method we could of transmitting values from one generation to another, we would probably not fasten on schools as we now know them.

6. Is what is aimed at something that it is important for everyone to have (or to achieve, be exposed to, etc.)?

Here the answer seems to be both yes and no. Perhaps, as I have suggested in places, there are some values, constituting a common core of morality, that ought to be passed on to everyone. But the more richly we fill in our picture of morality the less possible it will be to say, in a plural society, that the same should be transmitted to everyone (and, consequently, the less reason for using the resources offered by compulsory schooling for achieving this transmission). It is more arguable that what everyone needs in a plural society is the ability to reflect on and discuss values.

7. Is what is aimed at something that has a justified place in education because of its sheer importance, regardless of the other questions above?

I suggested in Chapter 2 that conceivably we might judge one aim (for example, avoiding global environmental disaster) so important that we could justifiably put all our efforts into attempting to achieve it. Some people may think that the dangers of moral breakdown of society are such that all possible efforts, in schooling and in any other way, should be devoted to avoiding such breakdown. We ought not to be too easily persuaded by that. Suppose we could try to gear schooling above all to transmitting the values that would prevent moral breakdown (assuming, of course, that we knew which values these were and how to transmit them). We would still need to ask ourselves: how great a danger is there of moral breakdown anyway?[13] If the danger is very great, is it likely that anything schools could do would prevent it? If the danger is not great, are there not other things that schools would be better employed in doing? As we saw in Chapter 2, there are many other values that education is concerned with, besides those that we may reckon to be fundamental to morality. If the transmission of moral values were at the expense of science and the arts, humanities and technology, would we be better off in the end?

8. Can what is aimed at be pursued without violating any moral values in the process?

I have suggested that the transmission of values, so far as we can make sense of the idea, need not involve indoctrination. Yet so long as we think in terms of the transmission of values, there is the danger that our concentration will be on whether a certain end result is achieved – whether the values we set out to transmit are in fact received at the other end. If that is what we are concentrating on, the danger that we will slip into using morally illegitimate means will never be far behind.

Given all these questions, to my mind the value of even thinking in terms of 'the transmission of values' is, at best, unproven. There is a strong case, I suggest, for concentrating on what schools can do best. What they can do best, perhaps, even given the recognized importance of ethos and example, is to teach things of a broadly cognitive nature. Putting people through school may or may not lead to their becoming people of a different kind, but we should have some confidence that schools *can*, and sometimes do, lead people to a knowledge and understanding that, without formal schooling, they would probably not have developed. If this is a valid point about schools in general, then its validity is not altered when it is values we have in mind.

My argument is that in a plural society there is a greater need than ever for people, not just to have values but to have an understanding of values – their own and other people's. Given compulsory schooling, we do in fact have the possibility of promoting a greater depth and breadth of understanding about values than any society so far has perhaps achieved (for in a more homogeneous society, in which most values are widely shared, these values are also likely to go relatively unquestioned, and so there will be less depth of reflection).[14] So, while recognizing that some will still wish to see teachers primarily as transmitters of values or developers of virtues, I shall come back, in the next chapter, to the idea that values education should after all be a matter above all of education, where that is taken to involve knowledge, understanding and rational thought.

[1] Snook (1972); Spiecker and Straughan (1991); Haydon (2006b) Chapter 5.
[2] To be accurate, we must also be supposing, if we are to speak of the teacher transmitting this value, that the pupils would not have come to hold this value were it not for the influence of this teacher; and that is something that it would be very difficult in practice to be sure of.
[3] In the first edition of this book, written before the outcome of the National Forum deliberations was known, I wrote that notions such as 'respect for persons' and 'toleration of cultural differences' would probably figure on an agreed list. This, not surprisingly, turned out to be the case.
[4] See Haydon (1993b).
[5] Aristotle's own account is in his work known as the *Nicomachean Ethics* (often published in translation just as *Ethics*), Books 2 and 3. There have to be more complex accounts of some of the virtues we have names for, such as temperance and courage, because we would not speak of temperance or courage at all if the person concerned did not in some sense recognize a temptation or a danger respectively. The temperate person, for instance, does refrain from indulging certain inclinations; but, roughly, on one account he or she takes some positive pleasure in that self-restraint, while on there other there might be only reluctance.
[6] See, e.g., Carr (1991); Tobin (1986, 1989); White (1996); Carr and Steutel (1999); McLaughlin and Halstead (1999); Noddings and Slote (2003).

[7] A point that was put forcefully in a different era by Bereiter (1974).

[8] See MacIntyre (1981), Chapter 16 on the variety of lists of virtues in different cultures and historical periods.

[9] See, e.g., Gutmann (1989); Galston (1989); Macedo (1990); White (1996).

[10] John Rawls's distinction between 'political liberalism' and 'comprehensive liberalism' is important for the following discussion. See Rawls (1993) and Rawls (1999).

[11] For more on the ethics of violence and non-violence see Haydon (1999b).

[12] This is not entirely unrealistic. It could be argued, for instance, in the case of Germany or Japan after the Second World War, that these societies did to some degree make a fresh start, in that some of the values that had found expression in militarism were not to be transmitted to rising generations. More morally ambivalent examples are provided by some of the formerly communist societies of Eastern Europe, where with hindsight we may think there were both positive and negative aspects to the decline of the values associated with communism.

[13] What would count as the moral breakdown of a society? One famous example, but concerning a very different sort of society, is that among the Ik people in East Africa, reported by the anthropologist Turnbull (1973). I have said more about this in Haydon (2006b).

[14] See Haydon (1995).

Chapter 12

Values Education: Teachers as Educators

Thinking for oneself?

Historically, the idea that moral education is about the transmission of a given set of values is perhaps the most venerable. But having concentrated on that notion in the previous chapter, I want now to look at approaches that assign a large role to rational thought and understanding.

At first sight the approach that lies at the opposite end of the spectrum from the simple transmission model is the hands-off 'policy' that in effect eschews any involvement of formal education in people's values at all. (Some liberal-minded people are attracted to this idea, but it is difficult to sustain it for long.) It can at least be said for this approach that, in avoiding the transmission of anything in particular, it avoids deliberate indoctrination and recognizes the diversity of values in modern society; but it does that only in a passive way. It does not help people to live with the diversity in any positive way. In so far as its message is one of 'do your own thing' it may even make harmony within a society less likely by the fact that it increases diversity. It does nothing, for instance, to prevent people growing up with racist values and the disposition to promote them through violence. (Perhaps you will object at this point that the hands-off approach to individual values ought to be coupled with the promotion of tolerance and commitment to non-violent ways of resolving conflict; but then, since it would be trying to influence people's values in these ways, it would no longer be a hands-off approach.)

I said that 'at first sight' the hands-off approach appears to lie at the opposite end of the spectrum from the transmission model, because in its actual result for the individual the hands-off approach may not be so different from the deliberate transmission of values. Individuals may grow up with one conviction or another, or with no clear or consistent values at all, but it does not follow, simply because formal education has taken a hands-off approach, that people have made up their own minds about their values. Their values will certainly have been influenced in one way or another by factors in their upbringing and environment, factors that they may themselves be unaware of. They will, perhaps unwittingly, have received some values even if no one has set out deliberately to transmit them. Their values will not necessarily be ones that they have freely endorsed, any more than if someone had set out deliberately to indoctrinate them.

The hands-off approach has not, I suspect, recommended itself to many teachers who have tried to think through their position on values. For even if teachers want to avoid inculcating substantive moral values, they do mostly believe that certain things are important, including people's ability to think for themselves – in other words, independence of thought or, in one of its aspects, autonomy.[1] In effect I have just argued that autonomy is not well served by the hands-off approach. It requires, rather, that people make their decisions with some measure of understanding and with a degree of rationality, rather than with no reason or with irrelevant reasons. Many educators, then, have favoured an approach that encourages people to *think* about their values. Indeed, to many teachers such an approach may seem obviously right. But it still needs defending, in part because the value of people thinking for themselves is not a value that everyone in contemporary societies accepts; there are groups that do not have a tradition of encouraging reflection about their own values. We will have to see whether encouraging people to reflect on their values can be justified to people who do not share *this* value. We may in the end have to rely on pragmatic arguments concerning the great importance of reflection within a plural democratic society.

There is room for different conceptions of what is involved in encouraging people to reflect on their values. One that was popularized at one time in the USA is 'Values Clarification', by which individuals are encouraged to identify and reflect on their own values.[2] This certainly goes beyond the hands-off approach, for rather than saying that values are not the business of education, it entails a great deal of explicit attention to values. I think we can agree that it is important for individuals to be clear about their own values – both the content of their values and the significance the values have for them – because without this kind of self-understanding, discussion between people holding different values is unlikely to be much more than a stand-off between different positions, and the participants may be at cross-purposes without realizing it. Notice that there is no implication here that the significance and explanation of an individual's values are to be found solely within that individual. If one's central values have been assimilated from a particular tradition, then to understand that fact, and to have some depth of understanding of one's own tradition, will itself be an important part of understanding one's own values.

Here I am concerned, not with the specific programmes promoted under 'Values Clarification' but with the idea that the *only* educational approach to values might be enabling and encouraging individuals to be clear about their own values. This approach in itself will be trying *not* to influence pupils towards holding certain values rather than others. It does not entail, for instance, that the teacher should express disapproval of expressions of racist values. Proponents of values clarification may well expect that such values would not survive the process of clarification. But if that turns out to be true, it will not be because clarification in itself will undermine racist values (there is not necessarily anything *unclear* about such values; they may appear rather clear-cut just because they are crude and simplistic) but because the clarification may bring with it a degree of critical reflection on the individual's own values.

One kind of critique that a person may undertake of their own values, and which formal education is well-placed to help people with, involves seeing whether they can all fit together consistently. A useful notion here is that of 'reflective equilibrium', which was named, though probably not invented, by the American political philosopher John Rawls.[3] People's values can come with any degree of abstractness or concreteness, generality or specificity: anything, say from the most abstract appeal to respect for persons and tolerance, to the most concrete opinions that a particular sort of behaviour is or is not acceptable. Rawls argues that I can seek consistency by moving back and forth between the particular and the general. Where I become aware of inconsistency I can modify my ideas at either level, changing what seems more peripheral and holding firmly to what appears central or fixed, until I arrive (if I ever do) at a point where all my views hold together: at this point we can say that reflective equilibrium has been reached.

If individuals have been able to reflect on, and if necessary modify their moral views, to the point where they are fully aware of them and can say that they all hang together, then that would certainly constitute a pretty thorough clarification.[4] It could enable people in the process to overcome any inner conflict that they may have been feeling as a result of discrepancies between their values. Of course, it may be that few people, moral philosophers included, ever achieve a completely self-consistent set of values. Nevertheless, the idea of reflective equilibrium (not necessarily under that name) may be one that education can promote, and in so doing make a contribution towards enabling people to have greater self-understanding about their own values.

Thinking the right way?

This kind of awareness of his or her own values and moral beliefs is likely to lead the individual at some point to ask 'Which views are right?' and 'How can I know?' (These questions are especially likely to arise when inconsistencies emerge. But even if someone has been brought up with a completely consistent set of values, rooted perhaps in a unified tradition of thought, it is still in principle possible to ask whether there is any way of showing that the beliefs involved are right.) Here we come back to the question I considered in Chapter 3 and again in Chapter 7: whether there is some right way of thinking about moral questions that can lead to determinate answers. There have been a number of approaches to moral education, proposed especially by philosophers, which, while retaining the idea that individuals should think for themselves about values and come to their own conclusions, have also stressed that the individuals' thinking should be rational, and have gone on to say something more specific about what distinguishes rational from irrational thinking in the field of values. One of these philosophers of education in Britain, John Wilson, argued that there are ways of thinking morally – amounting, in Wilson's own word, to a methodology – that can be taught quite specifically in timetabled lessons.[5] In the USA, Kohlberg, basing his approach to moral education on his research into developmental stages in moral thinking (see Chapter 6), argued that while it was not possible directly to teach people to think in the way that his own arguments favoured, it was possible to provide people with 'cognitive stimulation' that would help to move their own thinking from one stage to the next so that they would move more rapidly and further along the developmental ladder that culminates in Stage 6 thinking.

These rationalistic approaches claim to eschew the inculcation of particular positions on substantive issues; instead, they leave individuals free to come to their own conclusions. But at the same time, they want to see individuals reasoning in a way that, if followed through consistently, will lead to certain results rather than others. Richard Hare, in many articles, supported substantive positions on the basis of the form of critical moral thinking that he advocated, and he also claimed that, with sufficient time and information, different people applying the same method would converge on the same answers.[6] Kohlberg seems to have taken a similar view: he argued, for instance, that Stage 6 reasoners would be opposed to capital punishment.[7] What this illustrates (regardless of your own views on capital punishment) is that if a form of moral education, rather than telling people what to believe on particular issues, encourages or teaches them to think about moral issues in a specific way, that form of education will not be neutral with regard to the particular issues. That should not by itself be a reason for rejecting this kind of approach to moral education. After all, *if* there is such a thing as a correct, or uniquely rational, way of thinking about moral issues, we would surely want people to be able to think in that way – and indeed, want them to *want* to think in that way – and we should expect that it will lead to certain answers rather than others. In line with my argument in the last section of Chapter 7 above, we can say that if people did the thinking appropriately, the answers they came to *would* be the right answers (or as close to the right answers as it is humanly possible to get); but we would be enabling people to come to the answers for themselves rather than imposing them.[8]

Before we look at what such a way of thinking might involve I need to say more in reply to critics who would reject altogether the idea that there is one appropriate way of thinking about moral matters. To use yet again the distinction between content and significance of moral positions, it is clear that the approaches advocated by writers such as Kohlberg, Wilson and Hare are not neutral on the *significance* of moral ideas – on conceptions of what moral values are and how they work. In the first place, of course, to encourage people to believe that they must think about moral questions so as to come to their own decisions is already to go against any view that would expect people to defer to the authority of their elders or of scripture. What such writers would probably say on that point (influenced by Kantian ethics) is that an attitude of reliance on authority is not one of morality at all. So far as morality is concerned (the argument would go) these writers are not being partisan. They are talking about a way of thinking that, as a matter of language and logic, is the right way of thinking about moral questions. This does not mean that a particular set of answers to moral questions is being inculcated, any more than the teacher of mathematics is inculcating a particular set of answers to calculations.

But among those who would not dispute that people need to be able to do their own thinking, there are still, as we saw in Chapter 6, different conceptions of the kind of thinking that this would involve. In particular, we looked there at the distinction between the 'justice' and 'care' orientations. It is worth repeating that the proponents of the care orientation are not advocating an unthinking or unreflective approach to life, but that they do have a different understanding of the kind of thinking that is appropriate. The justice orientation requires the ability to take what its advocates might call an objective, rational view of a situation, which involves in turn a degree of detachment from the situation; whereas the care orientation does not attempt any detachment, but responds to the perceived situation from within, in all its concrete reality. This distinction was developed initially in response to the recognition that the kind of thinking that Kohlberg argued for revolved around the notion of justice. On the face of it, any approach that suggests there is a 'rational methodology' (Wilson's phrase) to be followed in moral thinking is aligning itself with the justice rather than the care orientation.

It may seem, then, that we have to settle the question of whether we should promote the justice orientation or the care orientation before we can usefully say more about 'methodologies' of moral thinking. In Chapter 7 I argued, in effect, that the justice orientation should not be dispensed with; now I want to argue that quite apart from any arguments for the intrinsic superiority of one way of thinking or the other, there are good reasons for education to concern itself with both. One reason is the kind of liberal concern that we have encountered before, that we should always be careful about promoting a specific way of thinking when there are defensible alternatives. A concern with the educational development of the individual as one who is capable of thinking autonomously would suggest that having both orientations available is a more desirable goal. Since the evidence suggests that most people are capable, with prompting, of taking either perspective, the educational task here may be not so much one of actually teaching anything as of giving practice in contexts in which people can themselves reflect on the ways on which they are thinking.[9]

Another reason why it may be desirable for any individual to be able to work within either orientation is that the different orientations may be appropriate to different sorts of situation. The majority of academic discussion has focused on interpersonal moral problems rather than on broader social and political issues. Feminist writings have persuasively argued that in many ways the personal is political: issues of power and domination, writ large at the level of a whole society, penetrate even the closest personal relationships. What is less clear is how far the political on the large scale can be approached through ways of thinking that seem to have their home in the personal. While an individual woman faced with the decision of whether to have an abortion may well find, as we saw in Chapter 6, that thinking in terms of rights seems alien and inappropriate, whereas thinking in terms of relationships and responsibilities comes naturally, the political question – which is still at the same time a moral question – of what the law on abortion should be for a whole society seems to call more naturally for the abstractions of rights and justice.

It might be said, in response, that what seems to be naturally called for is a function of the way the large-scale political realm has been shaped, predominantly by men, through the justice and rights orientation. It is as clear in the large-scale realm, as it was in the fable of the moles and the porcupine, that appealing to justice is not necessarily a road to harmony. The similarities between that fable and the condition of two ethnic or religious groups fighting for control over a single territory, each claiming to have justice on its side, may be more than merely accidental. On the other hand, there are many situations in which appeals in the language of the care orientation, especially if addressed by outside observers to those actually involved, and if not at least coupled with a recognition of evident injustice, would sound very hollow and perhaps

patronizing.[10] In any case, if there are to be laws and general policies at all (and perhaps they could be avoided only in the most
thoroughly devolved and anarchistic society of small and almost
self-sufficient face-to-face communities), they have to be framed in
general terms and cannot be designed so as to be always responsive to the nuances of particular and individual circumstances.
The challenge, on the large-scale political level, is to design institutions in such a way that legislation and policy-making is sensitive
to the values represented by the orientation of caring. This only
reinforces the point that citizens of a democracy should have
access to both orientations, and should be able to move from one
to the other.

A further reason why it is desirable for individuals to be able to
work within either perspective is that in this way understanding of
the values of others will be increased. However much a person
tends to work within the justice orientation, he (or, less often, she)
will come across people whose focus is that of caring, and vice
versa. When we take into account the point already stressed, that
understanding is necessary across cultures, the need for people not
to be confined within one way of thinking becomes all the clearer.

We can quite legitimately, then, see it as part of the role of values education to give people an acquaintance with systematic ways
of thinking about moral questions, without implying that this is, or
should be, all there is to the moral life. What might such ways of
thinking be?[11] Any likely candidate, I think, will involve the idea of
universalizability, though not necessarily under that label
(Kohlberg speaks of reversibility, a closely related notion[12]).

The underlying idea, which we have encountered before in the
context of Kant's ethics, is that the perspective of morality is in a
sense an impartial perspective. If something is right for me to do
when I am in this position (perhaps standing to benefit from some
course of action), and you are in that position (perhaps standing
to lose), then (unless there are special considerations that rightly
make a difference) the same thing would be right for you to do if
the positions were reversed. This means that, when I am contem-
plating an action that I know will make someone else worse off,
there is always a challenge I can put to myself (or that others could
put to me). I am in effect saying to myself: 'I think it is all right for
a person in this position (which happens at the moment to be my
position) to act this way towards someone in that position (which

happens at the moment to be your position)'. Now I try to imagine what it would be like to be in the other person's position, on the receiving end. I know I would not like it, but I might just try to shrug off that realization. The real challenge is that I have to ask myself, recognizing what it is like to be on the receiving end, 'Am I really prepared to endorse this as a moral position? Am I really prepared to stick to the idea that it is all right for a person in my position (which could be anyone) to act like this towards a person in that position (which could, at least in my imagination, be me)?' It is not simply a matter of being aware of what one would or would not like if one were in the other person's shoes, but of trying to be consistent in one's own thinking.[13] The capacity for consistency, and the tendency to be concerned about consistency, are among the attributes that education has to promote.

Notice, now, that to think in this way is not, after all, to commit all the faults that critics have seen as integral to the justice perspective. It does not mean that I try to put myself in some privileged detached position, nor that I set up very simple general rules that I hold to rigidly. On the contrary, it demands that I think myself into what it is like to be each of the people affected by what I do, in this concrete situation. In a matter of personal relationships that may involve all the awareness and sensitivity that any advocate of the care orientation could expect. But it also demands that I make the effort to distance myself from what might be only my own inclinations or prejudices.

Thinking with content: knowledge and understanding

So far in this chapter I have looked at ways in which education may enable and encourage people to think for themselves, both in understanding their own values and in thinking about what they are to do. There is also a large role for education in promoting knowledge and understanding, both about values in general and about the values of others within a plural society in particular. The field here is large, so I shall not try to give a comprehensive review of it, but only to illustrate its importance.

First, as I mentioned in Chapter 8, there is a role for the study of values, and of morality in particular, from the perspectives of, for instance, sociology and psychology, as well as that of philosophy (which has provided the basis for much of this book). Perhaps as an explicit and systematic study this might come in only at the upper levels of secondary schools, but there is much that could be done at earlier ages if teachers had sufficient relevant knowledge themselves. Second, and more specifically, there is understanding of the particular varieties of moral outlook that are important within one's own society. The need for knowledge *about* people's values adds importantly to the liberal emphasis on rational autonomy. The liberal aim that individuals should be able to make up their own minds on questions of values, and to make their own choice of ways of life, does require some knowledge and understanding of the possible values and ways of life that are available, but only to the extent that the possibilities are real options for the individual concerned. But in a plural society, I would argue, it is important for people to have knowledge and understanding of ways of life that are lived and values that are held by others within one's society, even if these are not live options for oneself. An example will illustrate the point. A teenage girl, brought up in a family with progressive liberal views about equality of the sexes, will not, so far as her own freedom of choice is concerned, need any knowledge of what it is like to be a girl brought up within a strict Muslim tradition that expects conformity to a differentiation of male and female roles; for that kind of life, founded as it is within a wider social and religious context, is not a live option for her. But if the educational aim is not (or not only) that each should choose for herself, but that each should have some understanding of the lives of others in the same society, then the girl will need some understanding of the Muslim standpoint.

Promoting knowledge and understanding relevant to life in a plural society is readily compatible, as an aim, with the aim of promoting tolerance which we looked at in Chapter 11. It is not *necessarily* true that in understanding more about someone's beliefs or their reasons for acting as they do, you will be more tolerant of them; but on the whole this is likely to be the case. Here again the significance of tolerance is larger than it would be if the moral autonomy of the individual were the only aim. Autonomously choosing individuals need to have tolerance of a range of moral standpoints only in the sense that they must be able to entertain different possibilities in an unprejudiced way, while deciding which ones to adopt. Once they have made their decision, it will not be inconsistent if they reject intolerantly, when they are held by others, the values that they have rejected for themselves. (Those who have made a 'leap of faith' into a religious commitment are not necessarily going to be tolerant afterwards of those who have not made a similar leap.)

In addition to the hope that individuals are less likely to act intolerantly towards each other if they have a greater knowledge and understanding of each other's positions, the argument for educating people about the variety of values operating within their own society is that such understanding is necessary to participation as a citizen in a multicultural society. Particular issues, of course, which arise at particular times, are of vital public concern for a few months or even years, and then fade into the historical background. In the first edition of this book I took as an illustration the Muslim protests over the book *The Satanic Verses* (1988), which led to a *fatwa* proclaimed against its author Salman Rushdie. I drew on a discussion by the British Muslim commentator Tariq Modood who pointed out that Western liberal thinkers, whose notions of tolerance and respect for other cultures were inevitably strained by that episode, were using a conceptual scheme, in terms of offence and blasphemy, that misconstrued the nature of the Muslim objections. Since the publication of *The Satanic Verses* relations between Muslims and non-Muslims have been further tested by two wars in Iraq, by the activities of professed Islamic terrorists in New York, Bali, London and elsewhere, by the publication in European newspapers of cartoons lampooning the prophet Muhammed, and in other ways too. Of course the details of particular controversies can only be ascertained at the time or later with historical hindsight; there is ample scope for such study in schools, both in the context of citizenship education and as history. At the same time, to understand what is at stake in any of these controversies, and to evaluate what is at stake without prejudice, requires a knowledge and understanding both of liberal values and of Islamic values.

The general point, then, is that understanding differences over values in a plural society requires a considerable amount of knowledge. The only way that knowledge is likely to be acquired by substantial numbers of people is through formal education. The kind of knowledge involved is not something that can be put across just as information, partly because, as so often, it involves differences not just in the content of moral views but in the significance of moral concepts to those who hold them. Within some cultural perspectives, for instance, there are notions of honour at stake that are hardly familiar within Western liberal thinking. In effect there can be a further kind of moral perspective or orientation in play: besides the orientations of care and of justice, this is one that asks whether the honour of one's family or one's religious community is being upheld. As with other moral orientations, it can hardly be understood without the ability to some degree to appreciate how things look from the inside of such a perspective. To understand the perspectives of others we need not just information, but further explanations and examples. We need to think about these and to see where they do or do not relate to anything that is part of our own experience. In doing this we need to exercise some imagination, and also critical reflection: the two are complementary. The educational task, then, is a challenging one, and one that all citizens should hope that teachers will be willing to take on.

Thinking with others: discussion and dialogue

Most teachers will recognize that discussion in the classroom can be a useful means towards a variety of educational ends. But before looking further at discussion within the context of formal education, it is worth stressing that, where values education is concerned, discussion is much more than a means to an end. That people should, throughout their lives, and in personal as well as public contexts, be willing and able to turn to discussion of their differences rather than stand-off or conflict, is itself one of the most important aims for values education. But rather than simply issue a plea for discussion, I want to stress that there is an ideal of reasoned discussion that is more difficult to achieve, and less commonly realized, than may be thought at first sight. Discussion may have a variety of aims, and the aim with which it is undertaken can make a difference to how it is pursued.[14]

At one end of the spectrum, what passes for discussion may be no more than an exchange of differing points of view. If this happens in a classroom, it may fulfil at least one learning aim: it can make people aware of the variety of views that exist, even among a group that may be relatively homogeneous. If this awareness comes about within a context of amicable interpersonal relationships, then some contribution may have been made towards tolerance also. But this will be a limited achievement and too low an aim for education if it does not lead on to something more searching. It can, too, lead to pupils taking a dismissive view of discussion about moral issues ('Oh no, not abortion/sexuality/treatment of animals again!').

If there is to be discussion that is more than an exchange of views, the first difference is that reasons have to be given for the views put forward. Where pupils are encouraged to think through the reasons for their views, so that they can defend them, this will have some educational value by helping people to clarify their own values; and may take them further in understanding others' points of views than the superficial exchange of opinions. But this is still a limited aim; and if discussion at this level is set up as debate, it can even be counterproductive from the point of view of promoting tolerance and reducing conflict. For it is characteristic of debate that two opposing sides are set against each other, and that each sets out to undermine the credibility of the other. This presupposes that the important differences can be assigned to just two camps (an appropriately military metaphor), and that a satisfactory outcome consists in one position winning: in which case an outcome that is satisfactory is ruled out from the start.

To establish the superiority of one's own point of view is by no means the only possible aim of participants in a discussion; in fact there is a sense in which someone who tries to do this is not really engaging in discussion at all, since such an aim presupposes that the person's own views cannot be altered. But where a person does not make that presupposition, discussion can be a way of testing their own views: others may point out inconsistencies or bring up counter-evidence that would not have occurred to the person unaided.

Another possible aim that can be shared by all participants in a discussion is to establish the truth about some matter. Some writers have characterized discussion, as distinct from debate, by just this mutually shared aim.[15] There are difficulties, though, in characterizing the aim of *moral* discussion in this way. Anyone who does not think there is, ultimately, a truth to be discovered on moral questions would on this basis be debarred from participation in moral

discussion. Though there are extreme forms of subjectivism or relativism – see Chapter 3 – that imply theoretically that no rational
discussion is possible, the fact that such discussion does go on
counts against those theories. On the other hand, if an objective
truth exists, in the first of the senses I distinguished in Chapter 3 –
a truth that is independent of what anyone thinks on the matter –
then even if all the participants come to an agreement, this will not
guarantee that they have found the truth.

There is at least one kind of context in which we would be able
to say that agreement by itself guarantees that the answer found is
right. Borrowing from Habermas's communicative ethics[16] we can
imagine a situation in which a dispute is seen, by all those
involved, as a matter of conflict of interests. If a context of dialogue can be realized in which all those whose interests are
affected are free to put forward proposed solutions, and equally
free to raise any objections they have to proposed solutions, then
any solution that emerges at the end to which no one has any further objection constitutes a solution to which there *are* no objections (since this solution will have survived all the objections of
those involved). If we can be sure that there is no objection to a
certain proposal, we can surely say that this *is* right. In such a case,
it is not that there is, already, a right answer which the discussion
may or may not discover, but rather that any answer that emerges
unscathed at the end of the discussion is by that very fact shown to
be right.

Real discussions, however, do not take place in ideal conditions
or with unlimited time available; and many moral issues are ones
in which some of the interests at stake are not directly represented
in the discussion, and in which at least some of the participants
may not see the problem in terms of *interests* at all (see Chapter 9
for examples). For that reason, the idea that discussion must be
aiming at the truth is not, in practice, a very helpful one. But we
do not have to accept that there are only two possibilities: that
either there is a truth that reasoned discussion will lead rational
people to agree on, *or* there can be no reasoned discussion of values. Another possibility is that participants in a discussion seek a
practical accommodation about what is to be done, while not necessarily trying to persuade each other of the truth of their respective positions. Though discussion in this sense is not aiming at
truth, it is by no means irrational or non-rational. Just as in a

search for truth, it requires understanding and articulation of the views of each participant, and the exploration of possibilities and objections.

It may be illuminating here to think again of the difference between the justice and care perspectives. As I pointed out in Chapter 6, the justice perspective tends to present difficult situations as conflicts of rights. If this perspective is assumed from the beginning, it may lend itself to the kind of debate in which each party is out to win. Or even if the parties do engage in a genuine discussion, seeking a common solution, they may assume that the solution must be one of two given alternatives. As viewed from the justice orientation, the issue between the moles and the porcupine is: who has right on their side? Whereas viewed from the care perspective, the question is a practical one: what, in the actual circumstances, given the different points of view and interests, is the best thing to be done? It is more likely that the moles and the porcupine would agree on the latter issue than on the former (especially if they have not been schooled to assume a bipolar view of discussion). All that was said in Chapter 5 about compromise is, of course, relevant here. To be able and willing to engage in discussion aimed at a practical accommodation is an important skill and disposition for citizens of a plural society, and is one that can be practised in schools, through discussion rather than bipolar debate.

Earlier I stressed the importance of knowledge and understanding of the variety of moral outlooks within one's society. Just as discussion may help to promote that kind of knowledge and understanding, so the possession of that knowledge and understanding may help to make particular discussions more productive. But any reasoned discussion is unlikely to happen if the conditions are not appropriate for it. It is widely accepted that discussion needs some ground rules; but I would add two further points. First, that different sorts of ground rules are appropriate to – indeed are partly what constitute – different kinds of discussion; and second, that ground rules need not themselves be sacrosanct. Within a classroom, the ground rules may initially have to be laid down by the teacher. But it should be part of the teacher's aim that pupils will come to recognize the point of the ground rules for themselves, and they are more likely to do this if they themselves have had a hand in setting them up. Some flexibility can be allowed, then: pupils may suggest rules for themselves and gain the experience of discussion within different frameworks of rules, reflecting on why some discussions seem to lead nowhere while others may achieve a resolution that leaves everyone feeling that they have gained something.

What the teacher needs is not so much an authoritative set of rules that he or she will lay down, as a repertoire of the sorts of rules that have been shown to make for constructive discussion. A good deal has been written about ground rules for rational discussion in general, and I shall not add to it here,[17] except to note that there is a philosophical tradition that provides many examples of rules that may be relevant in discussion of moral issues in particular. Some of them derive from the characteristic features of moral values that I mentioned in Chapter 3. Given an expression of a moral position, questions can be asked such as 'Does the person putting this view see it as an expression of personal preference?'; 'Are they taking other people's interests into account?'; 'Do they want to say that everyone should act in accordance with their view?'; and the familiar challenge 'What if everyone did that?' The last example shows that we are not talking here about the kind of rule that can be mechanically applied to substantiate some positions and filter out others; nor about rules that cannot themselves be challenged. To the question 'What if everyone did that?' it will sometimes seem appropriate to reply 'Not everyone will.' But when would that response be appropriate and when simply an evasion? This itself is something that can be discussed,[18] as can the question of whether moral positions must be universalizable (which would be denied by some advocates of a care orientation). These matters have been explored (but not resolved) by moral philosophers, but they do not need technical terminology or specialized knowledge, and there is no inherent reason why an ability to think about such matters should not be part of the education of everyone in a plural society.

Discussion of values requires more than formal ground rules; it also requires some conceptual clarification to be brought to bear on the range of possible positions. Philosophers and others have divided up and classified the various kinds of moral position and argument in many ways, some of which I have used in this book: for example, the distinctions between the justice and care orientations, and between consequentialist approaches (which hold that what matters is the promotion of the best consequences overall) and approaches that maintain that some kinds of action are required or ruled out independently of their consequences. The value of such distinctions is not that people should be able to play an academic game of pigeon-holing other people's views, but rather that to be able to locate someone's position within a conceptual scheme is an important part of understanding it. Debates over abortion or capital punishment, for instance, often reach deadlock because participants are arguing from conflicting assumptions, some holding that the decision should be made in terms of desired consequences, others seeking to apply an absolute principle about the taking of human life. To overcome the deadlock may require standing back and looking at the general issue between the conflicting assumptions.

One further point about the conduct of discussion: don't be afraid of the use of explicitly moral language. As I said at the end of Chapter 7, to state a view that some course of action is morally wrong, and to give reasons for the view, is not to condemn the person holding a contrary view. Where else, if not in discussion in school, will people learn that it is possible to have reasoned discussion about morality; that to say 'that's wrong' or 'this is what you ought to do' need not be an expression of personal preference or an uncritical adherence to tradition. If that kind of language is not used, in the context of a reasoned discussion, then, as I argued in Chapter 7, we cannot be sure even that morality will survive.[19]

---

[1] I noted in Chapter 7 that autonomy in its modern educational sense cannot be equated with Kant's understanding of autonomy. Independence of thought is only one aspect of autonomy in its contemporary sense, because autonomy may also include being able to act on the results of one's own thinking. If someone, through their own thinking, has come to have certain firm convictions, then what we call having the strength of one's convictions may be an aspect of that person's autonomy.

[2] See Kirschenbaum and Simon (eds) (1973).

[3] Rawls (1972: 20).

[4] Rawls would claim that it constitutes a justification too, and the only kind of justification we can have, but I shall avoid here the large issues raised by that claim.

[5] See Wilson (1990), Chapter 10.

[6] Hare (1992); and for the argument about convergence, Hare (1981), Chapter 12.

[7] Kohlberg (1981), Chapter 7.

[8] So far we have been assuming that the right kind of thinking is something that individuals can do for themselves. As we saw at the end of Chapter 7, we should not neglect the possibility that the right kind of thinking has to be a shared, collective process. This possibility will be relevant again in the final section of this chapter.

[9] The evidence also suggests that the distinction between the two perspectives will often not, in practice, be as clear-cut as it seemed to be in the story of the moles and the porcupine. Having made the distinction, we will often be able to recognize elements of both perspectives in someone's thinking on a given occasion. See Dancy (1992).

[10] See Wingfield and Haste (1987) for an investigation in which the different orientations were revealed in a political context. I am grateful to Helen Haste for discussion of the implications of the justice/caring debate.

[11] I have said more on this in Haydon (2000a).

[12] Kohlberg (1981), Chapter 5.

[13] It is Richard Hare who has given the most thorough and careful articulation of the idea I am trying to get across here. Philosophically it owes a lot to Kant. This way of thinking is, of course, related to the everyday appeals 'What if everyone did that?' and 'How would you like it if he did that to you?', but it is necessary to think through carefully what is involved in that sort of appeal, if people are not to be able to shrug it off with a simple 'So what?'. See Hare (1981), Chapters 9–11.

[14] I have said more on this in Haydon (2000b).

[15] See Bridges (1979); Wilson (1990).

[16] Habermas (1990b).

[17] See Bridges (1979); Habermas (1990a); Haydon (1993b); Haydon (2000b).

[18] Here in particular an acquaintance with Hare's arguments would be helpful to the teacher.

[19] See also Haydon (1999b: 124–126).

PART VI: VALUES IN THE TEACHING PROFESSION

The teaching profession, in England, has only recently begun to pay the explicit and systematic attention to values that one might expect a profession to pay. This seems to be true whether we are thinking of the preparation of teachers for their role in values education, or the part that any teacher may play in discussing and deciding on the issues of values that concern the profession collectively. This is, no doubt, a sweeping generalization, and one large and honourable exception to it exists in the area of equal opportunities, where the profession has often been ahead of public or political opinion. There is, too, a considerable attention to values in the literature on educational leadership, though it tends to be couched in its own jargon.

In this concluding part, which consists of one chapter, I want to look ahead, in broad terms, at what could and ought to happen. This chapter links with the question raised in Chapter 1 about the responsibilities of teachers as regards values: what responsibilities can the wider society reasonably expect teachers to shoulder, and how can teachers be helped to exercise the responsibilities that are reasonable? The right sort of professional education must be part of the answer, and the right sort of leadership must be another. So the chapter will include some brief consideration of both of these, in a way that will link these questions with some of the themes touched on earlier in the book.

Chapter 13

Valuing Teachers

Values in the curriculum

If I am right, in my argument in Chapter 12, about the amount of knowledge and understanding that schools can and should contribute to values education, then there is a considerable amount of knowledge and understanding about values that teachers themselves need to acquire. One response to this point could be to suggest that values education should be treated as a subject in its own right, and specialist teachers trained to teach it.[1] This would have the advantage of fitting the kind of pattern (especially for secondary education) that we have become used to, but it would also have distinct drawbacks: the difficulty of clearly identifying and delineating the subject in question, and the fact that it would be competing with other relevant subjects in the curriculum.

While the study of values, and within that of morality in particular, *could* be developed as a subject in its own right, the fact that it is not as yet established as a subject, at any rate in Britain, would raise practical difficulties. These would not be insuperable, but do constitute reasons for caution. Interdisciplinary work is never easy to establish, depending as it does on the capacity and willingness of people with roots in different disciplinary traditions to work together. In the case of the study of values, a case could be made for one particular discipline being in the forefront. This is the discipline that has been uppermost in this book, namely philosophy. Indeed the case could be made that if any subject with special relevance to values education were to be introduced into the curriculum, it should be philosophy in its own right.

There is already a movement – established for some years in the USA and in Australia, and gaining ground in Britain – for the teaching of philosophy in schools, at all ages and stages from early primary to A level.[2] Philosophy is not only about asking the deep and difficult questions; it is also concerned with the way one approaches questions, whether they are of cosmic importance or merely worrying to one individual. It is a way of approaching questions that tries to be as clear as possible about the concepts being used; which makes careful distinctions so as to avoid confusion and cross-purposes; which tries to be aware of alternatives to the ways of thinking that one is familiar with; which looks for underlying principles and asks whether they can be justified. Philosophy does have its own body of theories and texts, like any other subject, and it is perfectly possible for these to be studied by school students. But it is also possible to raise and discuss the questions of philosophy without advanced or specialized knowledge of theories and texts, which is the method that is being employed in primary schools, often through the use of stories and picture books.

One of the concerns of philosophy has always been the understanding of values and morality. Much of what I have been doing in this book is, I hope, recognizable as philosophy to readers who know something of the subject, but it is also important that the book did not carry a philosophy label on the cover. That might have put some people off; if you came to the book unaware that it was philosophy, you will have seen that the subject need not be esoteric. Of course, if people were introduced[3] to philosophical discussion from an early age, no one would think of the subject as esoteric.

So there is a case that could be made for introducing philosophy as a curriculum subject for everyone. But in the real world, any new addition to the curriculum has to find space alongside existing subjects. Since the first edition of this book was published, citizenship has come into the National Curriculum in England and Wales. Citizenship is certainly one area of the curriculum in which some value issues should be studied. Perhaps citizenship especially is the place in which attention should be given to whether, in a plural society, we do have some shared moral system. It would be a mistake to look to citizenship to cover all the aspects of values and morality that we have looked at in this book; some aspects would fit better under Personal Social and Health Education (PSHE).[4] The important point for the moment is that, while the English curriculum is still adjusting to the presence of citizenship, and while the relationship between citizenship and PSHE is still having to be worked out (they are effectively combined in most primary schools, while in secondary schools there is some pressure to keep them distinct), the time is not auspicious for advocating any new additions to the list of subjects, whether 'Philosophy' or 'Values'. Values should be studied, and a philosophical approach, among others, is needed. The challenge is to see how this can be done within the existing curriculum.

Educating the educators

If values are not to be – indeed cannot be – the preserve of any one part of the curriculum, then the task of preparing teachers to handle issues about values will not be a matter of training a group of specialists. All teachers need a considerable amount of knowledge and understanding about values. Such knowledge and understanding is not something that can be delivered didactically. Teachers need the opportunity to reflect on the kinds of ideas, distinctions and issues that have been raised in this book, to discuss such ideas, and to try them out in practice.

In the old style of teacher education (I am thinking now of Britain in, say, the 1980s) the obvious suggestion would have been to build some new content into initial training courses. But even if we assume that that would have been effective, it is not an option now when there are more routes into teaching and all routes involve more training on the job and less 'theoretical' input. New teachers, and those teachers in schools who are responsible for the training of new teachers, may have to do a lot for themselves (in-service education may, of course, have a lot to contribute as well). What I want to stress here is that, whatever the institutional context, opportunities both for individual reflection and for discussion between teachers are essential. In Chapter 12 I emphasized discussion as part of the educational process. How will teachers be able to facilitate and take part in educational discussion about values if they have not had the experience of engaging in such discussion themselves? What teachers need, after all, is not a passive assimilation of the kinds of ideas mooted in this book – any more than pupils need that. Pupils and their teachers need to be able to use these ideas, which means making sense of them in relation to the ideas one already has. Teachers, in facilitating discussion, should start from where the pupils are. Indeed, the teachers themselves, in learning to teach about values, will also be starting from where they are, with values of their own.

People may go into teaching for all sorts of reasons, but it would be surprising if people who have chosen to enter teaching did not bring with them some concern for the value of knowledge, understanding and skills, and some concern for the well-being and future prospects of children and adolescents. Often these values will have been developed over many years; people entering into teacher education are not, after all, naïve or uneducated. In many countries, to an increasing extent, they are already graduates when they decide to go into teaching, and many of them have not come directly from their own schooling through higher education into teacher education. They may have varied experience of working in other jobs, living in other countries, bringing up their own children, and more. To say to such people, in effect, 'These are the values you are going to transmit, and this is how to do it' (even supposing the techniques existed) would be patronizing. Where teachers are seen essentially as technicians delivering a predetermined content – even where that content is supposed to consist of values – the strategy may fail if we try to get them to transmit values that they themselves do not necessarily want to endorse. In any case, such a strategy fails to build positively on the enthusiasms, commitments and understandings that teachers already bring to their task.

To stress that teachers come into teaching with some of their values already formed is not to say that they should simply be left to get on with the job of values education – far from it. That people entering teaching have values of their own does not necessarily mean that they have thought a lot about these values, that they can readily articulate or defend them, or that they will know how to respond when encountering others with contrary values. In all these respects, the educators may themselves need educating. But, as in education generally, what is needed here is not the importing of something quite new, but a linking into the concerns already there. While student teachers and new teachers will usually be anxious about their classroom experience, and eager for practical advice, this does not prevent many of them from reflecting on the system they are entering, and asking how well it is serving young people.

On matters like this, as well as on everyday classroom concerns, both new and established teachers ought to be able from time to time to sit back, observe from the outside, and reflect, discuss,

revise and clarify their own views. For new teachers especially, at
least some of this should be done with others who are at the same
stage, and not just with experienced teachers who may be rather
more set in their ways and their views, and rather less prone to the
same worries.

The moves in Britain away from university-based teacher education and toward school-based training were motivated partly by a
rather inaccurate perception that education departments in uni-
versities and colleges were too much concerned with theory. But
in school-based training there is a danger that there will be too little space for reflecting, and for the kind of illumination that can
be provided by good theory – which does not have to abstract and
impractical. This is not to suggest that student teachers should be
subjected to seminar after seminar in which there is no agenda
other than an open-ended exchange of views about the aims of
education or about values. One problem with that is that, given a
shared interest in and concern about education, it can lead too
easily to an apparent agreement, whereas what may be more
worthwhile is to look seriously at differences. Though there may
be a greater degree of consensus on certain values among people
intending to be teachers than there is among the population as a
whole, it may be too easily assumed that the consensus extends
more widely than it actually does.

Teachers, values and equal opportunities

The fact that our society is a plural one means not only that teachers will be working in a context in which pupils and their parents
have different perspectives on questions of values, but also that
the values of teachers themselves will reflect this plurality. Even
while it is true that not enough recruits to teaching are being
drawn from certain sectors of society, especially some ethnic
minorities, there can still be a considerable diversity of religious,
cultural, political and ethnic perspectives represented within an
institution of teacher education or in a school.

Because of this diversity within the wider society, policies for
equal opportunities are vital within education. This is not a matter
of political fashion; the central reason for concern – itself an expression of values, of course – is that it is wrong for anyone's education,

career or life prospects to be hampered because the person happens to fit into a category that is viewed by others in society in a prejudiced, intolerant or, as many disabled people could testify, a patronizing way. It would be inconsistent, a bad example and unjust to new teachers themselves if this same central value, which ought to be realized in the education of pupils, were not also realized within the professional education of teachers.

One reason why it is difficult to put into practice even the best of intentions in the area of equal opportunities also explains why this is itself a fruitful area to focus on in encouraging new teachers to think about values: namely, that the issues – once one moves beyond superficial albeit important slogans – are by no means clear-cut. This is partly because people's values, including the values of teachers, differ where equal opportunities are concerned. If this is not recognized, one of the dangers (a danger of not preparing teachers as well as they ought to be prepared for their encounters with pupils' developing values, and a danger of injustice to teachers themselves) is that too much of what matters to some of the individuals in teaching will be overlooked. A consensus may be too readily assumed among tutors and new teachers: that there is unanimity, for instance, not just on the importance but on the interpretation of anti-racism and anti-sexism. And, as mentioned in Chapter 10, there is a widespread tendency in our secular society, reflected in many but not all institutions of teacher education, to think in altogether non-religious terms or to assume that a person's religion is a private matter.

But if all discussions are conducted in such terms, is due respect being shown to those persons – perhaps one or two in a seminar group – who do not agree? What, for instance, of the liberal consensus that a person's sexual orientation is no better a ground for disapproval or discrimination than skin colour or regional accent? There are people outside this consensus who would not see the cases as equivalent, and who, even if they are fully supportive of liberal toleration (as outlined in Chapter 5), have reasons of religious conviction for disapproval of certain practices. Not to let their voice be heard is to discriminate against them on account, indirectly at least, of their religion. Of course, it may be that in some other institutions, perhaps some with a strong religious affiliation, the positions are reversed, so that it is individuals whose sexual orientation is different from that of the majority who feel unable to speak in the face of a conservative consensus.

In teacher education, as much as anywhere, the fact that our society is far from homogeneous in its values is inescapable. There are additional reasons here why we should hope that the teaching profession will itself be multiethnic, multicultural and multifaith. One reason is the general equal opportunities consideration that nobody entering the teaching profession – or any other occupation – should be faced with special barriers because of their culture, religion or ethnic origin. A second reason, often mentioned, is that young people from ethnic minorities should have suitable role models. The third reason, less often noticed, is that teachers should have the chance among themselves, in their professional interaction, to discuss and conduct dialogue across different points of view and on the basis of different kinds of experience.

Whatever their background, teachers have to respond to diversity of values among the people they are teaching and among parents, some of whom may hold values with which a teacher profoundly disagrees. At the same time, teachers have to educate people in such a way that they will themselves be able to cope with conflicts of values within their society. If teachers are not able to face openly and with tolerance their own differences in values, they will hardly be able to help others to do so. This means that discussion among teachers, in which their own differences are honestly explored, ought to be an essential part of the expectations that the profession has of itself. Such discussion may well grow out of teachers' collective attempt to handle the particular issues that come up in a school, rather than out of more abstract discussions about values in general.

Some of the most productive discussions may themselves arise from the attempt to make an equal opportunities policy work, and to be transparent to all concerned. While student teachers should be expected to follow the equal opportunities policies of the schools in which they are working, this does not mean that they cannot think critically about such policies. (A similar point applies to the school's policy for pastoral care and for the delivery of curriculum areas in which values are central, such as PSHE and citizenship.) They should be encouraged to look at such policies and practices, discuss the principles behind them and their operation, and in the process express their own values and explore their areas of consensus and disagreement. The opportunity to do this in a structured way should be made available. This entails both a sufficient allocation of time and the availability of suitable facilitators, whether drawn from school or university staff. Meanwhile university departments of education (if they survive in Britain in anything like their present form) could give more prominence to research and teaching about the role of values in education, and especially to the still rather underexplored area of culturally and religiously based differences in our society as they affect education. Student teachers should be made aware that more systematic study of values is possible and that, though what can be done in initial teacher education is limited, there are further possibilities during inservice education.

Leadership: aims, purpose and vision

It is hardly necessary to say that much of the responsibility for seeing that values are taken seriously and put into practice within schools will fall on those in leadership roles. There is increasing attention to educational leadership worldwide, and with it a growing body of academic literature on the theme. Much of this literature refers to values, and some of it is specifically on the ethics of school leadership and management.

Perhaps we should treat with some caution the idea that there is a distinct field that can be called the ethics of educational leadership. The questions about values that face anyone seriously engaging in education face educational leaders as well; there is no distinct set of values for those who occupy leadership roles. Nevertheless, educational leaders do have the responsibility to see that educational and moral values are protected and promoted in their institutions; and sometimes that responsibility means that leaders and managers have to make difficult decisions that teachers without that responsibility are spared.

It is not possible here to do more than touch on a few points that will link some of the themes treated earlier in this book with the present chapter. I shall consider the responsibilities of educational leaders under the related headings of aims, moral purpose and vision.

There are some aims that all those who are in leadership roles[5] in institutions and organizations are likely to have in common: to maintain the institution or organization so far as possible in a flourishing condition, and to facilitate its successful achievement of its goals. What constitutes a flourishing condition, and what counts as success, will of course depend on the institution or organization in question. We should not expect a school to be in all respects analogous to, say, a manufacturing business, even if management theorists may see them as similar from certain theoretical perspectives. The aims of schools are different in some respects from those of any other organization, and to that extent the aims of leadership have to be different. This means that educational leaders need to pay close attention to questions and debates about the aims that schools should be pursuing; but there is no reason to think, just because someone is in a leadership role in a school, that their view of the aims of education has any privileged authority. There may be special skills required by leaders, and there may be particular qualities that make for a good leader, but questions about what the aims of education should be are questions on which no one has special expertise. What is perhaps a particular responsibility that goes with a leadership role is not to decide for oneself what the aims are going to be, but to have a clear view of the aims and to be able to communicate these to others.

Any aim can be pursued more or less efficiently, and efficiency, or effectiveness, is a notion very often heard in contemporary educational discourse. But efficiency is not all that matters. Even *if* the aim pursued is good, not all possible means towards it are justified. Some ways of achieving a given aim – ways, for instance, that override the rights of some members of the school, or that fail to show respect to others – may be ruled out on moral grounds. The same applies to anyone who is involved in pursuing the aim; teachers who are not in leadership roles are subject to the same moral constraints. But people in leadership roles, because of their special responsibilities, need to be especially aware of the moral dimension of what they are doing, and aware that they may be tempted to give first place to issues of efficiency and effectiveness at the cost of other values.

It is sometimes said that educational leaders need a *moral purpose*.[6] What does this notion convey, over and above the responsibilities of educational leaders to pay attention to educational aims?

One connotation is a negative but nevertheless an important one: that a leader's purpose must not be *immoral*. Of course, the great majority of educational leaders do not have immoral purposes, but cases are not unknown in which school leaders have used their position primarily for personal gain (fraudulently and beyond the remuneration to which they are entitled); or in which they have used it as an opportunity to degrade or abuse others. That an educational leader should respect the constraints of ordinary morality (morality in the narrow sense) is a minimal requirement (though as we shall see later this does not make the leader immune to some difficult moral dilemmas).

'Moral purpose' can also mean that the leader should be pursuing purposes that are morally admirable or morally required. This is not by itself saying more than that the leader should be pursuing educational aims (however we characterize those) since these are presumably aims that are desirable and probably morally obligatory (because a society surely has an obligation to see that its young people are educated; educational leaders are helping to carry out this responsibility on society's behalf).

Particular leaders may have more specific interpretations of the aims that they are pursuing; such interpretations overlap with the idea of *vision* that we shall consider next.

Perhaps the most distinctive use of the term 'moral purpose' is to characterize not the nature of the aim, but the quality of the motivation underlying the leader's pursuit of the aim. The idea of 'moral purpose' is saying that the leader should be morally motivated; that is, that their motivation should be not fundamentally selfish or egoistic but *altruistic*. In the eyes of some writers this means that the underlying motivation of educational leaders should be one of caring.[7] Of course, considerations of justice or fairness are important in the running of any organisation, and vital in an educational one where action is likely to be setting an example from which others will learn, for better or for worse. So an educational leader must be fair in his or her dealings with pupils and with staff. But a concern for fairness or justice will not usually explain why someone has gone into teaching, and from there into educational leadership in the first place. But the explanation may well be – perhaps especially for those who have gone on to become good educational leaders – that they have been motivated by a concern for young people and a desire to help them realize their potential. This provides the moral purpose that can give them the determination and persistence to overcome the difficulties that leaders inevitably face.

Moral purpose may give an educational leader a sense of direction, and the motivation to move in that direction. But a moral purpose does not in itself constitute a detailed view of the goal that is to be achieved. A rather different term may be needed to characterize such a goal. The term that for better of worse has been gaining ground in the discourse of educational leadership is *vision*. Educational leaders, and candidates for leadership roles, are expected to have a vision for their school. The notion of a vision seems to go beyond that of an aim or a purpose; a vision, as the term is being used in educational discourse, is a relatively concrete picture of what the school will be like.

Whether 'vision' is actually the best term in this context is questionable, given the other connotations of the word. A vision – in the sense in which, for instance, religious mystics may have visions – is not necessarily very clear. And if there is an idea at all of trying to achieve a vision, it may be as a distant aspiration. This fits oddly with the short-term emphasis of so much current policy thinking, and with the expectation of explicit goals and objectives. But perhaps the most serious question to be raised about the idea that an educational leader should have a vision for his or her school is whether there is a danger of the leader trying to impose this vision on others.[8] A strong theme in much of the educational leadership literature is that a vision shared within a school is much better than a vision that remains that of one person. And it can make a difference too how a vision comes to be shared: it is one thing for a leader to try to 'sell' his or her vision to the rest of the school; another for a shared vision to be built up through collaboration among the teachers.

We can also, of course, raise questions about the nature of the particular vision that may be motivating an educational leader. Is it a vision of an effective school where effectiveness is judged instrumentally in the light of standards laid down by external policy? Or is it essentially a vision of a good education that all the teachers in the school can endorse out of their own understanding of the values that are important in education?

Is it asking too much of teachers that they should be able to take responsibility for the aims they pursue and the values they put into practice? The answer to that question has a lot to do, as I shall suggest in the next and final section, with how we see the professional status of teachers.

Values and professional standing

It is sometimes said that one mark of a profession is its shared possession of a body of expertise and knowledge, such as the medical knowledge of doctors or the legal knowledge of solicitors.[9] The claims of teachers to professional status based on this criterion have proved somewhat controversial. There are those who will argue that, apart from relevant knowledge of the subjects being taught, there is no body of expert knowledge of 'teaching' equivalent to the specialist knowledge of medicine or law. There may be skills, as recent emphasis on competence models of training seems to assume, but the professional model in question speaks not of skills *per se* but of skills rooted in specialized and theoretically articulated knowledge. If in the case of teachers the idea of skills or competences, to be learned on the job, is detached from the notion of a body of expert knowledge and theory, then teachers are being seen more as technicians.

A second mark of a profession sometimes proposed is that it controls its own professional education. This is not at present the case for teaching in Britain, or indeed in many other countries. Of course, a profession will have a stronger case for controlling its own professional education to the extent that it has a collective sense of what that education should involve and what form it should take. But currently in Britain there is perhaps hardly a stronger sense of this within teaching than there is among the public at large.

A third possible mark of a profession is one that is perhaps influential among the general public, and for that reason often not clearly articulated. It is the sense, mentioned in Chapter 1, that a professional person maintains rather higher than ordinary ethical standards. It is true that this expectation is often accompanied by considerable suspicion about certain professions. In some cases their members may be seen as out to get power, status and income for themselves. That kind of charge could be made to stick, perhaps, against a minority of lawyers or certain medical consultants with private practices; it would seem laughable in Britain in relation to nurses or the average school teacher. In some people's eyes it may be that the very lack of prestige and high income makes the professional status of teachers or nurses dubious. But for others, the same factors will tell in favour of these groups, for there is an idea that the true professional is motivated by concerns other than income and status. In particular, it may be thought that the professional is motivated, at least in part, by altruistic concerns, and by the same token has to respect high ethical ideals.

But just what kind of demand does this idea make on teachers? Does it mean that teachers must be paragons of virtue? A good footballer or a good basketball player is not necessarily a good person. Must a good teacher be a good person? Some would say that anyone who is not a good person cannot be a good teacher. And some might suggest that if we could rely on teachers being good persons, little more would have to be said about the role of teachers in values education.[10]

I have already argued that, so far as values education is concerned, it is certainly not sufficient that teachers be good persons: there is a great deal that they need to be able to teach. Is it even *necessary* that they be good persons? It would be possible to overstate the answer to that question in either of two directions. On the one hand, if we say that a teacher must be a thoroughly good person in all respects, we need some standard by which to evaluate this goodness; and any such standard will be controversial. The more content we build into a conception of a thoroughly good person, the more it will be, in a plural society, some people's conception rather than everybody's. Besides, the higher we set the standard, the more difficult it will be to find enough teachers who can measure up to it. (I am not even entering here into the weighty problem of how any standard of morality or character could actually be applied within selection and professional education.)

On the other hand, if we were to say that all that can be required of teachers is that they have the necessary skills and competences, and that no moral demands are placed on them at all, we would be demanding less than is commonly expected of the members of other professions. Recognizing the large and potentially very damaging influence that the members of other professions can exercise on the layperson, the general public can reasonably ask that they respect certain ethical standards. In the same way, recognizing the potential influence for good or ill that teachers can exercise towards pupils, such an expectation is equally reasonable for them.

Some professions have responded to such public expectations, as well as to their own internal concerns, by formulating and promulgating a code of ethics. In Britain, teaching has been slow to catch up with other professions in this respect, but one thing that has changed in recent years (since the first edition of this book was published) is that there is now a General Teaching Council, and that this body has issued a Statement of Professional Values and Practice for Teachers. It is too early to be clear how much difference the existence of such a statement will make in practice; there is, as with other professional codes, a danger that it will be used as a reference point when a question of disciplinary action arises, but will otherwise be treated with benign neglect by most practitioners. It is doubtful in any case whether the possession of a code of ethics as such is the major factor in the public perception of a profession's ethical standing. The general public, even if it knows of the existence of such codes, is unlikely to know their details. Its moral expectations of the profession may have more to do with the sense, mentioned above, of what it is that motivates the professional: a sense that the professional is committed to certain ethical concerns. What might these concerns be?

Here it may be helpful to look at a kind of answer that, in essence, has existed at least since Plato: namely, that each profession has a particular goal, something of value that its practitioners aim at, and that this goal, or this recognized kind of *good*, is both what gives the profession its unity and what distinguishes it from others. In the case of medicine – perhaps the most clear-cut case – the goal is health, or at least life rather than death: the professionals are expected to have a shared commitment to this goal. In the case of law the goal, arguably, would be justice. In the case of religious ministry, it has been claimed that the goal is salvation.[11]

Pursuing the example of medicine further, it is important first to recognize that there are other professions besides medicine that are concerned with health, and that they will not all be concerned with it in the same way: nurses, for instance, may see themselves as concerned with the relief of suffering and the comfort of the whole person rather than the curing of disease; and there are increasing numbers of professionals in healthcare concerned more with prevention than curing of disease. For our purposes here though, I shall assume that the overriding goal of medicine is the curing of disease, and ask how such a goal is meant to function. For one thing, it provides the *raison d'être* for the profession as a whole: because the cure of disease is widely recognized as a goal worth aiming at, it is seen as good that there is a profession devoted to it.[12] There may be a sense too that this goal is aimed at for its own sake. The medical profession does not primarily, for instance, serve the goals of a flourishing economy, though it is true that by curing people's diseases it will often enable them to return to work or to work more productively; essentially, the profession aims at the restoration of health as a worthwhile end in its own right. The goal is also one that can be shared across national boundaries, and this is part of what constitutes the identity of a profession whose members can identify themselves as its members, independently of where in the world they work. By reference to this shared goal, for instance, it is possible for doctors in any part of the world to criticize the actions of those who put their medical expertise at the disposal of partisan political goals (as in Nazi Germany or, for psychiatry, in the Soviet Union at one time). All this may be to some degree idealistic, but we need not deny that ideals may have some force for at least some professionals.

What, now, of teaching? Is there a central, shared good which will stand for teaching as health does for the healthcare professions and (arguably) justice for the law? The obvious answer is 'education'. Whether this answer will work depends on whether there can be a clear enough shared understanding of what education is. If so, then teachers can see themselves, and be seen publicly, as committed to the pursuit of education. This implicit commitment would form the basis for professional ethics, providing teachers with a reason why they should resist calls – whether from parents, industry or government – to serve ends, such as indoctrination or narrow technical training, that would be incompatible with the good of education. The same commitment would be the source of the standards that individual teachers would know they must not fall short of despite the day-to-day pressures of the job.

While this is a possible model, we cannot avoid asking whether teachers actually do share a conception of what constitutes the good of education. There is a conception available: it would be roughly the liberal conception once articulated by philosophers such as Richard Peters,[13] seen as being of value for its own sake rather than for instrumental ends. The problem is that neither teachers nor the general public may agree that the central and overriding goal to which they must be committed is education in this sense. My arguments in Chapter 2 suggested that there are many aims that can legitimately be pursued by schools. In some contexts, perhaps in a developing economy dependent for the moment on subsistence farming where the productivity of the land must be improved to avert the danger of famine, education in the full-blown liberal sense, for everyone, may seem at best a long-term goal, at worst an unnecessary luxury. At the very least there would be room for debate about this; and so there is even in wealthy countries.

The difference as regards to a central professional goal between teaching and what I called the most clear-cut case, medicine, may after all be only one of degree. Even within the medical profession there is room for debate about how its goals are to be conceived, about how health is to be defined, and even, as some of the controversy over euthanasia shows, over what counts as life. A shared sense of values in a profession like medicine will not be entirely a matter of agreeing on the specification of goals; it will be partly also the recognition of the importance of the debate and the willingness and capacity to engage in it. That is what much of medical ethics is about: not handing down answers but equipping professionals to handle the questions. (This is perhaps even more true of nursing ethics, where the goals in question have never even seemed so clear-cut.)

I suggest that the position for teaching is actually very similar. Teachers will not necessarily share a unified sense of what it is they are aiming at, or of what the standards are that they should apply to themselves. But part of what distinguishes the teaching profession from the general public, and part of what could give it a well-deserved professional standing in the public's eyes, ought to be not that the profession is a repository of society's values which its members transmit, but that the professionals are committed to engaging in the debate and are rather better equipped to engage in it than the general public.

[1] This response would fit well with John Wilson's advocacy of the teaching of moral methodology (see Chapter 12). It should be said that Wilson does not see this as the sole approach that schools should take to moral education. See Wilson (1990), Part 4.

[2] The organization SAPERE (Society for the Advancement of Philosophy and Reflection in Education; www.sapere.org.uk) is in the forefront of the promotion of philosophy in schools in Britain.

[3] 'Introduced' may be misleading. Advocates of philosophy with children have pointed out that young children seem naturally to ask the kinds of question that adults may label as 'philosophical'. For different views on this see Matthews (1980); Lipman (1991); White (1992).

[4] I have said more about the role of PSHE in relation to values in Haydon (1995).

[5] I am referring to 'those in leadership roles' partly to avoid suggesting that a leader is a special sort of person, and partly to avoid suggesting that for each school there is just one leader (the Head or Principal). In a school, especially a large school, there may be a considerable number of persons who have responsibilities in leading others, even if the overall responsibility rests with one person. I shall use the terms 'person in an educational leadership role' and 'educational leader' interchangeably.

[6] See especially Fullan (2003).

[7] The writings of Nel Noddings have been influential in this respect; see Noddings (1984), (1992); Nias (1999).

[8] Critical questions of this nature are raised by Bottery (1992) and by Sergiovanni (1994). For a more recent view of the importance of shared vision, with empirical evidence from a British context, see Gold *et al.* (2003).

[9] Some of the marks of a profession may be realized, in teaching, in some countries but not in others. For discussion of the professional status of teaching in a British context, at a time when that status was quite uncertain, see Downie (1990) and Pring (1993).

[10] Carr (1991: 256ff.) is relevant here, though Carr would not fully endorse the suggestion above.

[11] This argument is made by Koehn (1994).

[12] But see Illich (1976) for a contrary view.

[13] See note 4 to Chapter 2.

References

Advisory Group on Citizenship (1998), *Education for Citizenship and the Teaching of Democracy in Schools* (The 'Crick Report'). London: QCA.

Aristotle (1954), *(Nicomachean) Ethics*. Oxford: Oxford University Press. (World's Classics edition; many other translations available.)

Barrow, R. (1981), *The Philosophy of Schooling*. Brighton: Harvester Wheatsheaf.

Barrow, R. (2005), 'On the duty of not taking offence'. *Journal of Moral Education*, 34, 3.

Benedict, R. (1946), *The Chrysanthemum and the Sword: Patterns of Japanese Culture*. Boston: Houghton Mifflin.

Benhabib, S. (1992), *Situating the Self*. Cambridge, UK: Polity Press.

Bereiter, C. (1974), *Must We Educate?* Englewood Cliffs, NJ.

Berger, P. (1983), 'On the obsolescence of the concept of honour'. In Hauerwas, S. and MacIntyre, A., *Revisions: Changing Perspectives in Moral Philosophy*. Notre Dame, ID: University of Notre Dame Press.

Berlin, I. (1969), *Four Essays on Liberty*. Oxford: Oxford University Press.

Blackburn, S. (1984), *Spreading the Word*. Oxford: Oxford University Press.

Blackburn, S. (1993), *Essays in Quasi-Realism*. Oxford: Oxford University Press.

Blackburn, S. (1998), *Ruling Passions*. Oxford: Oxford University Press.

Bottery, M. (1992), *The Ethics of Educational Management*. London: Cassell.

Bramall, S. and White, J. (2000), *Will the new National Curriculum live up to its aims?* London: Philosophy of Education Society of Great Britain (Impact no. 6).

Bridges, D. (1979), *Education, Democracy and Discussion*. Windsor: NFER-Nelson.

Carr, D. (1991), *Educating the Virtues*. London: Routledge.

Carr, D. (1995), 'Towards a distinctive conception of spiritual education'. *Oxford Review of Education*, 21, 1.

Carr, D. and Steutel, J. (1999), *Virtue Ethics and Moral Education.* London: Routledge.

Clark, S.R.L. (1993), *How to think about the earth: philosophical and theological models for ecology.* London: Mowbray.

Cupitt, D. (1980), *Taking Leave of God.* London: SCM Press.

Dancy, J. (1992), 'Caring about justice'. *Philosophy,* 67, 262.

Dawkins, R. (1976), *The Selfish Gene.* Oxford: Oxford University Press.

Day, J. (1989), 'Compromise'. *Philosophy,* 64, 250.

Dewey, J. (1916), *Democracy and Education.* New York: Free Press.

Downey, M. and Kelly, A.V. (1978), *Moral Education: Theory and Practice.* London: Harper and Row.

Downie, R. (1990), 'Professions and professionalism'. *Journal of Philosophy of Education,* 24, 2.

Downie, R. and Telfer, E. (1969), *Respect for Persons.* London: Allen & Unwin.

Dworkin, R. (1993), *Life's Dominion: An Argument about Abortion and Euthanasia.* New York: HarperCollins.

Fletcher, J. (1966), *Situation Ethics.* London: SCM Press.

Foot, P. (1978), *Virtues and Vices.* Oxford: Blackwell.

Freeman, A. (1993), *God in Us: A Case for Christian Humanism.* London: SCM Press.

Fullan, M. (2003), *The Moral Imperative of School Leadership.* Thousand Oaks, Ca.: Corwin Press.

Galston, W. (1989), 'Civic education in the liberal state' in N. Rosenblum (ed.) (1989) *Liberalism and the Moral Life.* Cambridge, Mass.: Harvard University Press.

Galston, W. (1991), *Liberal Purposes: Goods, Virtues and Diversity in the Liberal State.* Cambridge: Cambridge University Press.

Gilligan, C. (1982), *In a Different Voice: Psychological Theory and Women's Development.* Cambridge, Mass.: Harvard University Press.

Gilligan, C., Ward, J., and Taylor, J. (1988), *Mapping the Moral Domain.* Cambridge, Mass.: Harvard University Press.

Gold, A., Evans, J., Earley, P., Halpin, D. and Collarstone, P. (2003), 'Principled Principals? Values-driven leadership: evidence from ten case studies of "outstanding" school leaders'. *Educational Management and Administration,* 31, 2.

Gutmann, A. (1989), 'Undemocratic education' in N. Rosenblum (ed.) (1989), *Liberalism and the Moral Life.* Cambridge, Mass.: Harvard University Press.

Habermas, J. (1976), *Legitimation Crisis.* London: Heinemann.

Habermas, J. (1990a), 'Discourse ethics: notes on a program of philosophical justification', in S. Benhabib and S. Dallmayr, F. (1990), *The Communicative Ethics Controversy.* Cambridge, Mass.: MIT Press.

Habermas, J. (1990b), *Moral Consciousness and Communicative Action.*

Cambridge: Cambridge University Press.

Halstead, M. (1992), 'Ethical dimensions of controversial events in moral education', in M. Taylor and M. Leicester (eds.), *Ethics, Ethnicity and Education.* London: Kogan Page.

Hampshire, S. (1983), *Morality and Conflict.* Oxford: Blackwell.

Hare, R. M. (1981), *Moral Thinking.* Oxford: Oxford University Press.

Hare, R. M. (1992), 'How did morality get a bad name?', in Hare, R. M., *Essays on Religion and Education.* Oxford: Oxford University Press.

Hart, H.L.A. (1961), *The Concept of Law.* Oxford: Oxford University Press.

Haydon, G. (1977), 'The "right to education" and compulsory schooling'. *Educational Philosophy and Theory,* 9, 1.

Haydon, G. (1993a), 'Moral education and the child's right to an open future'. *International Journal of Children's Rights,* 1,1.

Haydon, G. (1993b), 'Values education in a democratic society'. *Studies in Philosophy and Education,* 12, 1.

Haydon, G. (1993c), *Education and the Crisis in Values: Should we be Philosophical about it?* London: Institute of Education.

Haydon, G. (1994), 'Conceptions of the secular in society, polity and schools'. *Journal of Philosophy of Education,* 28, 1.

Haydon, G. (1995), 'Thick or thin? The cognitive content of moral education in a plural democracy'. *Journal of Moral Education,* 24, 1.

Haydon, G. (1998), 'Between the common and the differentiated: reflections on the work of the School Curriulum and Assessment Authority on values education'. *The Curriculum Journal,* 9, 1.

Haydon G (1999a), 'Behaving morally as a point of principle: a proper aim of moral education?' in Halstead, M. and McLaughlin, T. (eds), *Education in Morality.* London: Routledge.

Haydon, G. (1999b), *Values, Virtues and Violence: Education and the Public Understanding of Morality.* Oxford: Blackwell.

Haydon, G. (2000a), 'What scope is there for teaching moral reasoning?' in R. Gardner, J. Cairns, J. and D. Lawton, (eds), *Education for Values.* London: Kogan Page.

Haydon, G. (2000b), 'Discussion of values and the value of discussion' in M. Leicester, C. Modgil and S. Modgil (eds), *Education, Culture and Values,* Vol. 3. London: Falmer.

Haydon, G. (2004), 'Educational aims and the question of priorities', in J. Stoltman, J. Lidstone, and L. DeChano (eds), *International Perspectives on Natural Disasters.* Dordrecht: Kluwer.

Haydon, G. (2005), *The Importance of PSHE: A philosophical and policy perspective on Personal, Social and Health Education.* London: Philosophy of Education. Society of Great Britain (Impact series no. 10).

Haydon, G. (2006a), 'On the duty of educating respect: a response to Robin Barrow'. *Journal of Moral Education,* 35, 1.

Haydon, G. (2006b), *Education, Philosophy and the Ethical Environment.* London: Routledge.

Hirst, P. (1974), *Moral Education in a Secular Society.* London: University of London Press.

Hobbes, T. (1968), *Leviathan.* Harmondsworth: Penguin (first pub. 1651).

Hume, D. (1888), *A Treatise of Human Nature.* Oxford: Oxford University Press (first pub. 1739).

Illich, I. (1973), *Deschooling Society.* Harmondsworth: Penguin.

Illich, I. (1976), *Limits to Medicine.* London: Boyars.

Kant, I. (1927), 'On a supposed right to tell lies from benevolent motives' in T. Abbott (ed.), *Kant's Critique of Pure Reason and Other Works on the Theory of Ethics.* London: Longman (first pub. 1797).

Kant, I. (1948), *Groundwork of the Metaphysic of Morals.* Translated in H. Paton (1948), *The Moral Law.* London: Hutchison (first pub. 1785).

Kirschenbaum, H. and Simon, S. (eds) (1973), *Readings in Values Clarification.* Minneapolis: Winston Press.

Kittay, E. and Meyers, D. (eds) (1987), *Women and Moral Theory.* Totowa, NJ: Rowman and Littlefield.

Koehn, D. (1994), *The Ground of Professional Ethics.* London: Routledge.

Kohlberg, L. (1981), *The Philosophy of Moral Development.* San Francisco: Harper & Row.

Kymlicka, W. (2002), *Contemporary Political Philosophy*, 2nd ed. Oxford: Oxford University Press.

Lipman, M. (1991), *Thinking in Education.* Cambridge, Mass.: Harvard University Press.

Lukes, S. (1985), *Marxism and Morality.* Oxford: Oxford University Press.

Lyons, N. (1988), 'Two perspectives: on self, relationships and morality', in Gilligan, C., Ward, J., and Taylor, J. (1988), *Mapping the Moral Domain.* Cambridge, Mass.: Harvard University Press.

McCarthy, T. (1978), *The Critical Theory of Jurgen Habermas.* London: Hutchison.

Macedo, S. (1990), *Liberal Virtues: Citizenship, Virtue and Community in Liberal Constitutionalism.* Oxford: Oxford University Press.

MacIntyre, A. (1981), *After Virtue: A Study in Moral Theory.* London: Duckworth.

McLaughlin, T. (1987), '"Education for all" and religious schools', in G. Haydon (ed.), *Education for a Pluralist Society: Philosophical Perspectives on the Swann Report.* London: Institute of Education.

McLaughlin, T. (1992), 'The ethics of separate schools', in M. Taylor and M. Leicester (eds), *Ethics, Ethnicity and Education.* London: Kogan Page.

McLaughlin, T. (1999), 'Beyond the Reflective Teacher', *Educational Philosophy and Theory*, 31, 1.

McLaughlin, T. and Halstead, M. (1999), 'Education in character and virtue', in Halstead, M. and McLaughlin, T. (eds), *Education in Morality*. London: Routledge.

Matthews, G. (1980), *Philosophy and the Young Child*. Cambridge, Mass.: Harvard University Press.

Meyers, D. (1987), 'The socialized individual and individual autonomy', In Kittay, E. and Meyers, D. (eds), *Women and Moral Theory*. Totowa, NJ.: Rowman and Littlefield.

Midgley, M. (1979a), *Beast and Man*. Brighton: Harvester Wheatsheaf.

Midgley, M. (1979b), 'Gene-juggling'. *Philosophy*, 54.

Midgley, M. (1991), *Can't We Make Moral Judgements*. Bristol: Bristol Press.

Milgram, S. (1974), *Obedience to Authority*. London: Tavistock.

Mill, J. S. (1962a), *An Essay on Liberty*. In Warnock, M. (ed.), *Utilitarianism*. London: Fontana.

Mill, J. S. (1962b), *Utilitarianism*, in Warnock, M. (ed.), *Utilitarianism*. London: Fontana.

Modood, T. (1992), *Not Easy Being British*. Stoke-on-Trent: Trentham Books.

Mott-Thornton, K. (1998), *A Common Faith: Education, Spirituality and the State*. London: Ashgate.

National Advisory Group on PSHE (1999), *Preparing Young People for Adult Life*. London: DfEE.

National Curriculum Council (1993), *Spiritual and Moral Development: A Discussion Paper*. York: NCC (reissued by SCAA 1995).

Nias, J. (1999), 'Primary Teaching as a Culture of Care', in J. Prosser (ed.), *School Culture*. London: Paul Chapman.

Noddings, N. (1984), *Caring: A Feminine Approach to Ethics and Moral Education*. Berkeley: University of California Press.

Noddings (1992), *The Challenge to Care in Schools: An Alternative Approach to Moral Education*. New York: Teachers College Press.

Noddings, N. and Slote, M. (2003), 'Changing notions of the moral and of moral education' in Blake, N., Smeyers, P., Smith. R., and Standish, P. (eds), *The Blackwell Guide to the Philosophy of Education*. Oxford: Blackwell.

Norman, R. (1987), *Free and Equal*. Oxford: Oxford University Press.

Peters, R.S. (1966), *Ethics and Education*. London: Allen & Unwin.

Plato (1995), *The Republic*. Harmondsworth: Penguin. (Many other translation available.)

Pring, R. (1993), 'Is teaching a profession?' Paper given at Annual Conference of the Philosophy of Education Society of Great Britain.

Raphael, D. (1998), 'The intolerable', in S. Mendus (ed.), *Justifying Toleration: Conceptual and Historical Perspectives*. Cambridge: Cambridge University Press.

Rawls, J. (1972), *A Theory of Justice*. Oxford: Oxford University Press.

Rawls, J. (1993), *Political Liberalism.* New York: Columbia University Press.

Rawls, J. (1999), *The Law of Peoples.* Cambridge, Mass.: Harvard University Press.

Ridley, M. (2003), *The Origins of Virtue.* London: Penguin.

Ross, W. (1930), *The Right and the Good.* Oxford: Oxford University Press.

Ross, W. (1939), *The Foundations of Ethics.* Oxford: Oxford University Press.

Scanlon, T. (1982), 'Contractualism and utilitarianism', in A. Sen and B. Williams (eds), *Utilitarianism and Beyond.* Cambridge: Cambridge University Press.

Scanlon, T. (1998), *What We Owe to Each Other.* Cambridge, Mass.: Harvard University Press.

Schama, S. (1995), *Landscape and Memory.* London: HarperCollins.

Schon, D. (1983), *The Reflective Practitioner.* London: Temple Smith.

Sergiovanni, T. (1994), *Building Community in Schools.* San Francisco: Jossey-Bass.

Shaw, G. (1987), *God in our Hands.* London: SCM.

Singer, P. (1976), *Animal Liberation.* London: Jonathan Cape.

Singer, P. (1981), *The Expanding Circle.* Oxford: Oxford University Press.

Singer, P. (1996), *Rethinking Life and Death: The Collapse of Our Traditional Ethics.* New York: St Martin's Press.

Smart, J. and Williams, B. (1973), *Utilitarianism For and Against.* Cambridge: Cambridge University Press.

Snook, I. (ed.) (1972), *Concepts of Indoctrination.* London: Routledge.

Snook, I. and Lankshear, C. (1979), *Education and Rights.* Melbourne: Melbourne University Press.

Spiecker, B. and Straughan, R. (eds), (1991), *Freedom and Indoctrination in Education.* London: Cassell.

Standish, P. (1997), 'Fabulously absolute', in Smith, R. and Standish, P., *Teaching Right and Wrong: moral education in the balance.* Stoke-on-Trent: Trentham.

Talbot, M. and Tate, N. (1997), 'Shared values in a pluralist society?', in Smith, R. and Standish, P., Teaching Right and Wrong: moral education in the balance Stoke-on-Trent: Trentham.

Taylor, C. (1982), 'The diversity of goods', in A. Sen and B. Williams (eds), *Utilitarianism and Beyond.* Cambridge: Cambridge University Press.

Tobin, B. (1986), 'Development in virtues'. *Journal of Philosophy of Education*, 20, 2.

Tobin, B. (1989), 'An Aristotelian theory of moral development'. *Journal of Philosophy of Education*, 23, 2.

Turnbull, C. (1973), *The Mountain People.* London: Jonathan Cape.

Von Fuerer-Haimendorf, C. (1967), *Morals and Merit.* London: Weidenfeld & Nicolson.

Waldron, J. (1984), *Theories of Rights.* Oxford: Oxford University Press.

Waldron, J. (1993), *Liberal Rights.* Cambridge: Cambridge University Press.

Walsh, P. (1993), *Education and Meaning: Philosophy in Practice.* London: Cassell.

Warnock, G. (1971), *The Object of Morality.* London: Methuen.

White, J. (1982), *The Aims of Education Restated.* London: Routledge.

White, J. (1990), *Education and the Good Life.* London: Kogan Page.

White, J. (1992), 'The roots of philosophy', in A. P. Griffiths (ed.), *The Impulse to Philosophise.* Cambridge: Cambridge University Press.

White, J. (1995), *Education and personal well-being in a secular universe.* London: Institute of Education.

White, J. (ed.) (2004), *Rethinking the School Curriculum: Values, Aims and Purposes.* London: RoutledgeFalmer.

White, P. (1996), *Civic Virtues and Public Schooling.* New York: Teachers College Press.

Williams, B. (1981), 'Conflict of values' in *Moral Luck.* Cambridge: Cambridge University Press.

Williams, B. (1985), *Ethics and the Limits of Philosophy.* London: Fontana.

Wilson, J. (1972), *Practical methods of Moral Education.* London: Heinemann.

Wilson, J. (1975), 'Moral education and the curriculum', in M. Taylor (ed.), *Progress and Problems in Moral Education.*

Wilson, J. (1990), *A New Introduction to Moral Education.* London: Cassell.

Wingfield, L. and Haste, H. (1987), 'Connectedness and separateness: cognitive style or moral orientation?' *Journal of Moral Education,* 16, 3.

Wringe, C. (1981), *Children's Rights.* London: Routledge.

Index